Governing the Euro Area in Good Times and Bad

Governing the Euro Area in Good Times and Bad

Dermot Hodson

OXFORD
UNIVERSITY PRESS

OXFORD
UNIVERSITY PRESS

Great Clarendon Street, Oxford OX2 6DP

Oxford University Press is a department of the University of Oxford.
It furthers the University's objective of excellence in research, scholarship,
and education by publishing worldwide in

Oxford New York

Auckland Cape Town Dar es Salaam Hong Kong Karachi
Kuala Lumpur Madrid Melbourne Mexico City Nairobi
New Delhi Shanghai Taipei Toronto

With offices in

Argentina Austria Brazil Chile Czech Republic France Greece
Guatemala Hungary Italy Japan Poland Portugal Singapore
South Korea Switzerland Thailand Turkey Ukraine Vietnam

Oxford is a registered trade mark of Oxford University Press
in the UK and in certain other countries

Published in the United States
by Oxford University Press Inc., New York

First published 2011

British Library Cataloguing in Publication Data

Data available

Library of Congress Cataloging in Publication Data

Data available

Typeset by SPI Publisher Services, Pondicherry, India
Printed in Great Britain
on acid-free paper by
MPG Books Group, Bodmin and King's Lynn

ISBN 978–0–19–957250–2

1 3 5 7 9 10 8 6 4 2

For Emma and William

Preface

The film, *The Italian Job*, ends with one of the great moments of jeopardy in cinema history. Having stolen $4 billion in gold bullion, a gang of thieves makes its getaway in a bus that wends its way through the mountains above Turin. When the driver misjudges a turn, the bus ends up balancing on the edge of a cliff, with the thieves down one end and the gold down the other. After some minutes pass, the ringleader, played by Michael Caine, steps forward and says, 'Hang on a minute lads, I've got a great idea!' with which the film's final credits roll.

This book concludes with its own moment of jeopardy for the euro area. Having seen their banks lose more than €500 billion in the worst financial crisis since the Great Depression and come through the steepest recession in recent memory, euro area members find themselves on the slow road to recovery. When several countries misjudge the effects of this turmoil on their public finances, the euro area ends up in a sovereign debt crisis facing a choice, in the minds of some commentators at least, between the centralization of economic policy and the potential collapse of the single currency. After some months, European Union (EU) leaders step forward with plans to enhance economic policy coordination and establish a permanent crisis resolution mechanism for the euro area, as financial market fears continue to mount.

Before it comes to this cliffhanger, this book explores the governance of the euro area from the launch of the euro in 1999 to the sovereign debt crisis that struck in 2010. Its point of departure is that Economic and Monetary Union (EMU) represents a radical departure from the EU's traditional modus operandi, the Community method. Under the Community method, as the old adage goes, the Commission proposes and the Council disposes. Under EMU, in contrast, the Commission patrols and the Council cajoles when it comes to economic policy coordination, while the European Central Bank (ECB) controls monetary policy.

What follows is an attempt to understand how EMU has fared in the absence of the Community method and what this means for three overarching debates about the governance of the euro area and the EU more generally. The first of these debates concerns the sustainability of the single currency without a more centralized approach to economic policy. The second one sees

EMU as a trial run for new modes of policymaking in other areas of EU decision-making. The final strand of debate is interested in the euro area's ability to exert influence in the international arena and what this means for the EU's ambitions to be a global actor.

The book's point of arrival, so to speak, is that the euro area's experimental approach to economic governance has yielded some rather surprising results. Efforts at economic policy coordination in the euro area, it finds, have fallen short, but not necessarily because of EMU's decentralized approach to economic policy. Informal dialogue between euro area finance ministers, for example, functioned fairly well until the Eurogroup's working methods were gradually formalized, bringing its fixed-term president into conflict with the ECB and into competition with the European Council. The stability and growth pact, likewise, suffered not only from a lack of enforcement at the EU level but also problems of compliance at the member state level as a result of deficiencies in national budgetary institutions.

A surprising element of euro area governance for students of EU policymaking is the ECB's evolution as a political actor. The Bank's reluctance to embrace European integration when it perceives a threat to price stability, in particular, is at odds with standard assumptions about EU institutions' commitment to ever closer union. EMU also reveals the scope and limits of so-called new governance, with the Broad Economic Policy Guidelines (BEPGs) showing value-added as an overarching instrument of coordination, but failing to bite as an instrument of peer pressure. That this failure was due, in part, to the BEPGs' lack of legitimacy in national political arenas comes as a blow to those who hoped that new governance, with its sensitivity to member states' sovereignty over economic policy, would circumvent such problems.

The global financial crisis may have laid bare the limitations of economic policy under EMU but it also showed EU member states' surprising capacity for collective action in international financial institutions and fora. The landmark leaders' summits of the Group of 20 in 2008 and 2009 were a high point in this regard, arising as they did from the EU's efforts to encourage an international response to the financial crisis. The first decade of EMU also witnessed a proliferation of informal, bilateral dialogues on macroeconomic policy between the EU and third countries. These dialogues have, for the most part, delivered little more than information exchange between EU officials and their counterparts. An exception is the euro area's concerted efforts to promote greater flexibility in the euro/renminbi exchange rate, which have demonstrated member states' ability to speak with one voice, even if Chinese authorities have been reluctant to listen.

None of these findings suggest that the crisis confronting the euro area is anything other than an existential one. They do challenge claims, however, that EMU's ills are due alone to its decentralized approach to decision-making and the corollary that EMU's cure lies in the centralization of economic policy in the euro area. Be this conclusion right or wrong, EU member states seem in no mood to countenance the Community method in response to the global financial crisis. It remains to be seen what form a permanent crisis resolution mechanism will take and whether it will be approved, but the ideas for enhancing economic policy coordination put forward in late 2010 look set to extend rather than end the euro area's experimental approach to economic governance.

Acknowledgements

It took months to write this book but more than a decade spent thinking and writing about the euro. Along the way, I have learned a great deal from talented teachers and communautaire colleagues. Those to whom I am most indebted include Brian Ardy, Marco Buti, Daniel Daco, Servaas Deroose, Eric de Souza, Bob Hancké, Joost Kuhlmann, Hartmut Lehmann, Joni Lovenduski, Deborah Mabbett, Ivo Maes, Imelda Maher, David Mayes, Nigel Nagarajan, Klaus Regling, Jim Rollo, Waltraud Schelkle, David Soskice, and David Styan. Iain Begg has been a major influence over the years and deserves particular thanks. Helen Wallace provided a great deal of intellectual inspiration for this book, for which I am truly grateful.

Any errors in this book are mine alone, but some of its more interesting ideas were inspired by colleagues who commented on draft papers at various stages in various venues. Thanks, in particular, to Kenneth Armstrong, Stijn Billiet, Patrick Crowley, Mark Pollack, Imelda Maher, David Mayes, Manuela Moschella, Manuel Palazuelos-Martinez, Uwe Puetter, Lucia Quaglia, Zbigniew Truchlewski, Richard Washington, and two anonymous referees. My students at Birkbeck and the College of Europe also helped to think through many of my half-formed thoughts on Economic and Monetary Union.

Three institutions made a big difference to the writing of this book. The first is the British Academy, which covered the costs of fieldwork in Brussels and Beijing to learn about new forms of economic diplomacy (Award Number: SG: 52237). The second is Birkbeck College, which made possible a visit to Washington, DC, to conduct interviews at the International Monetary Fund and granted research leave to complete this manuscript. The third is Oxford University Press, which offered encouragement, flexibility, and a first-rate editor, Dominic Byatt.

Many people provided moral support during the writing of this book. Those who struck the right balance between asking how it was going and not asking when it would be finished include Aidan, Carron, Paula, Gay, Deirdre, Simon, Andrea, John, Eddie, Val, Orit, Motti, Glynnis, Kate, Rob, Kim, and Angela. Mark provided operational support for trips to Beijing and Washington, DC. My parents, Kevin and Noreen, offered an invaluable hotline to the unfolding financial crisis in Dublin.

Acknowledgements

This book is dedicated to my wife, Emma, without whom I might not have begun writing, and my son, William, without whom I would not have finished.

Dermot Hodson
London
December 2010

Contents

List of Figures

List of Tables

1

Introduction: New Adventures in EU Policymaking

Though this be madness, yet there is method in't.
William Shakespeare

Few areas of European Union (EU) policymaking have come to embody European integration more closely than Economic and Monetary Union (EMU). The euro, which was launched in January 1999, has variously been described by the heads of state or government that had a hand in its creation as 'the process by which European integration became irreversible' (Kohl 2002: 11), 'one of the three pillars of the new monetary order' (Mitterrand 1988), and 'a Federal Europe by the back door' (Thatcher 1990). Amid such hopes and fears, it is easy to forget that the euro is an instance of EU policymaking that is far from typical, departing as it does from the so-called Community method.

This book explores how EMU has fared in the absence of the Community method from the launch of the euro in 1999 to the onset of the euro area's sovereign debt crisis in 2010. In so doing, it brings evidence to bear on three key questions in contemporary debates about the governance of the euro area in particular and the EU in general: Is the single currency sustainable in the absence of a more centralized approach to economic policy? What conclusions can be drawn from EMU about the search for alternatives to the Community method? What lessons can be learned from the euro area's external relations for the EU's ambitions to be a global actor in its own right?

Before getting down to business, it is important to make clear what the Community method is and how EMU differs from it. There is no commonly agreed definition, but the best known one is found in the European Commission's White Paper on European Governance (Commission 2001*a*: 8). According to this definition, the Commission's primary role in the Community method is to propose policy and legislation and to represent the EU in international negotiations. The Council of Ministers and the European Parliament, meanwhile, adopt legislative and budgetary acts, with decisions by the former typically based on a qualified majority vote. Responsibility for policy execution, finally, falls to either the Commission or national authorities, with the Court of Justice tasked with upholding the rule of EU law throughout.

Scholarship on the Community method puts stress on different aspects of this definition. Scharpf (1988, 2006) concentrates on decision-making within the Council and warns that the Community method will preserve the status quo because of the difficulties of reaching agreement on reform among member states with diverse preferences. Majone (2005, 2009) emphasizes the Commission's agenda-setting powers, noting its monopoly over decisions about when the EU should act and what legal form that action should take. Scott and Trubek (2002: 2) highlight the hard-law character of the Community method, with its tendency 'to produce binding legislation and executive acts at the EU level, and for these to impose more or less uniform rules for all Member States'.

Perhaps the most commonly cited example of the Community method in action is the original common agricultural policy (CAP). In a pioneering study of the CAP's creation, Lindberg (1965: 62) used the term 'Community method' to describe the 'hard bargaining and horse trading' among agricultural ministers over the negotiation of approximately 300 binding and uniformly applicable regulations. The Commission, Lindberg argued, played a decisive role in these negotiations by using its right of initiative to recommend a final settlement that was acceptable to member states and appealing to key agricultural interest groups.[1]

External trade is perhaps the best example of the Community method in action today (Wallace 2010: 94). The Commission alone can recommend that the EU open negotiations on trade agreements with third countries or international organizations (Article 207 Treaty on the Functioning of the European Union [TFEU]). If the Council agrees, then it falls to the EU executive to conduct negotiations on behalf of the Union in close consultation with the national officials who make up the trade policy committee (ex Article 133 committee). The Council retains the final say over the adoption of any agreement resulting from these talks, subject, in most cases, to the consent of the European Parliament.

Policymaking under EMU is based not on a single style of decision-making but on new modes of EU policymaking that differ in varying ways from the

[1] More recent scholarship on the CAP questions whether the Community method still applies in this area given, *inter alia*, the entrenched role of agricultural interest groups (Roederer-Rynning 2010).

Community method. In their discussion of new modes of EU policymaking, Scott and Trubek (2002) distinguish between 'new old governance' and 'new governance'. The first of these labels applies to cases that 'show elements of continuity with the Community method' (Scott and Trubek 2002: 2). The second applies to approaches that rely on some or all of the following working methods: (*a*) novel approaches to participation and power-sharing between governmental and non-governmental actors; (*b*) coordination and dialogue between actors at different tiers of government; (*c*) diverse and decentralized policy solutions; (*d*) a deliberative approach to problem solving; (*e*) the use of flexible and revisable guidelines that are closer to soft than to hard law; and (*f*) experimentation and knowledge creation through benchmarking and multilateral surveillance (Scott and Trubek 2002: 5–6).

Monetary policy under EMU comes closest to new old governance. Like the Community method, it involves the delegation of policymaking powers to a supranational institution with the right to formulate opinions, deliver recommendations, and make regulations on certain policies that fall within its sphere of competence (Article 127 TFEU). Unlike the Community method, it entails the creation of a new supranational institution, the European Central Bank (ECB), which has the first and final say over the definition and implementation of monetary policy (Article 127 TFEU). The Council has no say in monetary matters, although it does share responsibility for exchange rate policy with the ECB (Article 219 TFEU). The Parliament plays an even less conspicuous role, being permitted to do little more than invite senior ECB officials to appear before the legislature's Committee for Economic and Monetary Affairs. In keeping with the Community method, the Court of Justice is responsible for ensuring the rule of law in relation to the Bank's activities. In this context, the ECB can litigate and be litigated against before the Court (Protocol 4 Article 35 TFEU).

Economic policy under EMU, in contrast, relies on a distinctly decentralized approach to decision-making that shares most of the characteristics of new governance. Member states are ultimately responsible for the formulation and implementation of their economic policies, although they have agreed to coordinate these policies via the broad economic policy guidelines (BEPGs) and the stability and growth pact. The BEPGs are a set of soft law guidelines on the economic policies of member states and the EU that are designed to encourage benchmarking and the exchange of best practice (Article 121 TFEU). They include a set of country-specific recommendations on macroeconomic and microeconomic policies that take account of the diversity of member states' economic circumstances and characteristics. Countries that breach the BEPGs or otherwise jeopardize the smooth functioning of EMU face no more than peer pressure in the form of non-binding recommendations. The stability and growth pact reinforces the treaty's prohibition on budget deficits in excess of 3 per cent of GDP (Article 126 TFEU) and encourages member states to pursue country-specific objectives for borrowing over the medium term. Member states that break these limits face non-binding recommendations for the most part, although financial penalties and fines can be employed in extremis.

The Commission plays a curtailed role in relation to policy coordination under EMU. Its primary responsibilities are to monitor member states' economic policies, draw up the first draft of the BEPGs, and sound the alarm when member states violate the BEPGs or the stability and growth pact. The Commission alone can propose disciplinary measures against errant member states but the decision to issue recommendations or impose financial penalties and fines is formally taken by the Economic and Financial Affairs Council (Ecofin). In practice, Ecofin's role is overshadowed by the Eurogroup, an informal body of finance ministers that fosters deliberation over shared policy challenges and dialogue with the ECB over the monetary and fiscal policy mix. Given the soft law character of such coordination, there are, likewise, limited opportunities for the Court of Justice to intervene in this policy process. The Parliament is informed of key decisions taken in relation to the BEPGs and the stability and growth pact, but this has traditionally been a pro forma exercise. The Lisbon Treaty leaves the door ajar for a more active role by the Parliament by making decisions relating to regulations governing the conduct of multilateral surveillance subject to the ordinary legislative procedure (Article 121 TFEU).

The external dimension of EMU, finally, lies somewhere between new old governance and new governance. The ECB can participate in international monetary institutions and is responsible for representing the euro area on matters of international cooperation that relate to monetary policy (Article 6, Protocol 4 TFEU). Without prejudice to this provision, euro area finance ministers can vote by qualified majority to establish a unified representation in international financial institutions and conferences (Article 138 TFEU). That this decision is taken on the basis of a proposal from the Commission gives the EU executive agenda-setting powers on international issues but it cannot count on speaking on behalf of the euro area. The Treaty leaves open the question of who will represent the euro area in international financial institutions and conferences and what form a unified representation will take.

Having defined the Community method and explained how EMU differs from it, the remainder of this chapter sets the scene for the subsequent discussion. The first section provides some historical context by asking why EMU's architects were so adverse to the Community method. The second provides economic and political context by showing why the euro area's experimental approach to governance matters for contemporary debates about EMU and the EU more generally. The final section introduces the book's approach and gives a brief overview of its central arguments.

1.1 EMU and the Community method

This book is about the consequences rather than the causes of EMU's unorthodox approach to economic governance. This is neither the place, therefore, for a history of EMU's creation (see Dyson and Featherstone 1999) nor a review of the extensive literature on the economic and political dynamics that led to the launch of the single currency (see Sadeh and Verdun 2008). A little historical context is necessary, however, to make sense of what follows. To this end, this section considers some (but not all) of the reasons why the Community method did not feature more prominently when it came to designing the institutions and instruments of euro area governance.

The decision to delegate euro area monetary policy to the ECB rather than the Commission, it would seem, owes much to the institutional influence of national central banks. A sometimes forgotten fact is that the Rome Treaty gave the Commission a right of initiative in relation to (some aspects of) monetary policy. It called, in particular, on the Commission to submit recommendations to the Council to promote collaboration between central banks on matters related to the balance of payments (Article 105 Treaty establishing the European Economic Community (EEC)). The Commission wasted little time in making use of this provision, with (unsuccessful) plans for a European Reserve Fund in November 1958 and the Marjolin memorandum on monetary union in October 1962 among the earliest examples in this regard (Maes 2006).

By the time that member states were ready to have a serious discussion about EMU, the Commission had effectively ceded its right of initiative on monetary policy to national central banks (Maes 2006). Cooperation between EEC central bank governors, which had taken place on an informal basis since January 1958, was formalized in May 1964 with the creation of the Committee of Governors of the Central Banks of EEC member states. Though the Committee of Governors, as it was known, was created at the request of the Commission, national central bank representatives succeeded in keeping the EU executive at arm's length by gathering not in Brussels but in the margins of the Bank for International Settlements in Basel and excluding the Commission's observer from certain discussions (Andrews 2003).

The Committee of Governors played a key role in the preparation of the Werner Report, a plan for EMU prepared by the Luxembourg Prime Minister, Pierre Werner, following a request by EEC leaders at the Hague Summit in December 1969. That national central bankers used their influence to protect their bureaucratic position is suggested by the Werner Report's call to delegate control over credit and liquidity policy not to the Commission but to a European Monetary Fund (Werner 1970). The latter, it concluded, would be led by national central bank governors, in effect upgrading the Committee of Governors to the status of an EEC institution.

The Werner Plan was abandoned amid the economic and financial turmoil that followed the collapse of the original Bretton Woods system in 1971 and the oil crisis of 1973, but the Committee of Governors remained in the ascendancy on monetary matters. Having played a key role following the launch of the European Monetary System in 1979 (Andrews 2003: 959), national central bank governors were invited in 1988 to draw up fresh plans for EMU under the chairmanship of Commission President Jacques Delors. Scholars are divided on how much sway Delors held in this group (see Moravcsik 1998: 436; Dyson and Featherstone 1999: 706–20), but central bankers' influence is plain to see in the report's call to create an independent European System of Central Banks, to be comprised of a central monetary authority and national central banks.

The Maastricht Treaty, which entered into force in November 1993, stuck closely to the Delors Report's vision of monetary policy, with the Committee of Governors effectively drawing up the legal statutes of the ECB in the Intergovernmental Conference (IGC) on EMU (Dyson and Featherstone 1999: 386). Holding its last meeting in December 1993, the Committee of Governors was absorbed into the Council of the European Monetary Institute in January 1994, which in turn was transformed into the Governing Council of the ECB in May 1998. The last of these bodies took charge of euro area monetary policy in January 1999, thus cementing the role of national central banks in EMU's governance architecture.

Of the many reasons that have been offered to explain the decentralization of macroeconomic policies under EMU, national interests are probably the hardest to ignore. For Moravcsik (1998), Germany's interests were paramount in shaping EMU's institutional design because the EU's most populace member state had most to lose from giving up a currency with an unparalleled track record of price stability. For this reason, Moravcsik argues, German authorities were in a position to demand concessions in both the Delors Report and the IGC on EMU. Top of Germany's wish list was the desire to secure a credible commitment to anti-inflationary policies, which explains the very high degree of autonomy granted to the ECB. Next on the list was a set of institutional conditions to reinforce the stability of the single currency, including binding limits on government borrowing, prohibitions on EU financing of member state debt, and an approach to macroeconomic policy coordination that remained limited in scope and on a strictly intergovernmental footing.

The Delors Report delivered for Germany. EMU, it insisted, would 'require a degree of autonomy in economic decision-making to remain with individual member countries and a balance to be struck between national and

Community competences' (Committee for the Study of Economic and Monetary Union 1989: 17). Though it remained vague on precisely what this balance should be, the Delors Report sketched the broad contours of what would become EMU's approach to policy coordination, calling for binding rules on government borrowing and measures to allow the Council of Ministers to 'determine the broad lines of economic policy, while [accepting that] the implementation would be left to the national governments and the Commission in their respective areas of competence' (Committee for the Study of Economic and Monetary Union 1989: 27).

There was little appetite in the IGC on EMU for extending the Commission's right of initiative in relation to economic policy, but there were competing visions of the Council of Minister's role in policy coordination (Moravcsik 1998: 44). France envisaged an activist Ecofin working with the European Council to set broad guidelines for economic, monetary, and exchange rate policies and represent EMU on the world stage (Howarth 2007). These plans, Pisani-Ferry (2006) acknowledges, were a fairly transparent ploy to put in place political oversight of the ECB from a country that had reluctantly accepted the principle of central bank independence as the price to be paid for securing a single currency. Germany's plans for policy coordination under EMU were altogether more modest, calling for Ecofin to issue non-binding orientations on economic policy (Dyson and Featherstone 1999: 411).

In the end, the Maastricht Treaty's provisions on policy coordination offered concessions to both sides (Pisani-Ferry 2006). Germany protected its red lines on public finances by securing prohibitions on excessive budget deficits (Article 126 TFEU) bolstered by a no-bail out clause to prevent the EU or another member state from being liable for or assuming the commitments of national, regional, or local governments (Article 125 TFEU). France secured nothing like the gouvernement économique that it had sought, but the Treaty offered a token in the form of the non-binding BEPGs (Article 121 TFEU). The Treaty, finally, split the difference on the external dimension of EMU by allowing the Council to establish a unified representation in international financial institutions and fora without making concrete plans to do so (Article 138 TFEU).

Subsequent modifications to EMU's system of economic governance followed a similar pattern. The stability and growth pact started life as a set of proposals by the German Finance Minister Theo Waigel for making automatic the sanctions foreseen under the excessive deficit procedure. Though this attempt to curtail Ecofin's discretion over the enforcement of the stability and growth pact failed, the final agreement went some way towards speeding up and clarifying the excessive deficit procedure (Heipertz and Verdun 2010: 5). The launch of the Eurogroup in December 1997, likewise, stemmed from French Prime Minister Lionel Jospin's determination to revive the idea of gouvernement économique. That this body was built on informal working methods was a concession to Germany, which saw closer coordination between euro area finance ministers as a potential threat to the independence of the ECB (Puetter 2006).

A final factor to bear in mind is that EMU's creation coincided with a crisis in the Community method. This crisis, as Majone (2009: 35) puts it, refers to a situation in which the 'permissive consensus' over European integration gave way to 'a revolt of the masses'. Signs of this shift are plentiful, with the five referenda in the space of sixteen years in which voters have rejected proposed treaty changes and the secular decline in turnout since direct elections to the European Parliament were introduced in 1979 among the most striking examples.

The cure for this crisis is harder to identify than its symptoms. In its White Paper on European Governance, the Commission argued that reinvigorating the Community method, *inter alia*, by extending the European Parliament's legislative powers, strengthening the Commission's executive role, and clarifying the Community's competences, was essential to address 'the widening gulf between the European Union and the people it serves' (Commission 2001*a*: 7). Majone (2009: 31), in contrast, sees the EU's traditional modus operandi as part of the problem, criticizing the Community method for breaching the fundamental principles of parliamentary democracy and the separation of powers by giving the Commission 'a monopoly of legislative initiative... considerable executive powers and quasi-judicial responsibilities'.

EU leaders responded to the issues raised in the White Paper on European Governance by establishing a Convention on the Future of Europe to prepare a first draft of a Constitutional Treaty. Hopes of a short constitutional settlement gave way to a long constitutional stalemate after first French and then Dutch voters rejected the proposed treaty changes in mid-2005 (Wallace et al. 2010: 496). The decision to cut and paste all but the most controversial aspects of the Constitutional Treaty into the Lisbon Treaty served only to highlight the gulf between the EU and its leaders, as did the fact that the Treaty was ratified only after a second referendum in Ireland and controversial last-minute concessions to Poland and the Czech Republic. In spite of all this fuss, large swathes of EU policymaking remain unchanged under the Lisbon Treaty (Wallace et al. 2010: 496). Though it extends the Commission's right of initiative and the European Parliament's legislative powers in some areas (e.g. police cooperation and judicial cooperation in criminal matters) and changes the EU's institutional architecture in others (e.g. by creating the post of full-time President of the European Council), the Community method remains as it was in most cases.

Against this backdrop, it is hardly surprising that EU leaders were reluctant to push for a further transfer of powers over economic policy during

EMU's first decade. Although the European Council raised expectations at Laeken by inviting the Convention on the Future of Europe to consider ways to strengthen economic policy coordination (Council of the European Union 2001*a*), neither the drafters of the Constitutional Treaty nor those of the Lisbon Treaty were prepared to propose major changes to policymaking in the euro area (see Puetter 2007). Such was member states' reluctance to consider treaty changes at the outset of the global financial crisis, indeed, that EU leaders invited the González Group in December 2007 to put forward ideas on 'strengthening and modernizing' the European economy under the proviso that such measures should be 'within the framework set out in the Lisbon Treaty' (Council of the European Union 2007*a*).

Viewed from this vantage point, EMU's experimental approach to economic governance is sometimes seen as a pragmatic choice by policymakers forced to work within the legal provisions established, in essence, by the Maastricht Treaty. For Buti et al. (2003: 101), the decentralized approach of the stability and growth pact reflects member states' limited taste for political integration in this particular domain. McNamara and Meunier (2002: 868) apply a similar logic to EMU's external representation, suggesting that member states' reluctance to create a single chair in international organizations reflects 'the contradictory pulls of international power and national sovereignty'. Cohen (2008*a*: 52) puts the same point more forcefully when he argues that the euro area's fragmented system of external representation is symptomatic of the fact that 'after a decade of living with the euro national identity still trumps collective interest'.

1.2 The wider context

This book is interested in euro area governance not for its own sake but for the evidence that it brings to bear on three debates about policymaking in the euro area and the EU. The first of these debates concerns the sustainability of the single currency without a more centralized approach to economic policy. Arguments for greater centralization in the macroeconomic sphere point to the risk of cross-country spillover from excessive deficits (Buti et al. 2001) and unsustainable debt (Beetsma and Uhlig 1999) if euro area members are left to their own devices. Arguments against echo the theory of optimum currency areas by emphasizing the need for a more active use of national fiscal policies in the face of asymmetric shocks (HM Treasury 2003) and warn of the risks to price stability if coordination between finance ministers results in political pressure on the ECB to loosen monetary policy (Beetsma and Bovenberg 1995). The case for supply-side coordination underlines the added importance for euro area members of financial market integration and, where adjustment to asymmetric shocks is a problem, product and labour market reforms (Bean 1998). The case against insists that member states adjust to shocks in different ways and warns of the dangers of imposing one-size-fits-all reforms on heterogeneous product and labour markets (Tabellini and Wyplosz 2006).

Viewed from this perspective, economic policymaking under EMU seeks to strike a balance between the pros and cons of policy coordination. The stability and growth pact, for example, imposes uniform limits on short-term government borrowing as well as country-specific medium-term budgetary objectives. The logic of the pact is that member states meeting their medium-term objectives can, in principle, allow budgetary stabilizers to take effect in a typical economic downturn without running up excessive deficits that could endanger economic stability in the rest of the euro area (Artis and Buti 2000). The informal working methods of the Eurogroup, likewise, can be seen as an attempt to foster a dialogue between finance ministers and the ECB without jeopardizing the autonomy of the former or the independence of the latter. The BEPGs, meanwhile, encourage structural reforms for the smooth functioning of EMU while leaving member states to tailor reforms to the specificities of national product and labour markets (Deroose et al. 2008).

EMU's arrangements for policy coordination met with a steady stream of disapproval from economists during EMU's first decade. The stability and growth pact was criticized by some for being too restrictive vis-à-vis fiscal stabilization (Calmfors 2003) and by others for being too lax from the point of view of fiscal discipline (Wyplosz 2005), with one of the few points of consensus among such commentators being that the reforms to the pact agreed in March 2005 did not help matters much. The EU's efforts at supply-side coordination were also controversial. The pace of structural reforms after the introduction of the euro was too slow for many economists, with some interpreting the persistence of cross-country growth and inflation differences in the years that followed as a sign that member states were not adjusting to asymmetric shocks (Honohan and Lane 2003). For others, the BEPGs went too far by encouraging reforms that were ill-suited to the institutional complementarities inherent in national economic models (Amable 2009).

Without doubt, the biggest test to date of EMU's approach to policy coordination has been the global financial crisis and its after-effects. On occasion, euro area members' capacity for cooperation during the worst banking crisis to hit Europe since the 1930s and the steepest recession in recent memory has exceeded expectations. A high point in this regard was the coordinated bank rescue plan agreed by euro area heads of state or government in October 2008, which pledged €2 trillion to recapitalize and, if necessary, take shares in European banks (Quaglia 2009*a*). At others times, economists' predictions of a collective action problem at the heart of EMU seem to have been borne out. The worst news came from member states on the geographic periphery of the euro area, with Spain, Greece, Ireland, and Portugal posting budget deficits in excess of 9 per cent of GDP in 2009 (Commission 2010*a*: 200).

Financial market concerns focused, in the first instance, on Greece, which found itself on the brink of sovereign default after its budget deficit for 2009 was revised from 3.7 to 15.4 per cent (Commission 2010*a*: 200). Fears that Greece would default on its debt and that the resulting fiscal crisis would spillover into highly indebted euro area members created considerable uncertainty in financial markets in late 2009 and early 2010. Matters were made worse by the long months of equivocation before euro area heads of state or government finally agreed, in May 2010, on a joint EU–International Monetary Fund (IMF) rescue package for Greece.

Hot on the heels of this decision came the launch of a joint EU–IMF initiative offering up to €720 billion in loans and credit guarantees for EU member states facing financial difficulties. The IMF agreed to contribute up to €220 billion to this package with €60 billion coming from a newly created European financial stabilization mechanism and the remaining €440 billion coming from a newly created European financial stability facility. Ireland was first to avail of these funds, opening talks with the EU and IMF in November 2010 after the burden of supporting its stricken banks became too much to bear. The result was a €85 billion financial support package, including €22.5 billion from the European financial stabilization mechanism and €17.7 billion from the European financial stability facility, with the rest funded through the IMF, bilateral loans from Denmark, Sweden, and the United Kingdom, and contributions from the Irish Treasury cash buffer and the country's National Pension Reserve Fund (Eurogroup and Ecofin Ministers 2010).

This sovereign debt crisis has yet to run its course and it remains to be seen how and, indeed, whether EMU will survive. In the short term, a key question is whether the crisis might provide an opportunity for a more centralized approach to economic policy in the euro area. EU leaders' decision to convene a taskforce under the leadership of the President of the European Council, Herman Van Rompuy, to consider 'all options to reinforce the legal framework' surrounding EU economic governance in March 2010 was closely watched for this reason (Heads of State or Government of the Euro Area 2010). The Commissioner for Economic and Monetary Affairs, Olli Rehn, fuelled speculation in June 2010 when he called for reforms to EMU's economic sphere that 'respect and reinforce the Community method' (Rehn 2010). Following the publication of the Van Rompuy Taskforce's final report in October 2010, EU leaders agreed to take forward legislative proposals for strengthening the stability and growth pact and other aspects of euro area governance by mid-2011 and to consider a limited change to the

Lisbon Treaty by mid-2013 so as to establish a permanent crisis resolution mechanism (Council of the European Union 2010*a*).

The euro area's experimental approach to economic governance is also of interest to EU scholars. The ECB is, as Pollack (2003: 392) puts it, 'the most spectacular example of supranational delegation in the European Union since the EEC Treaty of 1957'. In rational choice terms, EMU provides an opportunity to observe a supranational agent in its adolescence and to compare its emerging preferences with those of traditional agents, such as the Commission and the Court of Justice, as well as with those of its principals, the member states. The ECB is, as the same time, an example of the trend towards delegation to function-specific agencies in EU policymaking (Wallace 2010). The bank's very high degree of statutory independence, it is true, makes it different from bodies such as the European Agency for the Management of Operational Cooperation at the External Borders (FRONTEX), the European Food Safety Authority (EFSA), and the European Defence Agency (EDA), but it can still serve as a useful point of reference in comparative studies of EU agencies (Williams 2005).

EMU also occupies a privileged place in studies of new governance. The BEPGs are, as discussed in Hodson and Maher (2001), a forerunner to the open method of coordination, which was launched by the European Council at Lisbon in March 2000. At this meeting, EU leaders adopted the lofty goal of creating 'the most competitive and dynamic knowledge-based economy in the world, capable of sustainable economic growth with more and better jobs and greater social cohesion' (Council of the European Union 2000). Like the BEPGs, the open method involves the setting of overarching objectives for the EU as a whole, which are then translated into country-specific targets. Both instruments rely on benchmarking through qualitative and quantitative indicators and the exercise of peer pressure through non-binding recommendations. If the BEPGs can, by virtue of these similarities, shed light on the dynamics of new governance, then the same can be said of the Eurogroup. The creation of the latter, as Puetter (2006) argues, was a conscious attempt by finance ministers to escape the bias towards formal bargaining under the Community method in favour of an informal, deliberative working method. The evolution of the Eurogroup is thus of central importance for understanding how the deliberative ideal of new governance works in practice.

Last but not least, euro area governance is also relevant to wider debates about the EU's global role. A recurring theme in the International Political Economy (IPE) literature is the link between currencies and international power (Kirshner 1995; Andrews 2006). Whereas studies in this field once focused on sterling's fall from grace in the post-war period (Cohen 1971; Strange 1971), there has been growing attention in recent years to the rise of the euro and its implications for the dollar's pre-eminent international position (Cohen 1998; Zimmermann 2004). Economists see the rise and fall of international currencies as an essentially economic phenomenon. IPE scholars see a role for politics too. Helleiner (2008), for example, contrasts the conscious attempts by US policymakers to cultivate an international role for the dollar through the creation of the Federal Reserve System in 1913 with the benign neglect showed by Germany and Japan towards their respective currencies in the 1960s and 1970s.

Scholars who are sceptical about the euro's challenge to the dollar have been quick to point the finger at the euro area's decentralized approach to economic policy. Helleiner (2008), for one, highlights the absence of a unified fiscal authority as a stumbling block to the creation of a centralized and integrated financial market, which he views as a key requirement for a currency with international standing. Cohen (2008*a*: 50) also draws attention to the euro area's fragmented system of external representation, which he claims, at best 'compounds confusion about who is in charge' and at worst 'condemns the euro area to lasting second-class citizen status since it limits its ability to project power on monetary matters'. This argument, as Cohen acknowledges, echoes McNamara and Meunier (2002: 850), who question the euro area's influence in international monetary matters '[a]s long as no "single voice" has the political authority to speak on behalf of the euro area, as the US Secretary of Treasury does for the American currency'.

For Cohen (2008*b*), the rise of the euro is just one of several shifts taking place in the international distribution of monetary power. Another is the accumulation of global imbalances between countries with large and persistent current account deficits, most noticeably the United States, and those with sizeable current account surpluses, especially China and oil-exporting countries. Another still is the emergence of new international fora involving industrialized countries and rising powers such as Brazil, Russia, India, and China. A case in point is the Group of 20 (G20) leaders' summits, which assumed centre stage during the global financial crisis as the heads of state or government of industrialized and 'systemically significant economies' met in search of a coordinated response to the unfolding economic turmoil. How the euro area, with its fragmented system of external representation, has responded to these changes is essential for understanding EMU's place in this new economic order. It also speaks to wider debates about the EU's emergence as a global actor. That students of EU foreign policy have paid scant attention to the single currency is surprising given that the EU's 'geopolitical comparative advantage', as Moravcsik (2009) calls it, lies in civilian rather than military power, with economic influence abroad a key indicator of the former.

1.3 The approach and argument of this book

Scholars have always been struck by the shock of the new; the study of policymaking in the EU is no exception. Few concepts in this field have received more attention since the mid-1990s than new modes of EU policymaking and none are more contested. A recurring criticism of new governance, in particular, is that policy coordination without binding constraints is in danger of producing little more than cheap talk (Borrás and Greve 2004; Hix 2005; Pollack 2005). Another is that new governance fails to understand the 'institutional complexity of EU policy and law' (Chalmers and Lodge 2003: 17) and that it could do more harm than good to the traditional role of EU institutions (Hatzopoulos 2007). Even those who are sympathetic to the 'governance turn' in EU studies warn against treating new modes of policymaking 'as the magic solution to the EU's performance problem' (Kohler-Koch and Rittberger 2006: 37).

These criticisms notwithstanding, further investigation into new modes of policymaking is a matter of exigency for two reasons. Firstly, new modes of policymaking are an empirical reality that has left few areas of EU activity untouched. Fields as diverse as pension reforms (de la Porte and Nanz 2004), social inclusion policy (Armstrong 2010), occupational health and safety (Smismans 2008), civilian crisis management (Menon and Sedelmeier 2010), and fundamental rights (de Schutter 2004), for example, all have characteristics that are common to new governance. Secondly, the crisis in the Community method has hardly dissipated since it inspired scholars to think about new modes of policymaking in the mid-1990s. Majone (2009), indeed, argues that the crisis has intensified, *inter alia*, because of the stiff resistance encountered by the Commission in exercising its right of initiative in areas such as services liberalization, increased heterogeneity in socioeconomic conditions, and divergent policy preferences as a result of the EU's enlargement from fifteen to twenty-seven member states.

Another recurring criticism is that the study of new modes of EU policymaking is based on unsound methods. Hix (1998), for example, laments the tendency of new governance scholars to treat the EU as *sui generis* and EU decision-making as something that cannot be reduced to rational choice. This book responds to this line of criticism by putting euro area governance in comparative context where possible and by showing that new modes of policymaking can be studied from a variety of theoretical perspectives using insights from the study of EU politics, comparative political economy, and IPE.

Broadly speaking, this study situates EMU in its widest possible institutional context by linking policymaking in the euro area to national, EU, and global governance. Part I emphasizes the interplay between two institutions tailor-made for EMU, the ECB and the Eurogroup, and the EU's legal order. Part II considers the interaction between two key instruments of euro area governance, the stability and growth pact and the BEPGs, with the machinery of national policymaking. Part III explores European influence on the world stage, discussing the role played by the EU and the euro area in multilateral settings and in bilateral dialogues with third countries.

'The primary weakness of EU studies today, Moravcsik (1997) wrote, is not a lack of theoretical innovation. To the contrary, numerous sophisticated theoretical conjectures exist to explain most important aspects of integration. The primary weakness of EU studies is instead its unwillingness to subject theories to potential disconfirmation through rigorous empirical testing'. It is in the spirit of this statement that this book resists the temptation to build another theory of EMU in favour of a theory-testing approach that confronts specific hypotheses about euro area governance from the copious conceptual literature on this topic with fresh empirical evidence.

Chapter 2 looks at the ECB's evolution as a political actor from a rational choice institutionalist perspective. Presenting case studies of ECB policy on anti-fraud, Treaty changes, economic coordination, and financial supervision, it assesses claims that the Bank shares the same pro-integrationist tendencies as traditional EU institutions.

Chapter 3 explores the rise and fall of the Eurogroup as a deliberative body. Charting this forum's gradual formalization since 1998 and its declining effectiveness as a forum for macroeconomic policy coordination before and during the global financial crisis, it revisits competing theoretical claims about the informal working methods on which the Eurogroup was founded.

Chapter 4 offers a comparative political economy perspective on compliance with the stability and growth pact during EMU's first decade. Exploring data on electoral regimes and fiscal policy in euro area members, it challenges political institutionalist claims that EMU's fiscal rules provide a better institutional fit for countries that bind the governing coalition to fiscal contracts than those that rely on institutionally strong finance ministers to fulfil this role.

Chapter 5 draws on scholarship concerning the effectiveness of international sanctions to understand the BEPGs' limits as an instrument of peer pressure. It focuses, in particular, on the credibility of Ecofin and the Commission as sanctioning institutions, the precision of the sanctioning criteria underpinning the BEPGs, and the impact of EU peer pressure in domestic political arenas, using Article 121(4) recommendations against Ireland in February 2001 and Greece in May 2010 as case studies.

Chapter 6 revisits claims about the euro area's fragmented system of external relations in multilateral settings in the light of the global financial crisis. Focusing on the involvement of the EU and euro area in the G20 and the IMF Executive Board, it offers a case study of European influence during the most turbulent period for the international economic system since the Great Depression.

Chapter 7 assesses the influence of the EU and the euro area in bilateral settings. Drawing on the literature on international economic policy coordination and statecraft, it seeks to understand why the EU has initiated bilateral macroeconomic dialogues with some countries but not others. It also compares the euro area's efforts to encourage a reform of China's exchange rate policy to those of the United States.

Chapter 8 summarizes the key findings of the preceding chapters and considers their implications for contemporary debates about policymaking in the EU and the euro area. It concludes with an overview of the proposals for strengthening economic governance presented by both the Commission and the Van Rompuy Taskforce in late 2010 and considers whether the ideas contained within or the planned revision of the Lisbon Treaty could belatedly pave the way for the Community method under EMU.

Having mapped out where this discussion is headed, it is only fair to give some indication of where it will arrive in relation to the three questions posed at the beginning of this introductory chapter: Is the single currency sustainable in the absence of a more centralized approach to economic policy? What conclusions can be drawn from EMU about the search for alternatives to the Community method? What lessons can be drawn from the euro area's external relations for the EU's ambitions to be a global actor in its own right?

The (short) answer to the first question is that policy coordination in the euro area has yielded mixed results, but not necessarily because of EMU's decentralized approach to economic policy. Member states' patchy track record of compliance with the stability and growth pact, it is argued, is due not only to shortcomings in EU budgetary surveillance but also to serious deficiencies in national budgetary institutions. The Eurogroup, likewise, fell short as a forum for fostering an exchange of views between finance ministers and the ECB, but not because of its informal working methods. If anything, it was the gradual formalization of this body during EMU's first decade that undermined its dialogue by politicizing the relationship between the Presidents of the Eurogroup and ECB and fuelling bureaucratic tensions with the European Council. Overall, EMU's future may be clouded in uncertainty by the global financial crisis, but that of its decentralized approach to economic policy is not. For better or worse, the reforms to euro area governance envisaged by the Commission and the Van Rompuy Taskforce in the wake of the crisis are unlikely to strengthen the Community method to any great extent. The governance implications of possible changes to the Lisbon Treaty to establish a permanent crisis resolution mechanism, meanwhile, remain to be seen.

The answer to the second question is that EMU has demonstrated the scope and limits of new modes of policymaking in the EU. The ECB's opposition to initiatives for enhancing European integration in cases where it sees a threat to price stability jars with standard assumptions about what EU institutions want. An implication of this finding is that delegation to function-specific agencies may be one way for member states to ensure that they do not get 'more Europe' than they bargained for. The limits of new modes of policymaking in the EU are exemplified by the BEPGs, which showed some value-added as an overarching instrument of coordination but failed to bite as an instrument of peer pressure. This is because non-binding recommendations under Article 121(4) lacked credible sanctioning institutions, precise sanctioning criteria, and legitimacy in the domestic arena. This last point is a blow to new governance since it suggests that the EU's legitimacy is open to question irrespective of whether it has a significant policymaking role or not.

The answer to the third question is that the euro area and the EU exhibited an unexpected degree of influence on the international stage. Member states showed themselves to be capable of speaking with one voice in bilateral settings by establishing macroeconomic dialogues between the EU and a host of third countries. The Eurogroup, meanwhile, found its voice over China's controversial exchange rate policies and sent a high-level mission to Beijing in November 2007 for the first in a series of talks with Chinese leaders. The EU also showed a capacity for collective action in multilateral settings, with member states working closely together at the G20 leaders' summits at the height of the global financial crisis. In the IMF, EU member states exerted collective influence on the terms of the financial assistance provided to Hungary, Latvia, and Romania during the global financial crisis. EU member states were, it is true, initially divided over the IMF's role in the financial rescue of Greece but this was due to differences between member states rather than a lack of coordination between European representatives at the Fund.

Part I
New Institutions

2

The ECB as a Reluctant EU Institution

We are with Europe but not of Europe.
We are associated but not compromised.

Winston Churchill

The European Central Bank (ECB) is an integral part of Economic and Monetary Union's (EMU) experimental approach to economic governance. One of only two institutions tailor-made for the euro area – the Eurogroup, the focus of Chapter 3, being the other one – the Bank enjoys exclusive competence over monetary policy (Article 3 Treaty on the Functioning of the European Union [TFEU]) and is responsible for, among other things, conducting exchange rate operations, holding foreign exchange reserves, promoting the smooth operation of payment systems, and contributing towards member states' efforts to secure financial stability (Article 127 TFEU).

A great deal has been written about what kind of central bank the ECB is, with the consensus being that it enjoys a higher degree of statutory independence and attaches more weight to the pursuit of price stability than most other monetary authorities (Canzoneri et al. 1992; De Haan et al. 2005; Quaglia 2008). Opinion is divided on what this means for EMU with some warning of a lack of accountability, openness, and transparency in euro area monetary policy (Buiter 1999) and others arguing that the ECB should be judged chiefly on its ability to deliver price stability (Issing 1999).

Much less has been written about what kind of European Union (EU) institution the ECB is. A number of scholars conceptualize the ECB in rational choice institutionalist terms as an agent that takes charge of monetary policy on behalf of a collective principal, the member states (Campanella 2000; Elgie 2002; Howarth and Loedel 2005). For Pollack (2003: 392), the ECB 'is without doubt the most spectacular example of delegation in the European Union since the EEC Treaty of 1957'. The eight-year nonrenewable term of office served by members of the ECB Executive Board – Commissioners serve five-year renewable terms compared with six years for Judges and Advocates General of the Court of Justice – gives the Bank, he argues, a 'remarkable' degree of independence compared to other EU institutions (Pollack 2003: 393).

Although the tendency of supranational institutions to favour a more pro-European agenda than member states is central to rational choice institutionalist accounts of EU policymaking, scholars working in this tradition have largely overlooked the ECB's preference for European integration. An exception to this rule is Heisenberg and Richmond (2002). Based on a review of EMU's first two years, the authors conclude that the ECB's preferences for European integration are stronger than those of the member states on several key issues, including the need for EU involvement in financial supervision and fiscal coordination. In spite of this fact, Heisenberg and Richmond cast doubt on the ECB's capacity for agency in these areas, in part because the Treaty allows limited scope for a further transfer of competences in the domain of economic policy.

This chapter seeks to bring more evidence to bear on this debate through a review of the ECB's evolution as a political actor since the launch of the euro. Its central argument is that the ECB has proved to be a reluctant EU institution that has, in many cases, resisted attempts to enhance the Community dimension of EMU. The reason for this reticence, it is argued, is that the Bank's preference for 'more Europe' is contingent on its overriding commitment to price stability. Bureaucratic politics between the ECB and national central banks (NCBs) may also have played a role. This conclusion challenges the idea that supranational institutions are hardwired to support the European project and raises questions about whether this tendency is unique to the ECB.

The remainder of this chapter is divided into four sections. The first reviews Pollack's argument concerning what EU institutions want and considers reasons why the ECB might be different in this respect. The second section presents a series of short case studies that examine the ECB's preferences for further integration in a variety of contexts. The third section discusses the implications of these findings for scholarship on the ECB. The final section concludes with some thoughts on what this might mean for wider debates about what supranational agents want.

2.1 What the ECB wants

A hypothesis at the heart of Pollack's seminal work, *Engines of European Integration*, is that EU institutions prefer 'more Europe'. By this he means that EU institutions can be 'characterized by a common preference for greater competences for themselves and for the European Union as a whole, including both the liberalization of the European internal market *and* the re-imposition of social regulations from the European level, and that these organizations represent their preferences consistently vis-à-vis other actors despite the presence of internal conflicts within each organization' (Pollack 2003: 39).

Drawing on the literature on policymaking in the EU and the United States, Pollack (2003: 36) considers a number of reasons as to why supranational institutions might be positively disposed towards European integration. Firstly, it is assumed that the Commission is a competence maximizer, which, like other bureaucratic actors, will support schemes that enhance its power and influence. Secondly, there may be an element of self-selection in the recruitment procedures for supranational institutions, with individuals who support European integration more likely to participate in open competitions. Thirdly, the socialization effects of working for EU institutions and living in Brussels or Luxembourg could produce a convergence in views in favour of arguments supporting 'more Europe'.

There are a number of reasons why the ECB might not mimic the pro-integrationism of other EU institutions. In the first place, the ECB has a much narrower mandate than its supranational siblings (Williams 2005). Under the Treaty, the Commission's overarching aim is to promote 'the general interest of the Union' (Article 17 Treaty on European Union (TEU)) while the Court of Justice is required to 'ensure that in the interpretation and application of the Treaties the law is observed' (Article 19 TEU). The ECB, in contrast, is required to maintain price stability and without prejudice to this goal to support the general economic policies in the Union (Article 207 TFEU). The phrase 'without prejudice' is crucial here as it establishes a lexicographic ordering between the Bank's objectives, meaning that support for general economic policies is not permissible unless price stability is first secured (Driffill and Zeno 2004).

The precision of the ECB's price stability mandate, as Heisenberg and Richmond (2002: 204) recognize, makes it harder for the ECB to justify a competence-maximizing strategy, particularly when steps towards further integration cannot be easily reconciled with the pursuit of price stability. Even though the ECB is free to choose its own definition of price stability, financial markets will be quick to punish policies that fuel inflation. In this sense, the ECB may enjoy a higher degree of independence than other EU institutions, but the Bank has more to lose if it is seen to exploit such independence for its own ends.

Another reason why the ECB might be circumspect about the need for 'more Europe' is that it is unlikely to be subject to the same self-selection and socialization effects as other EU institutions. To the extent that the former matters, the ECB's practice of recruiting economists with PhDs from leading universities in Europe and the United States means that a shared belief in economic precepts rather than a commitment to ever closer union is more likely to bind its staff together. This trend could be compounded by the fact that all members of the ECB's Executive Board and almost all members of its senior management have a background in national central banking. Insofar as socialization effects count, the fact that the ECB is headquartered in Frankfurt reduces the frequency of contact between its officials and their counterparts in Brussels or Luxembourg.

The ECB's comparatively decentralized governance structure is another reason to expect its preferences for European integration to differ from those of other EU institutions. Whereas the College of Commissioners, the highest body in the EU executive, is bound to act in the general interests of the Community (Article 245 TFEU), no such obligation applies to the six members of the ECB Executive Board, who are in charge of the day-to-day running of the Bank. Responsibility for, *inter alia,* formulating monetary policy and executing the ECB's advisory role falls to the Governing Council, which includes not only the members of the Executive Board but also, as discussed in Chapter 1, the NCB governors of euro area members. This advisory role is significant for matters relating to European integration because it is the primary means through which the ECB adopts opinions on matters relating to 'European cooperation', including treaty changes. Since decisions in the Governing Council are based on a simple majority vote and taken on a one-person-one-vote basis, this means that the collective weight of NCB governors significantly outweighs that of ECB Executive Board members.

Although the NCB governors cannot channel the views of their government – they are subject to the same prohibition on seeking or taking instructions from third parties as ECB Executive Board members (Article 130 TFEU) – they would not necessarily be expected to pursue a pro-integrationist agenda. For one thing, NCBs in some member states retain significant policymaking powers in certain areas (e.g. financial supervision) and so have a vested interest in preserving national competences. Furthermore, the fact that NCBs are embedded within, what Snyder (1999: 76) refers to as, 'different national political systems and political cultures' means that attitudes towards European integration in the Governing Council are unlikely to be uniform.

2.2 The ECB and European integration

Wim Duisenberg (2002*a*), the first President of the ECB, described the euro as 'tangible proof... of the vision and ambition of the founding fathers of the European integration process, which continues to bring the people of Europe closer together by fostering economic integration'. Jean-Claude Trichet (2003), who succeeded Duisenberg in November 2003, has been equally effusive in his praise for European integration, arguing that the euro is 'a strong symbol of Europe... [that] makes the world "identify" Europe and helps Europeans to identify with Europe'. While public statements such as these, and there are many to choose from, are suggestive of support for European integration in general, the ECB has been less enthusiastic about specific plans for strengthening the Community dimension of EMU. This section looks at four episodes in the ECB's evolution as a political actor that bring home this point.

2.2.1 Anti-fraud policy

An early glimpse of the ECB's self-image as a supranational actor came in the unlikely domain of EU anti-fraud policy. The facts of this case surround a decision by the ECB Governing Council in October 1999 to guard against financial irregularities in the activities of the Bank (ECB Decision 1999/726/EC). Specifically, the ECB decided to create its own independent anti-fraud Committee to reinforce and monitor the activities of the Bank's Directorate for Internal Audit. According to this decision, the Directorate for Internal Audit remained 'responsible for conducting administrative investigations within the ECB', but it was instructed to keep the anti-fraud Committee abreast of its activities, which in turn was required to report regularly to the ECB Governing Council, the Bank's external auditors, and the Court of Auditors (ECB Decision 1999/726/EC).

The timing of this decision was controversial, coming as it did a matter of months after the resignation of the College of Commissioners following an investigation into financial mismanagement. Among the steps taken by the Commission in response to this scandal was the establishment of an independent European Anti-Fraud Office (OLAF) in April 1999 (Commission Decision 1999/352/EC, ECSC, Euratom). An inter-institutional agreement between the European Parliament and the Council of Ministers in May 1999 upgraded OLAF from a Commission watchdog to a Community one, noting that its investigative powers would apply to 'the institutions, bodies, offices and agencies established by, or on the basis of, the Treaties' (Regulation EC No. 1073/1999 Article 1).

In January 2000, the Commission, backed by the European Council, the European Parliament, and The Netherlands, challenged the ECB's anti-fraud measures on the grounds that they infringed the inter-institutional agreement on OLAF. Specifically, the Commission contested the ECB's assertion that the Directorate for Internal Audit alone was responsible for internal investigations within the Bank on the grounds that Regulation No. 1073/1999 extended OLAF's jurisdiction to all Community institutions. The ECB, the Commission insisted, was not exempt from this regulation, even though ECB Decision 1999/726/EC distinguished between the ECB's actions in the area of anti-fraud and those undertaken by the 'institutions of the European Communities' (Court of Justice Case C-11/00: para. 33).

In its defence, the ECB argued, *inter alia*, that the inter-institutional agreement on OLAF was neither applicable in this instance nor lawful. On the first of these points, the ECB claimed that it could not be counted as an institution, body, office, or agency of the Community and insisted on its financial independence (Article 282 TFEU). On the second point, the ECB sounded the alarm over its independence, warning that the 'mere threat' of an OLAF investigation 'is capable of bringing pressure to bear on the Members of the Governing Council or the Executive Board of the ECB and of jeopardising their independence when taking decisions' (Court of Judgement Case C-11/00: para. 118).

Though it may seem far removed from debates about the economic governance of the euro area, the OLAF case is a landmark one. Above all, it represents an attempt by the ECB to limit the scope of EU legislation on the grounds that such measures could undermine the credibility of the Bank's commitment to price stability. In so doing, the ECB adopted, what Goebel (2006: 600) called, an 'expansive... claim of autonomy from the Community framework'. This defence, Goebel suggests, owed an intellectual debt to the legal scholarship of Zilioli and Selmayr (2000: 622), who argued not uncontroversially that the Bank is a '"new Community" within the European Union's central pillar, which stands on an equal footing with the original three Communities'.

If the OLAF case illustrates the ECB's desire to remain aloof from the Community's legal order, then it also confirms the Bank's limited scope for agency in this regard. In July 2003, the Court of Justice ruled that Regulation No. 1073/1999 applied to the ECB and overturned Governing Council Decision 1999/726/EC and the internal anti-fraud measures that flowed from it (Court of Justice Case C-11/00). The Court of Justice also made it clear that 'the independence which the ECB enjoys... is strictly functional and is limited to the performance of the specific tasks conferred upon the ECB by the EC Treaty and the ESCB Statute', and that 'the fact it is independent does not have the consequence of placing the ECB beyond the reach of the rules of the Treaty' (Court of Justice Case C-11/00: para. 126).

2.2.2 Treaty reforms

The ECB's uneasy relationship with the EU's legal order was also plain to see during the Convention on the Future of Europe, which met between February 2002 and July 2003 to debate and draft the Treaty Establishing a Constitution for Europe. Although ECB President Duisenberg (2003*a*) gave his support to the overall aims of the Convention, he fought a rearguard action to insulate the Bank from the proposed treaty changes. As in the OLAF case, the key issue here was whether the ECB was separate from other EU institutions by virtue of its specific responsibilities in the area of monetary policy.

In May 2003, the Praesidium of the European Convention presented a draft version of the Constitutional Treaty listing the ECB as an EU institution alongside the European Parliament, the European Council, the Council of Ministers, the Commission, the Court of Justice, and the Court of Auditors (Article I-18, Title IV). Duisenberg (2003*b*) signalled his concern over these changes in a letter to the Chairman of the European Convention, Valéry Giscard d'Estaing. Although this letter noted that the Governing Council was not yet in a position to respond to changes concerning the ECB's status as an EU institution, Duisenberg was insistent that no changes in the substance of the ECB's institutional provisions should occur.

The European Convention's final draft of the Constitutional Treaty provided a partial concession to this point by placing the ECB under Chapter II, Title IV ('other institutions and bodies') rather than Chapter I ('the institutional framework'). This change did not go far enough for the ECB, which, as in the OLAF case, sought to clarify its unique institutional status. In September 2003, the Governing Council delivered an opinion on the Constitutional Treaty, which argued that the ECB should be 'differentiated from the "Union's institutions" by virtue of the bank's specific institutional features' (ECB 2003: para. 11). To this end, the Governing Council suggested that the headings of Title IV ('the Union's institutions') and Chapter I ('the institutional framework') be switched.

The fact that the ECB waited almost five months to deliver its formal opinion on the Constitutional Treaty can be partly explained by legal reasons; it did not make much sense for the Bank to express a view on the EU's institutional status until after the Court of Justice ruled on the OLAF case in July 2003. It may also have been due to tensions within the Governing Council between members of the ECB Executive Board and some NCB governors. Such tensions are suggested by the Bundesbank Governor's decision to go public with its own more hawkish line on the Constitutional Treaty after the ECB had adopted its opinion.

In a speech in November 2003, the President of the Bundesbank, Ernst Welteke (2003), warned of the 'unenviable dilemma of squaring the EU Constitution, which is desired in principle by all parties, with the institutional foundations of stable money'. Welteke also drew a clear link between the ECB's institutional status and its credibility as a central bank, arguing that sacrificing the *sui generis* character of the euro area's monetary authority 'may open the door to assigning objectives other than price stability'. A statement by the Executive Board of the Bundesbank endorsed the thrust if not the tone of this message, cautioning member states 'against receding to a situation which falls short of the achievements of the monetary constitution established by the Maastricht Treaty' (Bundesbank 2003).

The Bundesbank President's contribution to this debate was significant since it revealed concerns within the upper echelons of the ECB Governing Council that the Constitutional Treaty could undermine the credibility of the ECB's commitment to price stability. This attempt to preserve the ECB's existing competences is at odds with the traditional rational choice conception of supranational actors as competence maximizers in search of new channels of influence and power. As in the OLAF case, however, what the ECB wanted as a political actor and what it achieved were not one and the same.

The final version of the Constitutional Treaty, signed by the heads of state or government in October 2004, listed the ECB under Chapter II ('other Union institutions and advisory bodies') of Title IV ('Union institutions and other bodies). By August 2004, the ECB was resigned to its fate. In its monthly bulletin, the Bank insisted that the Constitutional Treaty preserved the *sui generis* status of the ECB and noted (somewhat sheepishly) that its independence 'was never in question' (ECB 2004: 61). Axel Weber (2004), Welteke's successor as Bundesbank President, had meanwhile adopted a less confrontational tone, warning against 'weakening the foundations of a stable euro through the backdoor in the European Convention's draft Constitution' but accepting that this matter was ultimately 'up to the politicians'.

The rejection of the Constitutional Treaty by French and Dutch voters in mid-2005 served only to embolden member states' efforts to clarify the ECB's institutional status. The first draft of the Lisbon Treaty, which was presented in July 2007, went further than the Constitutional Treaty by including the ECB alongside other EU institutions in Article 9(1). The ECB President, Jean-Claude Trichet (2007), voiced his objections to this revision in a letter to Portuguese Foreign Minister Manuel Lobo Antunes in August 2007, repeating the Governing Council's view that the ECB should be distinguished from other EU institutions by virtue of the bank's specific institutional provisions. In the end, the ECB's arguments failed to gain sufficient traction, with the result that the final draft of the Lisbon Treaty, which was signed by the heads of state or government in December 2007, placed the ECB squarely in the list of EU institutions (Article 13 TEU).

2.2.3 Economic policy coordination

The ECB's support for greater Community involvement in the area of economic policy has been more ambivalent. On the one hand, the euro area monetary authority has always acknowledged the need for economic policy coordination between euro member states. On the other hand, the ECB has reacted warily to calls for a significant strengthening of the Community dimension of economic policymaking. The Bank's concern for its independence and its defence of its price stability mandate appear, once again, to be the key factors behind its reluctance to embrace further integration in the euro area.

The ECB's fairly consistent position during the first ten years of EMU has been that economic policy coordination between euro area members is important for the smooth functioning of EMU. The Bank has offered a number of arguments in support of this view, including the need to ensure a coherent response to common economic shocks, to take account of the potential for spillover between euro area countries, and to promote coherence between national economic policies and the pursuit of price stability (see ECB 2008*a*).

The ECB has also championed a rigorous interpretation of EMU's fiscal rules and has, to this end, been a consistent critic of those member states that have failed to respect the stability and growth pact. In October 2002, for example, the ECB Governing Council issued a strongly worded rebuke of the Economic and Financial Affairs Council (Ecofin) for its 'failure to go along with the rules and procedures foreseen in the stability and growth pact', warning that its actions risked undermining 'the credibility of the institutional framework and the confidence in sound public finances of Member States across the euro area' (ECB 2002). This was followed in March 2005 by a statement in which the ECB Governing Council expressed 'serious concern' over Ecofin's plans to reform the stability and growth pact (ECB 2005*a*). In spite of such reservations, the ECB championed the revised stability and growth pact as an essential requirement for ensuring fiscal discipline under EMU (ECB 2008*a*).

Member states' efforts to coordinate structural reforms via the Lisbon Strategy have also been welcomed by euro area central bankers. In its annual report for 2000, the ECB welcomed 'the impetus given by the European Council to the economic reform process' (ECB 2001: 98). This message was repeated in March 2005, when the ECB expressed its full support for the 'ambitions of the renewed Lisbon strategy and . . . the efforts undertaken in that context by governments, parliaments and social partners' (ECB 2005*b*). In his remarks on the tenth anniversary of the euro, the ECB President, Jean-Claude Trichet (2008*a*), noted that 'the resolute pursuit of structural reforms in line with the Lisbon process' was among the most important challenges for the future of EMU.

The ECB's support for the stability and growth pact and the Lisbon strategy fits with euro area central bankers' core belief in the desirability of fiscal discipline and the need for structural reforms to enhance the flexibility of euro area product and labour markets and greater competition in price and wage setting (see Dyson 2008). Where plans to strengthen economic governance are perceived as a threat to price stability, the ECB has made clear its opposition. A case in point is the Bank's consistent stance against giving the Eurogroup a greater say in euro area governance, an idea that has been proposed in different ways and at different times during EMU's first decade by the likes of Oskar Lafontaine, Jean-Claude Juncker, and Nicolas Sarkozy (see Chapter 3). The ECB's typical response to such proposals is to argue that the Eurogroup serves an important function as things stand and that reform is unnecessary. A concern for price stability is never far from the surface, however, as reflected in comments by ECB Executive Board Member Jürgen Stark in January 2008 that the real motivation behind calls for stronger economic governance is 'to establish political influence on monetary policy in the euro area and thereby to undermine the independence of the ECB' (Stark 2008).

The point here is not that the ECB is opposed to the idea of 'more Europe' per se but that it is reluctant to consider schemes for stronger economic governance that contradict its commitment to price stability. Where such assurances are given, the Bank has shown itself willing to entertain the idea of a transfer of sovereignty that goes beyond the bargain struck at Maastricht. A case in point is the ECB President's tentative support for the German Finance Minister Wolfgang Schäuble's plans for a European monetary fund (Lambert 2010). Under this plan, member states at risk of sovereign default would be offered emergency liquidity support in return for 'stricter sanctions within the framework of budget deficit proceedings' (Schäuble 2010). Far from being a move towards fiscal federalism in the euro area, Schäuble's idea was more akin to a permanent crisis resolution mechanism for the euro area coupled with a stricter interpretation of the stability and growth pact (see Chapter 8). From this perspective, it was entirely rational for the ECB President to give his guarded support to such plans at a time when rising real debt burdens in member states such as Greece added to political pressure on the Bank to maintain low interest rates and, if necessary, pursue a higher rate of inflation over the medium term. Schäuble's proposal that the Eurogroup could provide support to stricken member states only with the approval of the ECB can only have sweetened this deal for Frankfurt.

The ECB was less enthusiastic about the recommendations on reforming EU economic governance tabled by the Van Rompuy Taskforce in October 2010. Taking Jean-Claude Trichet's membership of the Taskforce as a pretext, the ECB took the unusual step in June 2010 of publishing a set of informal proposals 'to make a quantum leap towards strengthening the institutional framework of EMU' (ECB 2010: 4). These proposals were broadly in line with the draft legislation tabled by the Commission in September 2010 (see Chapter 8), although the Bank went further by fleshing out details for a permanent crisis resolution mechanism to provide 'last-resort financial support for euro area Member States experiencing impaired access to private credit' (ECB 2010: 2). The ECB also called for quasi-automaticity in the implementation of financial penalties under the excessive deficit procedure. The Taskforce's refusal to back the ECB on this point and several others resulted in the inclusion of a footnote in the final draft of the Van Rompuy Report, which stated that Trichet did not subscribe to all elements contained within it (Taskforce to the European Council 2010: 14).

2.2.4 The ECB and financial supervision

Financial markets are one area where the ECB has unequivocally pushed for 'more Europe'. A preference for 'task expansion', Dyson (2008) notes, is suggested by the Bank's efforts to promote the smooth operation of payment systems in line with Article 127 TFEU. A key milestone in this respect was the ECB's launch in January 1999 of the Trans-European Automated Real-Time Gross Settlement Express Transfer System (TARGET), which was designed to facilitate transfers in euro between member states sharing the single currency and some other EU members (see ECB 2005*c*). More important still was the phased introduction in November 2007 of TARGET2, a more centralized arrangement that brings together national settlement systems under a single shared platform.

The ECB employed functional arguments to justify its efforts in this area, arguing that TARGET was paramount for the implementation of euro area monetary policy, the reduction of systemic risk, and the management of liquidity, and suggesting that TARGET2 was more cost-effective than a decentralized settlements system, particularly in the context of the EU's eastern enlargement. Bureaucratic politics may also have been at play within the European System of Central Banks (ESCB). Quaglia (2009*b*) emphasizes the decision to allow the Bundesbank, the Banque de France, and the Banca d'Italia to build and operate the single shared platform as being essential for ensuring NCB support for TARGET2. The ECB's policy on payment systems, she notes, was also consistent with 'budget-protecting' behaviour insofar as it allowed NCBs to redeploy officials away from areas of monetary policy that are now decided by the ECB.

The ECB's preferences for 'more Europe' are yet more striking in relation to financial supervision. As noted in the introduction, the Treaty gives the ECB a limited role here, allowing it to contribute towards member states' efforts to supervise credit institutions and promote the stability of the financial system (Article 127 TFEU). This has not stopped members of the ECB Executive Board, however, from seeking a more active role on supervisory issues. A little over a month after the launch of the single currency in January 1999, ECB Executive Board Member Tommaso Padoa-Schioppa (1999) expressed his conviction that EMU and the integration of euro area financial markets would eventually require the creation of a 'true and effective collective euro area supervisor'. Padoa-Schioppa stopped short, however, of recommending that the ECB should assume such responsibilities, arguing instead that cooperation between the Eurosystem and national supervisors would suffice in the first instance.

Wim Duisenberg (2002*b*) pursued a similar line in a speech to De Nederlandsche Bank in April 2002, calling for measures to 'strengthen cross-border and cross-sectoral co-operation between supervisors, to enhance convergence in supervisory practices and to reinforce collaboration between supervisory and central banking functions' (Duisenberg 2002*b*). Like Padoa-Schioppa, Duisenberg did not explicitly call for an expansion of the ECB's competences but instead argued that the Eurosystem should take the lead in promoting 'co-operation between central banks and supervisory authorities'.

From an economic point of view, it was more difficult for the ECB to justify its desire to play a greater role in financial supervision than in the creation of an integrated system of cross-border settlement. Whereas the latter is generally seen as essential for the smooth functioning of monetary policy, scholars are divided on the question of whether responsibility for maintaining price stability and financial stability should be delegated to the same institution (see Davies and Green 2008). For some commentators, there are informational advantages to be gained from conducting these tasks in tandem. Others argue that these tasks should be kept separate to ensure that central bankers focus on price stability alone and to insulate them from those who stand to gain or lose from more stringent financial supervision.

Given the diversity of supervisory arrangements that exist within the euro area, the ECB Executive Board has, not surprisingly, sought to keep its options open on this issue. Padoa-Schioppa (1999) challenged the view 'that one model is right and the other wrong' and insisted that '[b]oth can function, and do function, effectively . . . if appropriately managed'. Bini Smaghi (2009) belatedly came to the same view, suggesting that his prior concerns that financial supervision could undermine the credibility of monetary policy warranted reconsideration in the light of the financial crisis and that they, in any case, applied to 'central banks, which were not fully independent'.

Whether the ECB Executive Board was driven by functional arguments of this kind or self-interested attempts to maximize its competences, its efforts to assume a greater role in financial supervision were initially rebuffed by some NCB governors and national governments. For Dyson (2008), a desire to protect national competences explains why the Lamfalussy Process – an innovative approach to the adoption, implementation, and transposition of EU financial regulation launched in 2001 – delegated responsibility for fostering a convergence in supervisory practices to a new European Committee of Banking Supervisors rather than the ECB's Banking Supervision Committee.

By highlighting the limits of the Lamfalussy Process, the global financial crisis gave the ECB Executive Board another opportunity to press for a more prominent role in financial supervision. Initially, ECB President Trichet (2008*b*) was reluctant to be drawn on this issue, accepting that the current institutional framework could be improved in an interview with the *Financial*

Times in December 2008 but insisting that the ECB Governing Council had not formed a view on the need for radical change in this area. Internal divisions within the ECB Governing Council seem to have contributed to this hesitancy. Yves Mersch (2009), Governor of the Central Bank of Luxembourg, hinted as such when he acknowledged that the issue of financial supervision would entail 'a very difficult discussion' and that the Governing Council had 'not yet had a thorough, conclusive discussion on it'. By February 2009, the ECB formed a more unified position on this issue, which was outlined by a speech by Trichet (2009*a*) to the Committee of European Securities Regulators. 'The ECB and the Eurosystem', the ECB President noted, 'have the technical capacity to assume a stronger role in macro-prudential supervision', adding that an advisory role 'would be a natural extension of the mandate already assigned to us by the Treaty, namely to contribute to financial stability'.

Trichet, as always, chose his words carefully. By putting forward the ECB *and* the Eurosystem for this role, he made clear that the ECB Executive Board was not seeking a greater say over financial supervision at the expense of NCBs. By focusing on an advisory role, Trichet also made clear that he was not advocating the creation of new instruments and objectives that might interfere with the Bank's primary objective. The ECB, in other words, was seeking 'more Europe' but not in a way that threatened NCBs or the pursuit of price stability.

Trichet's remarks were also well timed, coinciding as they did with the deliberations of the de Larosière Group, a wise person's committee convened by Commission President José Manuel Barosso to put forward plans for the future of EU financial supervision. The de Larosière Group's final report, presented in March 2009, called for the ECB President to be installed as chair of a new European Systemic Risk Council (ESRC), which would take charge of 'an early warning mechanism' that would allow it to issue recommendations and opinions in the event of threats to financial stability in the EU as a whole (de Larosière Group 2009).

The fact that the ECB President (Trichet 2009*b*) expressed his support for the de Larosière Report was not surprising in light of his earlier comments on financial supervision. More significant was the vote of confidence given by the NCB governors to plans for the ESRC (see Noyer 2009; Weber 2009). Whether some NCB governors had a change of heart on this issue is not known, but their behaviour is consistent with bureaucratic politics explanations. By recommending that all members of the ESCB be represented on the ESRC, the de Larosière Report offered something to everyone. For those NCB governors who were concerned with preserving their competences over national supervisory arrangements, it ensured that they had a seat at the table. For those seeking a greater say over financial supervision, the report proposed that they retain the right to attend meetings of the ESRC or to send the head of the national supervisory agency instead.

Wanting 'more Europe' and getting it are, as Heisenberg and Richmond (2002) observe, not the same thing. In contrast to matters relating to payment systems, the Treaty gives the ECB little autonomy in relation to financial supervision. Article 127 TFEU allows the ECB to 'contribute to the smooth conduct of policies pursued by the competent authorities relating to . . . prudential supervision', but it ultimately falls to the Council, acting on a recommendation from the Commission, to decide to confer new competences to the Bank. The fact that this decision is based on unanimity has allowed EU member states, particularly those from outside the euro area, to resist a transfer of powers in this area to Frankfurt.

The European Council in March 2009 welcomed the de Larosière report as the 'basis for action' (Council of the European Union 2009*a*), but soon bowed to opposition from the United Kingdom and others against giving the ECB a say over financial stability beyond the euro area. The conclusions of the European Council in June 2009 consequently stated that the chair of the ESRC should be chosen from the ECB General Council (Council of the European Union 2009*b*). This seldom-seen body includes members of the ECB Executive Board and the NCB governors of all EU member states, meaning that the Governor of the Bank of England or the head of another central bank from outside the euro area could, in principle, serve as chair of the ESRC.

These compromises were reflected in the agreement on a new European financial supervisory framework for the EU agreed by Ecofin and the European Parliament in September 2010. Under this deal, it was agreed that the European Systemic Risk Board (ESRB), as it was renamed, would open for business in January 2001, and that the ECB President would chair this body for the first five-year term. Though this has given ECB a much more prominent role in this area of policymaking than has hitherto been the case, Ecofin and the European Parliament agreed that early warnings of risks to the EU's financial system issued by the ESRB would be legally non-binding, thus replacing de Larosière's quasi-supranational vision of financial supervision with an approach in which soft law looks set to dominate.

2.3 The ECB as an awkward case

The preceding section asked whether the ECB will, like other supranational institutions, choose 'more Europe' if given the opportunity to do so. The answer that emerges from the case studies covered is an equivocal one: in some instances, the ECB has sought a greater role for itself or the EU in economic policy, but in others it has vehemently opposed attempts to enhance the Community dimension of EMU.

Financial market policy is the principal area in which the ECB has conformed to rational choice institutionalist expectations about what EU institutions want. The euro area monetary authority has, it was shown, fostered an integrated approach to cross-border payments and assumed a decisive role in the process through the creation of TARGET and its successor, TARGET2. More significant still has been the ECB's attempts to gain a foothold in financial supervision in spite of its limited competence to do so under the Treaty. Members of the Executive Board, it was noted, have consistently made the case for greater ECB involvement in this domain, with the global financial crisis providing an opportunity to step up their campaign for 'more Europe'.

The ECB's attitude towards economic policy coordination in the euro area appeared more ambivalent. On the one hand, Frankfurt has been a vocal champion of the EU's efforts to promote structural reform under the Lisbon Strategy and fiscal discipline under the stability and growth pact. On the other hand, the ECB has been an outspoken critic of attempts to promote closer macroeconomic policy coordination in the context of the Eurogroup, with senior members of the ECB warning against attempts by politicians to exert influence over monetary policy.

The ECB has also sought to distance itself from the EU's legal order and the responsibilities of other supranational actors. This was evident in the OLAF case, which saw the ECB seek an exemption from inter-institutional cooperation on anti-fraud policy on the grounds that it was not, strictly speaking, an EU institution. A similar strategy was evident in relation to the Constitutional Treaty and the Lisbon Treaty, with the ECB arguing that it was part of the EU's institutional framework but not an EU institution.

The case studies covered in this chapter chime with some aspects of Heisenberg and Richmond's (2002) analysis of the ECB and challenge others. They concur with the authors' findings that the ECB, in spite of its remarkable degree of independence, has limited scope for exercising agency beyond the narrow domain of monetary policy. This was apparent, for example, in the Bank's ultimately unsuccessful defence of its institutional autonomy in both the OLAF case and the debate over treaty reform. Where this chapter differs with the authors is over their assumption that the ECB would choose 'more Europe' than member states if given the opportunity to do so. This may have been the case in relation to financial supervision and some forms of economic policy coordination, but the ECB appeared as an opponent rather than a proponent of further integration in the other cases explored.

The findings presented in this chapter also challenge Pollack's (2003) assertion that EU institutions share a 'common preference for greater competences'. The ECB's preference for 'more Europe', it would seem, is contingent on its preference for price stability. When the pursuit of greater competences for itself or the EU as a whole is perceived as reinforcing price stability (e.g. by promoting fiscal discipline or more flexible markets) or reconcilable with it (e.g. playing an advisory role on financial supervision), the ECB is willing to play along. When greater competences are perceived as a threat to price stability (e.g. by interfering with its mandate or political independence), the ECB prefers the status quo to further integration.

Bureaucratic politics within the ECB may also explain the Bank's contingent preferences. In the case study on treaty reform, the President of the Bundesbank was notably more outspoken than members of the ECB Executive Board, with the former warning about the tensions between the pursuit of ever closer union and price stability serving as a reminder that central bankers in the euro area may not be subject to the same self-selection and socialization effects as those working in the Commission and the Court of Justice.

The reluctance of the NCB governors to enhance the Bank's competences was also evident in the case of financial supervision. ECB Executive Board members' desire to increase their competence was resisted by those NCB governors seeking to maintain their grip over financial supervision at the national level. The reforms to EU financial supervision agreed in September 2010 were arguably more palatable for these players since they ensure that all NCBs, whether they are responsible for financial supervision or not, will be represented on the ESRB.

2.4 Conclusion

'We are with Europe but not of Europe. We are associated but not compromised'. Winston Churchill's famous remark on the United Kingdom's position in a united Europe could also be applied to the ECB's place in the EU's institutional order. There can be little doubt that the ECB is *with* Europe; those in the upper echelons of the Bank are never slow to support the goal of European integration and the euro's contribution to it. Whether the ECB sees itself as being *of* Europe is another matter, especially when it fears that price stability could be compromised in the process.

The case studies presented in this chapter challenge rational choice institutionalist claims that supranational actors generally favour 'more Europe'. On some issues, such as the coordination of fiscal policies and structural reforms, the ECB has sought a greater role for itself and/or the EU. On others, most notably cooperation in the area of anti-fraud, treaty reform, and macroeconomic policy coordination, the ECB has opposed attempts to enhance the Community dimension of EMU.

This variance, it would appear, is explained by two factors. Firstly, the ECB appears to support schemes to enhance its competences or those of the EU only when they do not prejudice the pursuit of price stability. Secondly, bureaucratic politics plays a role in the ECB Governing Council, with NCBs less keen on further integration, especially if it concerns areas in which national monetary authorities retain a policymaking role.

What are the wider implications of these findings for the themes of this book? On the one hand, it could be argued that the ECB is a *sui generis* supranational actor whose reluctance to embrace 'more Europe' reflects the acute importance of independence and credibility in the domain of monetary policy (Dyson 2008). On the other hand, the ECB's reluctance to go beyond its price stability mandate might mean that function-specific agencies – an increasingly common feature of EU policymaking in recent years – could be a means for member states to reap the benefits of delegation to the supranational level without getting 'more Europe' than they bargained for.

A more speculative question is whether the traditional engines of European integration might follow the ECB's lead in becoming more circumspect about the European project. Peterson (2008), for one, argues that the Commission is now less enthusiastic about the ideal of ever closer union than it once was. Faced with the challenge of decision-making in an enlarged Union and influenced by the intergovernmentalist tendency of José Manuel Barroso, the EU executive has, Peterson suggests, grown more wary of extending the scope of EU legislation. Further research on what supranational institutions want in a changing EU, it would seem, is warranted.

3

The Rise and Fall of the Eurogroup

I wish the meeting had been as good as the lunch.
Warren Christopher

The transformation of the Eurogroup is one of the most eye-catching elements in the evolution of euro area governance. This forum was launched in December 1997 after European Union (EU) leaders agreed that euro area finance ministers could meet informally in the margins of the Economic and Financial Affairs Council (Ecofin) to discuss policy issues of particular salience for Economic and Monetary Union (EMU). Since its first meeting in June 1998, the Eurogroup has been progressively formalized, acquiring a permanent secretariat, a fixed-term presidency, and a legal status under the Lisbon Treaty. The fact that the Treaty also allows member states that share the euro to adopt provisions specific to EMU (Article 136 Treaty on the Functioning of the European Union (TFEU)) and excludes non-euro countries from some decisions that are of particular relevance to euro area governance (Article 139 TFEU) confirms the Eurogroup's *de facto* decision-making powers, even if formal authority in this field still rests with Ecofin.

The 'creeping institutionalization' of the Eurogroup, as Chang (2009: 80) calls it, provides an opportunity to revisit debates about informal policy coordination under EMU. Jacquet and Pisani-Ferry (2001: 11), for instance, view the Eurogroup's initial informality as a barrier to coordination that prevented ministers 'developing a truly common vision [that] could shed light on the interaction between national economic policies and the common monetary policy'. Puetter (2006: 263), in contrast, sees the Eurogroup's informal working methods as an exercise in deliberative intergovernmentalism designed to foster 'a common understanding . . . of the coordination process' outside the formal structures of the Ecofin Council.

This chapter considers what impact the formalization of the Eurogroup has had on its contribution to the governance of the euro area. Its central argument is that formalization, though it has increased the influence of euro area finance ministers on some policy issues, has undermined the Eurogroup's value-added in two key respects. Firstly, the decision to appoint a president of the Eurogroup for a renewable term of office helped to politicize debates over the macroeconomic policy mix that previously took place behind closed doors. Secondly, the Eurogroup's emergence from the shadows has created tensions with some heads of state or government and encouraged the European Council to seek a more active role in economic policy coordination, especially in the context of the global financial crisis.

The remainder of this chapter is divided into four sections. The first section charts the gradual formalization of the Eurogroup since 1998. The second section asks what impact the Eurogroup's evolution has had on its effectiveness as a forum for economic policy coordination. The third section draws general lessons for our understanding of EMU governance in particular. The final section considers the Eurogroup's relevance for wider debates on EU policymaking in general.

3.1 The rise of the Eurogroup

In December 1997, EU heads of state or government adopted a resolution on enhanced economic policy coordination among the member states that were about to embark on Stage 3 of EMU. They called, in particular, for 'closer Community surveillance' of macroeconomic developments, budgetary positions, structural policies, and cost-price trends (Council of the European Union 1997). To achieve these aims, the European Council agreed, in the first instance, on need for 'the Council, the Commission and the Member States... to apply the Treaty instruments for economic policy coordination fully and effectively' (Council of the European Union 1997: para. 4).

Enhanced economic policy coordination, the resolution also agreed, required a threefold change to the way in which EU finance ministers did business. Firstly, informal meetings of Ecofin would pay close attention to the surveillance of macroeconomic and budgetary developments. Secondly, Ecofin would meet periodically in restricted sessions – that is, involving one minister and one advisor – to discuss issues such as macroeconomic surveillance. Thirdly, the ministers of euro area members could 'meet informally among themselves to discuss issues connected with their shared specific responsibilities for the single currency' (Council of the European Union 1997: para. 44).

Little time was wasted in enacting the third of these three points. On 4 June 1998, a little over a month after EU leaders agreed that eleven member states met the convergence criteria and should proceed to Stage 3 of EMU, the finance ministers of the embryonic euro area held their first meeting at

Chateau de Senningen in Luxembourg. Puetter (2006: 103), in what remains the most comprehensive study of the Eurogroup, describes the informal working methods established at this inaugural meeting as follows:

- Firstly, the Eurogroup lacked a firm basis in EU law insofar as it was convened on the basis of the European Council's December 1997 resolution on economic policy coordination rather than secondary law or a treaty provision.
- Secondly, euro area finance ministers steered clear of making formal decisions, thus preserving Ecofin's position 'at the centre of the economic coordination and decision-making process' (Council of the European Union 1997: para. 44).
- Thirdly, one finance minister and one advisor from each euro area member attended the first meeting, thus establishing the principle that the Eurogroup should meet in a restricted session.
- Fourthly, the attendance of ECB President Wim Duisenberg and Commission President Jacques Santer at the Eurogroup created an opportunity for behind-closed-doors discussions of the policy mix.
- Fifthly, the meeting was chaired by Austrian Finance Minister Rudolph Edlinger, thus creating the principle of a rotating presidency occupied by the member state holding the EU presidency or, as was the case during the UK presidency in the second half of 1998, the next euro area member in line for this position.
- Sixthly, officials from the Austrian finance ministry, with informal input from the Commission and the secretariat of the Economic and Financial Committee, organized the first Eurogroup session, thus confirming that the new body would not have a permanent administrative infrastructure.

Since it convened in Chateau de Senningen, the Eurogroup has experienced a gradual formalization of its working methods. A number of steps have, for instance, been taken to enhance administrative support for Eurogroup meetings (Puetter 2006). In July 1999, the Commission was invited to submit regular notes on the economic situation and budgetary surveillance to the Eurogroup via the Economic and Financial Committee and the Commission, thus giving EU and national officials a more prominent role in Eurogroup preparations. In April 2003, a newly created subgroup of the Economic and Financial Committee, known as the Eurogroup Working Group, was given overall responsibility for preparing, and ensuring follow-up to, policy discussions among euro area finance ministers.

Changes to the Eurogroup's organizational structures have gone hand in glove with greater responsibilities in relation to economic policy coordination. A key driver in this respect has been the strengthening of fiscal surveillance measures for euro area members under the stability and growth pact. Under the reforms to

EMU's fiscal rules agreed in March 2005, it was decided that the Eurogroup would carry out a 'horizontal assessment of national budgetary developments and their implications for the euro area as a whole... at least once a year before the summer' (Council of the European Union 2005*a*: 25). Such discussions took place in secrecy until the Eurogroup decided, in April 2007, to publish 'terms of reference' to be taken into account by member states in the formation of their budgets (Regling 2007). This exercise was a forerunner to the so-called European Semester, which has shifted the submission and assessment of member states' stability and convergence programmes to spring with a view to maximizing their impact on domestic economic policy decisions (see Chapter 8).

At the European Council in Nice in December 2000, EU leaders endorsed euro area finance ministers' 'intention to extend the range of mainly structural matters dealt with in this forum' with a view to enhancing 'the growth potential of the euro area' (Council of the European Union 2000: para. 33). The fact that structural reforms were seen as an issue for all EU member states – and hence as a matter for Ecofin and the European Council – might explain why the Eurogroup was slow to follow up on this intention. The relaunch of the Lisbon Strategy in March 2005, coupled with a concern for the supply-side causes of persistent macroeconomic imbalances under EMU, encouraged the Eurogroup to pay greater attention to structural reforms. The euro area chapter in the Commission's annual progress report on growth and jobs served as a focal point for its discussions on this topic.

Exchange rate policy is, in effect, a shared competence of Ecofin and the ECB. The latter is responsible for conducting foreign-exchange operations (Article 127 TFEU) but the former is empowered to formulate general orientations for exchange rate policy (Article 219 TFEU). In practice, Ecofin has been reluctant to issue formal recommendations on the exchange rate for fear that it might be seen as impinging on the independence of the ECB. Instead, the Eurogroup has developed an informal approach to exchange rate policy based on the adoption of 'terms of reference' by euro area finance ministers. Though these pronouncements carry no legal weight, they provide political cover for the ECB to carry out exchange rate operations. For example, the ECB's joint intervention in exchange rate markets alongside the US Federal Reserve and the Bank of Japan in September 2000, Frankfurt's first move of this kind, followed a Eurogroup communiqué, also the first of its kind, which stated that '[a] strong euro is in the interest of the euro area' (Eurogroup 2000).

The Eurogroup's rise has altered the balance of power between EU finance ministers from inside and outside the euro area. The Eurogroup has, as Pisani-Ferry (2006: 840) puts it, 'become a kind of caucus within the Council in which the important discussions... take place and lead to decisions that are thereafter endorsed by the wider Ecofin'. One illustration of this fact is the Eurogroup's role in brokering a deal over the reform of the stability and growth pact in March 2005 before this issue went to Ecofin. It was also suggested in UK Chancellor Gordon Brown's infrequent appearances at EU finance ministers' meetings after the Eurogroup was established and in the reforms to Ecofin's working methods launched in April 2006. The latter, launched by Austrian Finance Minister Karl-Heinz Grasser, looked suspiciously like an attempt to make Ecofin more like the Eurogroup by taking 'routine issues' off the agenda and encouraging an exchange of view on political and strategic issues (Federal Ministry of Finance 2006).

Perhaps the most significant step in the formalization of the Eurogroup to date was the decision to replace the rotating presidency with a more permanent arrangement. Under an agreement reached at Scheveningen in September 2004, it was agreed to bring forward (a slightly modified version of) a provision in the Constitutional Treaty to appoint a fixed-term president of the Eurogroup.[1] In addition to preparing, chairing, and reporting on Eurogroup sessions, the President was given responsibility for formulating meeting agendas, preparing a long-term work programme, and representing euro area members on the international stage.

Jean-Claude Juncker's appointment as the Eurogroup's first fixed-term president in January 2005 signalled euro area members' desire to have an experienced and recognizable figurehead at the helm. At the time, Juncker was entering his sixteenth year as Finance Minister of Luxembourg, giving him a longer institutional memory of EMU than any of his peers. The fact that Juncker was both Finance Minister and Prime Minister of Luxembourg at this time was not unusual for the Grand Duchy – Pierre Werner and Jacques Santer had combined both roles in the past – but it put him in the unique position among euro area members of occupying a seat on both the Eurogroup and the European Council.

The Lisbon Treaty further formalized the Eurogroup by giving it a legal status. A protocol annexed to the Treaty states that euro area ministers shall meet 'to discuss questions related to the specific responsibilities they share with regard to the single currency' (Article 1 Protocol 14 TFEU), recognizes the role of the Eurogroup presidency, and extends its term of office from two to two and a half years (Article 2 Protocol 14 TFEU). The preamble to the Protocol also calls for an 'ever closer coordination of economic policies within the euro area' and the need for 'special provisions for enhanced dialogue between the Member States whose currency is the euro, pending the euro becoming the currency of all Member States of the Union'.

[1] Technically, the Treaty lengthened the existing term and ended the principle of rotation, but 'fixed-term presidency' is more accurate than 'full-time presidency' or 'permanent presidency' since the Eurogroup chair is occupied neither exclusively nor in perpetuity.

Though it insists on the informal character of the Eurogroup (Article 1 Protocol 14 TFEU), the Lisbon Treaty gives *de facto* decision-making powers to euro area finance ministers. Article 136 TFEU, for example, calls on euro area members to adopt specific measures, including economic policy guidelines, to 'strengthen the coordination and surveillance of their budgetary discipline'. The Treaty also excludes EU member states that do not share the single currency from decisions relating to, *inter alia*, the adoption of the euro area-specific aspects of the Broad Economic Policy Guidelines (BEPGs), the imposition of financial penalties under the excessive deficit procedure, and decisions regarding the euro area's representation in international fora and conferences (Article 139 TFEU).

The Eurogroup's visibility increased soon after the Lisbon Treaty entered into force in December 2009. The Council Secretariat, for one thing, launched a new Eurogroup website containing public statements by the President, recordings of relevant press conferences, and details of legislative acts flowing from discussions by euro area finance ministers. Jean-Claude Juncker followed up in January 2010 with a series of measures for strengthening economic policy coordination on the eve of his reappointment for a fourth term as Eurogroup President (Juncker 2010). These measures included a commitment to make clear the positions of euro area finance ministers on certain policy issues; Eurogroup conclusions on intra-euro area competitiveness (Eurogroup 2010*a*); and terms of reference on exit strategies (Eurogroup 2010*b*) both adopted in March 2010 offered a taste of this new approach. Juncker also announced the establishment of a small secretariat within the Council of Ministers to assist with the practical preparation of Eurogroup meetings. Though the Eurogroup Working Group will continue to set the agenda for Eurogroup discussions, this move was symbolically significant since the absence of a permanent secretariat is, as Italianer (1999) notes, one of the hallmarks of informal approaches to policy coordination.

3.2 The fall of the Eurogroup

The formalization of the Eurogroup, Pisani-Ferry (2006: 840) suggests, 'has transformed [it] from a mere talking shop into what increasingly looks like a policy-making institution'. A case in point is a Eurogroup agreement in September 2005 to avoid unilateral cuts in VAT and duties in response to high fuel prices. This response, Pisani-Ferry argues (2006: 837), provided evidence of 'collective learning' within the Eurogroup, which had failed to prevent the uncoordinated and incoherent response of euro area members to high oil prices in 2000.

The Eurogroup's formalization has also helped euro area members to pursue their collective interests on the global stage, albeit with varying degrees of success. The practice of adopting terms of reference on exchange rate issues has produced a more coherent line on the euro's external value than was the case in the early days of the single currency (Commission 2008*a*: 24). The appointment of a fixed-term president has also made it easier for the euro area to speak with one voice in some international settings. Though the Eurogroup is excluded from meetings of the G20 finance ministers and central bank governors (see Chapter 6), Jean-Claude Juncker has been at the centre of the euro area's efforts to promote greater flexibility in China's exchange rate policy (see Chapter 7).

The Eurogroup's formalization has undermined its effectiveness in other respects. For one thing, it has grown less useful as a forum for fostering dialogue between euro area finance ministers and the ECB. Though the meaningfulness of this dialogue is a matter of debate – Puetter (2006) suggests that finance ministers are generally reluctant to confront the ECB President directly – Eurogroup Presidents have become outspoken about monetary policy decisions as the institutionalization of the body has gathered pace.

This may appear to be an unlikely claim in the light of Oscar Lafontaine's confrontational approach to the ECB during his tenure as Eurogroup President. Contrary to reports, however, the German Finance Minister did not publicly ask the ECB to cut interest rates; he had done so of the Bundesbank in October 1998 (Atkins and Norman 1998), but he limited his remarks to exchange rate coordination, the outlook for inflation, and the fiscal stance once Stage 3 of EMU was underway. Lafontaine seems, moreover, to have enjoyed limited support within the Eurogroup (Puetter 2006: 163) and the German government, with the second of these factors leading to his resignation as Finance Minister in March 1999.

Lafontaine's departure was, in any event, followed by a period of greater public harmony between euro area finance ministers and the ECB. Didier Reynders, who served a full year as Eurogroup President in 2001, did court controversy by letting his concerns over the economic outlook be known in advance of an ECB Governing Council meeting in April 2001. This incident, however, produced little more than Wim Duisenberg's renowned retort: 'You might say I hear but I don't listen' (Barber et al. 2001). Karl-Heinz Grasser's public remark at this time that an interest rate cut was long overdue was more serious, but the Austrian Finance Minister was roundly criticized by other Eurogroup members for failing to respect the independence of the ECB (Barber et al. 2001).

Relations with Frankfurt entered a new and more difficult phase following the appointment of the first full-time Eurogroup President in January 2005. Within days of taking office, Juncker let it be known that he favoured a 'fruitful dialogue' between the Eurogroup and the ECB and spoke of developing a partnership between finance ministers and central bankers (Atkins and

Parker 2005*a*). Juncker put the same point more bluntly in June 2005 when he called for Eurogroup members to be more 'forthright' in expressing their views to the ECB (Atkins 2005).

It did not take long for this more forthright approach to bear fruit. After a meeting of the Eurogroup on 7 November 2005, Juncker told journalists that finance ministers saw 'no second-round effects [and] no wage changes as a result of oil price developments' and that they had 'asked the ECB after a very thorough debate to bear that point in mind' (Atkins and Parker 2005*b*). Later that month, Juncker broke the Eurogroup's omertà over monetary policy by telling the European Parliament that euro area finance ministers saw the ECB's anticipated increase in interest rates as 'not particularly necessary' (Atkins et al. 2005).

Juncker's comments did not prevent Frankfurt from raising interest rates in December 2005, but they did reveal a serious breakdown in communications between the Eurogroup and the ECB. So too did Juncker's admission in June 2006 that he had sent a letter to ECB President Trichet calling for measures to 'foster a common understanding of the key policy challenges facing the euro area' (Atkins and Parker 2006). Among the ideas contained in the letter, Juncker noted, was the consideration of an enhanced dialogue on euro area issues between the ECB President, the Eurogroup President, and the Commissioner for Economic and Monetary Affairs.

The contents of the letter revealed by Juncker were fairly anodyne – Didier Reynders' call in 2001 for a similar arrangement was dismissed by Wim Duisenberg only on the grounds that the Eurogroup President did not, in his opinion, speak for all finance ministers (Committee on Economic and Monetary Affairs 2001) – but the manner of its revelation was not. The fact that Juncker chose to discuss his private correspondence with the ECB President before the European Parliament showed signs of strain between monetary and fiscal authorities. Juncker's disclosure that Trichet had not replied to the letter served only to strengthen this impression, as did the former's subsequent admission that relations with the ECB were subject to 'institutional tenderness' (Parker 2006*a*).

It is tempting to put this spat between the ECB and the Eurogroup Presidents down to personality, with Jean-Claude Juncker's sarcasm coming up against Jean-Claude Trichet's sobriety. There is reason to believe, however, that the formalization of the Eurogroup may also have been a factor. For one thing, the switch from a rotating to a fixed-term Eurogroup presidency removed a valuable reset button in relations between finance ministers and the ECB. Whereas Wim Duisenberg was rid of Lafontaine after three months and Reynders after one year, tensions between Trichet and Juncker carried on and on.

The timing of Juncker's more confrontational approach to the ECB undoubtedly owed something to the macroeconomic cycle – by mid-2005 it was clear that interest rate rises were in the offing for the first time since October 2000 – but it might also have been linked to an electoral cycle of sorts. Two days before the decision was taken in September 2006 to reappoint Juncker for a second term, the Eurogroup President made it clear that he was putting his name forward on condition that a more productive dialogue with the ECB could be established (Parker 2006*a*). Two days after his reappointment, Juncker called a ceasefire with the ECB and urged 'ministers not to be too outspoken on monetary policy' (Parker 2006*b*).

For his part, Juncker claimed that the media had exaggerated tensions between the Eurogroup and the ECB (Parker 2006*b*). This might be true, but an alternative reading of these events is that taking a more forthright approach to the ECB was the price of French support for a second term as Eurogroup President. Comments concerning the ECB emanating from Paris and Luxembourg certainly moved in lockstep during this period. Juncker's call in June 2005 for euro area finance ministers to stand up to the ECB, for example, came one day after the French Prime Minister had called for greater efforts to coordinate economic policies in the Eurogroup (de Villepin 2005).

A second major consequence of the Eurogroup's formalization is that it has created strains between finance ministers and some heads of state or government. An early indication of this trend occurred in July 2004 when the Italian Prime Minister, Silvio Berlusconi, attended the Eurogroup to present details of additional fiscal measures designed to keep government borrowing below the 3 per cent of GDP reference value. Berlusconi's charm offensive seemed to do the trick, with EU finance ministers deciding not to endorse the Commission's recommendation to issue an 'early warning' against Italy on the understanding that the proposed fiscal measures would be implemented (Council of the European Union 2004).

The Eurogroup's fiscal feud with France in mid-2007 had more significant consequences. As noted above, euro area finance ministers took the unprecedented step in April 2007 of issuing 'terms of reference' as part of its medium-term budgetary review. Under this agreement, several Eurogroup members, including French Finance Minister Thierry Breton, agreed to target their medium-term budgetary objectives by 2010, in what was seen as an attempt to demonstrate the credibility of the revised stability and growth pact. Sarkozy's election in May 2007 on a manifesto that promised to cut taxes by as much as €15 billion per year threw this agreement into doubt, prompting several Eurogroup members, including the Finance Ministers of Spain and Germany, to issue sternly worded warnings to the newly installed president concerning his country's obligations to the EU's budgetary rules (Hall and Parker 2007).

Sarkozy responded to these criticisms by inviting himself to the Eurogroup meeting in July 2007 to explain that France would postpone its target date for achieving its medium-term budgetary objective from 2010 to 2012. Whilst this decision dealt a blow to the Eurogroup's ambitions to be a forum for economic policy coordination, the fact that a sitting French president with a fresh democratic mandate was forced to explain himself to euro area finance ministers did not go unnoticed. Sarkozy himself acknowledged the unprecedented nature of this situation, but argued that France must show its sincerity on such matters before it could seek stronger forms of gouvernement économique (Sarkozy 2007*a*).

That finance ministers would not reign supreme in Sarkozy's conception of gouvernement économique was clear. In an interview with *Le Journal du Dimanche* on the eve of his Eurogroup appearance, the French President argued that the economy, growth, and jobs were the kinds of subjects that the heads of state or government of euro area members should be discussing (Ricard 2007). In the press conference that followed the Eurogroup meeting, Sarkozy acknowledged that he had raised the idea of a euro area summit with finance ministers and that he would be returning to this subject at a later date (Sarkozy 2007*b*).

The French President did not have long to wait, with the global financial crisis providing the perfect opportunity to put the Eurogroup in its place. A little over a month after turbulence in the US subprime mortgage market triggered worldwide liquidity shortages, Sarkozy issued a strongly worded criticism of the Eurogroup President for failing to show initiative on debates over the future of financial capitalism (Sarkozy 2007*c*). This was followed in January 2008 by calls for a euro area summit to deal with the worsening global financial situation. The idea of a euro area summit received short shrift from the German Chancellor, Angela Merkel, however, who expressed concerns about what message it could send regarding political interference in ECB monetary policy (Benoit 2008).

Undeterred, Sarkozy used France's presidency of the EU in the second half of 2008 to push for a reform of the Eurogroup. In July 2008, the French President outlined plans for strengthening the Eurogroup, including the creation of a permanent secretariat independent of the Commission and a structured dialogue between euro area finance ministers and the ECB. Although concrete proposals on these issues never materialized – reportedly because the French government recognized their divisiveness (Hall and Parker 2008) – Sarkozy saw and seized his opportunity to convene a summit of euro area heads of state or government after EU members of the Group of 8 (G8) had failed to formulate a coherent response to the international banking crisis that followed the collapse of Lehman Brothers.

The inaugural summit of euro area heads of state or government took place in Paris on 12 October 2008, with UK Prime Minister Gordon Brown making a surprise guest appearance at the invitation of the French President to outline British plans for a coordinated bank bailout. Sarkozy's summit was a success, paving the way for a pledge by EU members of up to €2 trillion to recapitalize and, if necessary, take shares in European banks. This plan, which was endorsed by the full European Council a week later, was far from perfect, but it is credited with bringing Europe's banking system back from the brink (Quaglia et al. 2009). From a governance perspective, the summit confirmed the rise of the heads of state or government at the expense of the Eurogroup. Jean-Claude Juncker was present in Paris but he remained in the wings as Nicolas Sarkozy and Gordon Brown ran the show (Quaglia 2009*a*).

The Eurogroup's waning influence was also evident at the European Council on 16 October 2008. At this meeting, it was agreed to establish a 'financial crisis cell' to facilitate information exchange, provide an early warning of further turbulence, and otherwise coordinate EU member states' response to unfolding events (Council of the European Union 2008*a*). The President of the Eurogroup was invited to join the cell along with the Presidents of the ECB and the Commission, but Juncker's influence on this body was diluted by the presence of the President of the European Council. Significantly, EU leaders also dispatched Nicolas Sarkozy and José Manuel Barroso but not Jean-Claude Juncker to the United States in October 2008 for talks with President George W. Bush on the search for a global solution to the financial crisis (see Chapter 6).

The concurrence of the financial crisis and France's presidency of the EU provided Nicolas Sarkozy with a unique opportunity to realize his vision of giving the heads of state or government a more prominent role in economic policy coordination. Mindful that his tenure as president in office of the EU was running out and that the leaders of the Czech Republic and Sweden, two member states from outside the euro area, would follow, Sarkozy volunteered to serve as 'president of the euro area' for at least a year, arguing that only the heads of state or government of member states sharing the euro had the authority to form a gouvernement économique (Chambraud et al. 2008).

Angela Merkel's lukewarm response ended Sarkozy's extraordinary bid for power but his particular vision of economic policy coordination lived on. In December 2008, EU leaders agreed on a coordinated fiscal stimulus package worth around 1.5 per cent of EU GDP. Although the EU's Economic Recovery Plan fell short of the US Recovery and Reinvestment Act (in terms of discretionary budgetary measures, at least), it was an unprecedented attempt by EU member states to coordinate aggregate-demand policies. This was followed in December 2009 by a European Council agreement to delay the withdrawal of fiscal stimulus measures to 2011 in view of the worsening economic outlook for 2010.

The hands-on involvement of the heads of state or government in economic policy coordination was also evident in response to Greece's fiscal crisis. Ecofin initially took the lead on this issue, declaring Greece to be in a state of excessive deficit in April 2009 after its budget deficit for 2007 was amended from 2.8 per cent of GDP to 3.5 per cent and giving notice to Greek authorities to undertake swingeing expenditure cuts in February 2010 after its budget deficit for 2009 soared (see Chapter 4). Euro area leaders were forced to step in, however, after credit rating agencies downgraded Greek debt in December 2009, raising the spectre of a sovereign default.

The first high-level discussions of Greece's fiscal predicament took place at the leaders' dinner of the European Council in December 2009, where Prime Minister George Papandreou briefed his peers about his country's public finances (Barber and Hope 2009). This was followed in February 2010 by an informal meeting of EU heads of state or government in Brussels, which declared euro area members' commitment to 'take determined and coordinated action, if needed, to safeguard financial stability in the euro area as a whole' (Heads of State or Government of the European Union 2010). Protracted discussions over the precise nature of this commitment concluded in another summit of euro area heads of state or government in May 2010, which approved a €110 billion joint EU–IMF financial rescue package for Greece (Council of the European Union 2010*b*).

The Eurogroup was by no means absent from the policy process that produced the financial rescue package for Greece. It was euro area finance ministers who took the lead in monitoring Greece's compliance with Council recommendations under the stability and growth pact; the terms of reference on Greece's stability programme adopted by the Eurogroup in March 2010 provide a case in point (Eurogroup 2010*c*). Euro area finance ministers also hammered out the fine details of the financial rescue package in a series of meetings that finally produced a deal at the Eurogroup on 3 May 2010 (Hope et al. 2010). It ultimately fell, however, to euro area heads of state or government to find political agreement on a way forward. Significantly, the meetings of euro area leaders in February and May 2010 were chaired by Herman Van Rompuy, who was installed as the first full-time President of the European Council in December 2009.

3.3 Explaining the Eurogroup's demise

The preceding analysis implies that the Eurogroup has become less effective as a forum for economic policy coordination as its working methods have been formalized. The acquisition of a permanent secretariat, a fixed-term presidency, and *de facto* decision-making powers has, it would seem, given euro area finance ministers greater sway over the surveillance of budgetary policies and structural reforms and, in some cases, a stronger presence on the international stage, but these gains have come at a price.

A key finding of this chapter is that the creation of a fixed-term Eurogroup presidency politicized finance ministers' dialogue with the ECB and opened the door on what was intended to be private discussions. The end of the rotating presidency, it was argued, removed an important safety valve between the ECB and the Eurogroup by allowing tensions between monetary and fiscal authorities to linger on. It also appears to have, on occasion, put pressure on the Eurogroup President to take a tougher line against the ECB. This finding speaks to Puetter's (2006) core point that the deliberative ideal of the Eurogroup's founding fathers was inextricably linked to the institution's informal setting. The more like an alternative configuration of Ecofin the Eurogroup has become, in other words, the more difficult it has been for finance ministers to engage in information exchange, problem-solving, and consensus building.

There are tentative signs that informal dialogue may be emerging outside the increasingly formal structures of the Eurogroup. In January 2007, ECB President Jean-Claude Trichet reportedly invited Eurogroup President Jean-Claude Juncker and Commissioner for Economic and Monetary Affairs Joaquin Almunia to Frankfurt for the first in a series of 'informal, irregular chats' on shared economic concerns (Parker 2007). The fact that this meeting went largely unnoticed in the press suggests that this might be a more favourable venue for a full and frank exchange of views than the Eurogroup.

Another key finding of this chapter is that the growing influence of the Eurogroup produced a backlash by some heads of state or government. Nicolas Sarkozy's disenchantment with the Eurogroup, which was plain to see in the preceding section, speaks to Pisani-Ferry's (2006) point that the economic governance of the euro area offers 'one bed for two dreams'. By this he means that the Keynesian vision of gouvernement économique that has periodically prompted French policymakers to push for the close coordination of economic policies and an activist approach to exchange rate policy since the Intergovernmental Conference (IGC) on EMU in 1991 has been consistently opposed by German policymakers, for whom price stability and the preservation of central bank independence are sacrosanct (see Chapter 1).

But Sarkozy's dream of economic governance is as intergovernmental as it is Keynesian. The French President, it was noted, was willing to explain his budgetary plans to euro area finance ministers in July 2007, but he refused to be bound by the terms of reference adopted by the Eurogroup. Likewise, his plans to overhaul the governance of the Eurogroup presented in July 2008 can be seen as a fairly transparent attempt to weaken the role of the Commission and the Economic and Financial Committee by establishing an autonomous secretariat. From this perspective, Sarkozy's frustration with the formalized Eurogroup is symptomatic not only of his manic modus operandi but also of traditional French approaches to EU diplomacy. The idea of a euro area summit, with its emphasis on bargaining between heads of state or government and a limited role for supranational institutions, is taken straight from the neo-Gaullist playbook. A similar strategy, indeed, is discernable in calls by Jacquet and Pisani-Ferry (2001) for the Eurogroup to become a collective executive body that is empowered to take decisions on euro area economic policy without being encumbered by the EU's legislative process. The authors, in other words, are critical of the Eurogroup's informality but they seek to formalize it outside the EU's institutional architecture.

On one level, it is unsurprising that the financial crisis allowed Sarkozy to move forward his plans for euro area governance. The European Council is the preferred vehicle for crisis management in the EU, meaning that finance ministers were always going to take a back seat to their political masters during the biggest economic challenge to face the Union to date. It seems unlikely that finance ministers will retake the wheel once economic conditions become less bumpy, however, not least because the Eurogroup faces competition from the new full-time President of the European Council. The first holder of this post, Herman Van Rompuy, has made no secret of his ambitions to play an active role in EU economic policy (see Van Rompuy 2010). That the heads of state or government are supportive of this approach is suggested not only in the lead role played by Van Rompuy during the euro area's sovereign debt crisis but also in the launch of the Europe 2020 strategy.

More important still was the decision by euro area leaders in March 2010 to invite the President of the European Council to head a taskforce on the future of the stability and growth pact and other aspects of economic governance. This move not only had symbolic importance – the Eurogroup President had, after all, traditionally led on these policy issues – but it also provided Van Rompuy (2010) with an opportunity to realize his vision of making the European Council 'something like the "gouvernement économique" of the Union'. Significant in this respect were calls in the Van Rompuy Taskforce's final report (see Chapter 8) for the Eurogroup to report to the European Council at critical junctures in EU economic surveillance, including instances in which member states fail to comply with the preventive arm of the stability and growth pact, breach the BEPGs, or otherwise jeopardize the smooth functioning of EMU (Taskforce to the European Council 2010).

3.4 Conclusion

At the European Council in Luxembourg in December 1997, EU leaders insisted that the finance ministers of euro area members could meet on condition that they respected '[t]he defining position of the Ecofin Council at the centre of the economic coordination and decision-making process'

(Council of the European Union 1997: para. 6). This principle was stretched to breaking point, however, as the Eurogroup acquired a permanent secretariat, a full-time president, and *de facto* decision-making powers during its first decade. With the entry into force of the Lisbon Treaty in December 2009, the Eurogroup further eclipsed Ecofin by acquiring a legal basis and the authority 'to adopt measures specific to those Member States whose currency is the euro' (Article 136 TFEU).

The formalization of the Eurogroup has allowed euro area finance ministers to exert collective influence at home and abroad, but it has undermined their impact on economic policy coordination in other respects. One consequence of creating a fixed-term presidency is that the Eurogroup has become less useful as a forum for encouraging a full and frank exchange of views between finance ministers and the ECB. A possible reason for this development is that the Eurogroup President has became more beholden to member states, some of whom wish to see Frankfurt held to political account.

The Eurogroup's stewardship of the stability and growth pact, moreover, fuelled tensions with some members of the European Council, with the President of France, in particular, pushing for greater involvement by the heads of state or government in euro area matters. The global financial crisis allowed Nicolas Sarkozy to put his plans into action by convening the first summit of euro area leaders in October 2008 to tackle the turmoil in the European banking sector. Though this development owed much to the Sarkozy's dynamism and the demands of the financial crisis, euro area finance ministers might not recover the exalted status that they once enjoyed in relation to the governance of the euro area. One reason is that the Eurogroup faces stiff competition from the new full-time President of the European Council, who has fought for, and won, a central role in economic policy coordination.

What is the wider significance of these findings for the themes of this book? For economists, the Eurogroup's fall raises concerns about a lack of informal ties between euro area monetary and fiscal authorities compared to their counterparts in other monetary unions. In the United States, as Meyer (2000) observes, the Chairman of the Federal Reserve and the Treasury Secretary hold breakfast or lunch meetings once a week (sometimes more often) and are in close contact by telephone. Similarly, informal contacts at the technical level are also well developed, with the Federal Reserve Governors inviting senior treasury officials to weekly lunchtime discussions of economic issues. Bini Smaghi and Casini (2000: 379) also found evidence of 'intense and frequent' dialogue between central banks and finance ministries in euro area members before the launch of EMU. Such dialogue, the authors note, ranged from technical discussion to high-level interaction and covered issues such as the economic and financial situation and, in some cases, major policy announcements, without any discernable impact on central bank independence.

Hayes-Renshaw and Wallace (2006: 42) suggest that the peculiar emphasis on policy coordination over legislation under EMU lends itself to informality. There are signs, however, that the informal working methods on which the Eurogroup was established have found favour in other area of EU policy. Informal meetings of the Council of Ministers for Justice and Home Affairs (JHA), for example, are frequently used to foster a common understanding of security issues not only between the representatives of member states but also between the EU and the United States. The US Secretary for Homeland Security Janet Napolitano, for instance, attended the JHA informal meeting in Toledo in January 2010 to discuss transatlantic cooperation on terrorism following a failed attack in Detroit on Christmas Day 2009.

Informal sessions have always taken place in the margins of the European Council – the decision to appoint Wim Duisenberg as the first President of the ECB was famously taken after a five-hour lunch between French President François Mitterrand and German Chancellor Helmut Kohl – but informal meetings of EU heads of state or government have become increasingly influential in recent years. UK Prime Minister Tony Blair's decision to invite EU leaders to a 'fireside chat' at Hampton Court in October 2005 was widely derided at the time but his attempt to escape the hard bargaining environment that characterizes meetings of the heads of state or government still resonates. The working methods of the European Council, indeed, were one of the first issues that Herman Van Rompuy raised following his appointment as full-time president of this body, inviting the heads of state or government to meet in more informal and intimate settings to facilitate a more open and productive exchange of views on pressing policy issues (Puetter forthcoming).

Part II
New Instruments

4

Profligacy, Prudence, and the Stability and Growth Pact

A man who pays his bills is soon forgotten.

Oscar Wilde

The euro area's experimental approach to economic governance involves new instruments as well as new institutions. By far the most important instrument is the stability and growth pact, a set of rules governing public sector borrowing in European Union (EU) member states. The corrective arm of the pact, which is set out in Council Regulation (EC) 1056/2005, establishes a timetable for enforcing the excessive deficit procedure, which in turn threatens members posting budget deficits in excess of 3 per cent of GDP with non-binding recommendations and, in certain circumstances, financial penalties and fines (Article 126 Treaty on the Functioning of the European Union (TFEU)). The pact's preventive arm, contained in Council Regulation (EC) 1055/2005, establishes country-specific budgetary objectives that member states pursue through annually updated stability programmes. The Economic and Financial Affairs Council (Ecofin) issues non-binding opinions on these programmes each year and can, in the event of a deviation from these objectives, issue a non-binding warning against the country in question.

To say that the stability and growth pact fared badly during the financial crisis would be a serious understatement. By mid-2010, government borrowing was above 3 per cent of GDP in all euro area members, with excessive deficit procedures underway against all countries in the currency zone except Luxembourg. Those on the geographical periphery of Economic and Monetary Union (EMU) were hardest hit, with Spain, Greece, and Ireland posting double-digit deficits, and Portugal lagging not far behind. Financial market concerns focused, in the first instance, on Greece, which found itself on the brink of sovereign default after its budget deficit for 2009 was revised from 3.7

to 15.4 per cent (Commission 2010*a*: 200). Attempts to restore confidence in Greek public finances through the corrective arm of the stability and growth pact failed to convince financial markets, leaving heads of state or government with little choice but to agree to a joint EU–International Monetary Fund (IMF) rescue package for Greece (see Chapter 6) followed by a reform of EMU's fiscal rules (see Chapter 8).

The jury is still out on precisely what caused the euro area's rapid reversal of fiscal fortune during the financial crisis. Ireland, which was forced to turn to the EU and IMF for financial assistance in November 2010 (see Chapter 6), was one of several countries to face a perfect storm of rising expenditure on troubled banks and falling tax revenues due not only to swings in the automatic budgetary stabilizers but also to the end of a prolonged housing boom during which the state coffers were filled with stamp duties. These developments left little room for a fiscal stimulus in Ireland, but the same is not true of all euro area countries. Stimulus measures in Germany were valued at 1.5 per cent of GDP in 2009 and 2.0 per cent of GDP in 2010, which lagged behind only China, Saudi Arabia, and the United States among G20 members (IMF 2009). Under such circumstances, it would be wrong to scapegoat the stability and growth pact for the euro area's fiscal problems; the United States and the United Kingdom, it should be recalled, also saw double-digit deficits at the height of the financial crisis (Commission 2010*a*: 200). The pact must shoulder some of the blame, however, not least in the light of Ecofin's decision in June 2007 to close an excessive deficit procedure against Greece in spite of, what transpired to be, widespread inaccuracies in the country's official statistics.

Of course, the stability and growth pact's problems began well before the global financial crisis. The reluctance of some member states to put their public finances on a sound footing during the economic upturn of 1999 and 2000 made excessive deficits hard to avoid once economic conditions slowed in 2001. A reluctance on the part of some EU finance ministers to contemplate the use of financial penalties against two of these transgressors, France and Germany, led to the suspension of the pact and, following an inconclusive ruling on this decision by the Court of Justice (Maher 2004), reforms to the preventive and corrective arms of the agreement in March 2005 (see Hodson 2009). Compliance with the revised stability and growth pact was variable. By mid-2008, government borrowing was below 3 per cent of GDP in all euro area members for the first time since euro notes and coins had been introduced, but only one-third of members had reached their medium-term budgetary objectives at this point (ECB 2008*b*: 56).

The stability and growth pact's shortcomings have inspired a steady stream of literature on the reform of EMU's fiscal rules (see Fischer et al. 2007 for a systematic overview of reform proposals prior to March 2005). Some contributors to this debate challenge the substantive focus of EMU's fiscal rules, with Blanchard and Giavazzi (2003), for example, calling for net public investment to be excluded from the calculation of budget deficit targets. Others call for a radical overhaul to the procedures underpinning the pact, with Wyplosz (2005), for instance, arguing that independent committees should carry out fiscal surveillance on a country-by-country basis. EMU's tenth anniversary and the financial crisis inspired a new wave of reform proposals, with calls by von Hagen and Wyplosz (2008) for a system of collective insurance through tax revenue sharing and Burda and Gerlach's (2010) suggestion of a surcharge on excessive public debt among the more interesting ideas in this emerging debate.

Less attention has been paid in the literature to the question of why some member states found it easier than others to comply with EMU's fiscal rules during the first decade of the single currency. The most systematic attempt at an answer comes from political institutionalism, an approach to the study of public finances that stresses a link between electoral regimes and budgetary institutions (see Hallerberg et al. 2001, 2009; Hallerberg 2004). The point of departure for political institutionalism is that countries electing single-party majority governments or coalitions in which the ideological space between governing parties is small typically delegate control of the budgetary process to strong finance ministers, while countries electing ideologically diverse coalitions usually rely on numerical rules or some other form of contract to enforce fiscal discipline. Simply put, political institutionalism's critique of the stability and growth pact is that countries belonging to the first of these groupings ('delegation states') will find it harder to comply with EMU's fiscal rules than those belonging to the second one ('contract states').

Proponents of political institutionalism arrive at this critique of the stability and growth pact from different directions. For Hallerberg (2004: 194), the pact 'is unlikely to benefit delegation states' and could do more harm than good if 'rigid rules from Brussels can undermine the finance minister's position'. Annett (2006: 15) echoes this point, arguing that the pact's emphasis on multiannual budgetary targets 'fits snugly with the numerical contracts approach associated with commitment states, but not so well with countries relying on domestic governance institutions'. Hallerberg and Bridwell (2008: 82) expect delegation states to 'face difficulties avoiding excessive deficits' because of their tendency to run a more flexible fiscal policy that is unconstrained by multiannual targets.

This chapter discusses the link between the stability and growth pact and national budgetary institutions during EMU's first decade. Its findings are threefold. Firstly, compliance with the pact among countries that are typically counted as delegation states varies during this period. Secondly, not all of these countries had a well-formed system of delegation in place during this period.

Thirdly, there is evidence that some delegation states are increasingly turning to numerical fiscal rules in the pursuit of budgetary discipline. These findings challenge political institutionalist claims that the stability and growth pact suits some member states more than others but chimes with its conclusions that domestic institutions matter for EU economic policy coordination.

The remainder of this chapter is divided into four parts. The first presents a broad-brush overview of compliance with the stability and growth pact in the period 1998–2007. The second discusses the institutional position of finance ministers in euro area delegation states. The third examines the growing use of numerical fiscal rules by delegation states during this period. The final section revisits these findings in the light of the financial crisis and draws conclusions for wider debates about economic policy coordination in the EU.

4.1 Fiscal governance and the stability and growth pact

The first step in this exercise is to classify euro area members according to their expected fiscal regime. In so doing, it is important to recognize that delegation and contract states are ideal types. In practice, it can be difficult to know how to categorize a given country, not least because electoral regimes and budgetary institutions evolve over time. With this caveat in mind, Table 4.1 cross-checks Hallerberg et al.'s (2009: 47) taxonomy for the twelve founding members of the euro area with a measure of ideological space based on Benoit and Laver's (2006) elite survey of party policies.[1] The latter gives a minimum score of 1 to parties that favour tax increases to pay for greater government services and a maximum score of 20 to those in favour of reduced government services to cut taxes. Ideological space is measured here as the difference between the scores of the most ideologically distinct parties in government on average over the period 1998–2007.

Viewed from this perspective, the link between fiscal and electoral regimes in euro area members is consistent with the central tenets of political institutionalism. Member states that tend to elect single-party majority governments – a case in point is Greece – or coalition governments made up of parties that have similar views on tax and expenditure policies – as exemplified by Germany – typically delegate a significant degree of control to finance ministers over the formulation and implementation stages of the budget. A fiscal regime of this kind is more problematic in member states that tend to elect coalitions in which parties are far apart on fiscal policy. This explains why countries such

[1] The focus of this discussion is on the euro area's founding members. See Hallerberg et al. (2009: 138–69) for a discussion of fiscal regimes in Central and Eastern European member states.

Table 4.1. Ideological space on tax and expenditure issues and expected fiscal regimes, 1998–2007

	Ideological space	Fiscal regime
Greece	0.0	Delegation
Portugal	0.0	Delegation
Spain	0.0	Delegation
Germany	2.5	Delegation
France	2.7	Delegation
Luxembourg	3.2	Contract
Italy	3.7	Delegation
Ireland	4.2	Delegation
Finland	4.8	Contract
Austria	5.0	Delegation
The Netherlands	7.0	Contract
Belgium	10.8	Contract

Note: Ideological space is the difference between the scores of the most ideologically distinct parties in government on average over the period.

Source: Ideological space based on Benoit and Laver (2006). Fiscal regimes taken from Hallerberg et al. (2009).

as Belgium and The Netherlands traditionally favour contracts as a means of pre-committing the government to medium-term budgetary plans.

Luxembourg and Austria are interesting cases. The former is an example of a country in which the ideological space within government fluctuates over time. Between August 1999 and July 2004, Jean-Claude Juncker's Christian Social People's Party (CSV) governed alongside the fiscally conservative Democratic Party. Thereafter, CSV joined forces with a group that preferred tax increases or expenditure cuts, the Luxembourg Socialist Workers' Party, with the result that the ideological space within the governing coalition increased from 1.2 to 5.3 (Benoit and Laver 2006). This might explain why Luxembourg adopted much more stringent fiscal rules during this period (Hallerberg et al. 2009). Austria is an example of a country in which the fiscal regime varies over time. During EMU's first year, the country was ruled by a grand coalition of the Austrian People's Party (ÖVP) and the Social Democratic Party of Austria, which had traditionally employed fiscal contracts. The ÖVP's alliance with the Freedom Party of Austria in February 2000 saw the ideological space within the governing coalition fall from 7.2 to 0.8 (Benoit and Laver 2006), which might explain the government's preference for delegation until the grand coalition was restored to power in January 2007.

The second step in this exercise is to compare the fiscal track record of the two groupings. Overall, there can be no denying the fact that net government lending was considerably higher in contract states than it was in delegation states between 1998 and 2007. Whereas contract states posted budget positions of close to balance or in surplus during this period, delegation states remained in deficit throughout (Figure 4.1). In view of this fact, it is

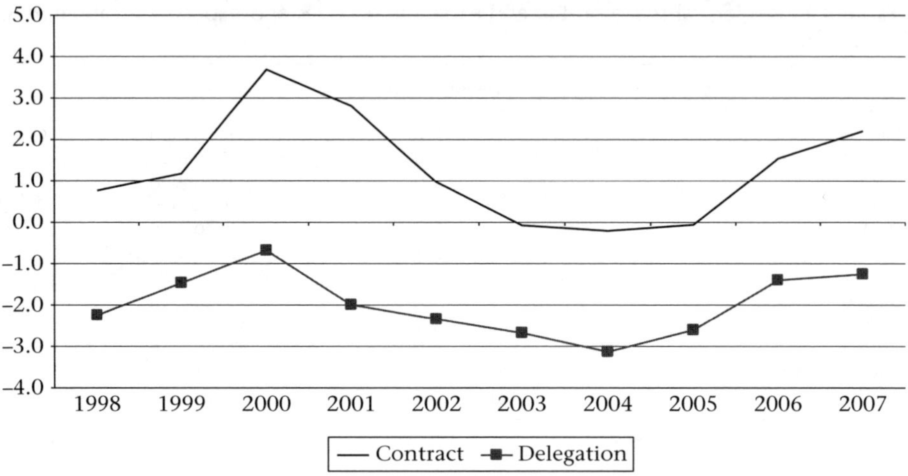

Figure 4.1. Net government lending in contract and delegation states, 1998–2007 (% GDP)

Source: DG Economic and Financial Affairs AMECO database.

Table 4.2. Compliance with the corrective arm of the pact, 1998–2007

	Date of Ecofin recommendation to end excessive deficit	Fiscal regime
Portugal	05 November 2002	Delegation
Germany	21 January 2003	Delegation
France	03 June 2003	Delegation
The Netherlands	02 June 2004	Contract
Greece	05 July 2004	Delegation
Italy	29 June 2005	Delegation
Portugal	20 September 2005	Delegation

Source: Fiscal regimes taken from Hallerberg et al. (2009).

unsurprising that delegation states were the worst offenders when it came to compliance with the corrective arm of the stability and growth pact. Of the six member states that were deemed by Ecofin to be in a state of excessive deficit during EMU's first decade, The Netherlands was the only one classified as a contract state throughout (Table 4.2).

A fact not widely acknowledged by proponents of political institutionalism is that three delegation states, Spain, Ireland, and Austria, achieved an impressive degree of fiscal discipline in EMU's first decade (Figure 4.2). Spain, which began the transition to delegation in the mid-1990s (Hallerberg 2004: 188), was fully compliant with EMU's fiscal rules during this period. Having posted a budget deficit in 1998, which was slightly above 3 per cent of GDP in hindsight, net government lending rose steadily thereafter to reach a surplus of slightly below 2 per cent of GDP in 2007. Ireland, which also delegated greater powers to its finance minister at this time (Hallerberg and Bridwell 2008: 76),

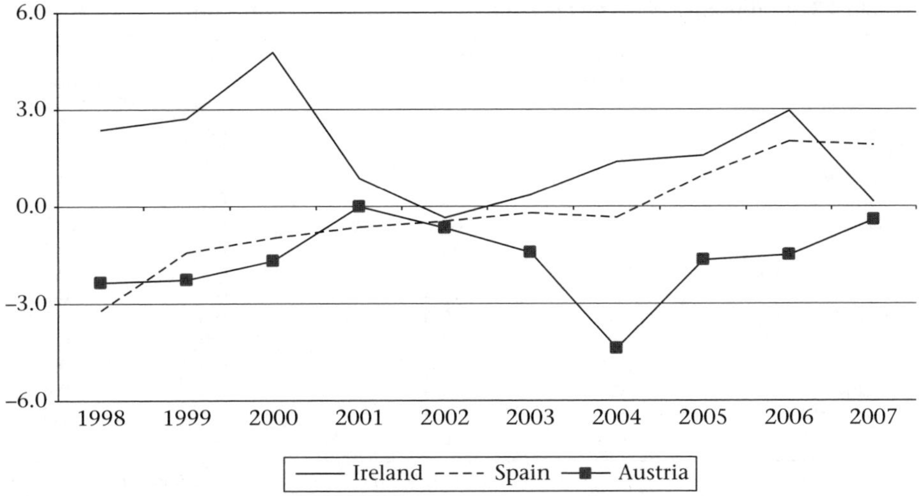

Figure 4.2. Net government lending in Ireland, Spain, and Austria, 1998–2007 (% GDP)
Source: DG Economic and Financial Affairs AMECO database.

was a more erratic fiscal performer – procyclical tax cuts and expenditure increases in the 2000 budget were deemed to have breached the Broad Economic Policy Guidelines (BEPGs) (see Chapter 5) – but it remained well within the limits set by the stability and growth pact. Austria, meanwhile, balanced its budget in the year after its aforementioned switch to delegation. Thereafter, it avoided problems of compliance in relation to the stability and growth pact, even though a Eurostat ruling on the treatment of a capital injection into the country's state railways saw an exceptional budget deficit of 4.1 per cent in 2004.

A similar story emerges as regards compliance with the preventive arm of the stability and growth pact. Prior to 2005, the Commission used minimal benchmarks to assess compliance with the pact's rules on government borrowing in the medium term. In essence, these benchmarks identified what net lending would need to be to allow budgetary stabilizers to take effect during a typical economic downturn without triggering an excessive deficit. These benchmarks varied from country to country, based on estimates of the sensitivity of budget balances to changes in the economic cycle (see Commission 2000: ch. 3). Overall, contract states had a better track record of compliance with these targets than delegation states, with the former meeting their minimal benchmarks 87.5 per cent of the time during the period 1998–2007, compared with a figure of 30 per cent for delegation states (Table 4.3). Not all delegation states fared the same, however. While Greece, France, Italy, and Portugal never once met their minimal benchmarks during EMU's first decade, Ireland and Spain (after 2003) complied more often than not.

Table 4.3. Compliance with the preventive arm of the pact, 1998–2007

	Minimal benchmark	Rate of compliance	Medium-term objective	Rate of compliance
Finland	−1.2	100.0	2.0	100.0
Belgium	−1.3	100.0	0.5	0.0
Luxembourg	−1.0	100.0	−0.8	90.0
Ireland	−1.5	90.0	0.0	70.0
Spain	−1.2	60.0	0.0	30.0
Austria	−1.6	60.0	0.0	0.0
The Netherlands	−1.1	50.0	−1.0 to −0.5	0.0
Germany	−1.6	30.0	0.0	0.0
Greece	−1.4	0.0	0.0	0.0
France	−1.6	0.0	0.0	0.0
Italy	−1.4	0.0	0.0	0.0
Portugal	−1.5	0.0	−0.5	0.0
Contract states	–	*87.5*	–	*47.5*
Delegation states	–	*30.0*	–	*12.5*

Note: Minimal benchmark (MB) and medium-term objectives (MTO) measured as lending (+) and borrowing (−) as percentage of GDP. Rate of compliance measured as percentage of EMU's first decade spent in compliance with the MB or MTO.

Source: Based on ECB (2008*b*: 56).

Under the reform of the stability and growth pact agreed in March 2005, member states agreed to adopt medium-term budgetary objectives. These targets took account not only of the cyclical sensitivity of budget balances but also variables such as debt dynamics, investment, and expenditure related to ageing populations (Commission 2006). Contract states had a more difficult time in meeting medium-term budgetary objectives than minimal benchmarks, possibly because the former were more ambitious, but they still fared better than delegation states. While countries in the first grouping complied with the pact's revised rules on medium-term government borrowing 47.5 per cent of the time, those in the second did so only 12.5 per cent of the time (Table 4.3). Spain and Ireland, once again, stood out from their fellow delegation states. The former had little problem in meeting its medium-term budgetary objective once it was formally introduced in 2005, with the latter compliant in all but one of EMU's first ten years.

In summary, the evidence considered in this section supports political institutionalism's hypothesis about the link between electoral regimes and fiscal governance but questions its claim that delegation states have been more profligate than their contract counterparts. Although excessive deficits were more common among delegation states than contract states during the period 1998–2007, there is a danger of overgeneralization. Ireland, Spain, and, to a lesser extent, Austria stand out as examples of member states that depended on strong finance ministers to enforce fiscal discipline and yet encountered few problems of compliance in relation to EMU's fiscal rules prior to the global financial crisis.

4.2 Finance ministers in delegation states

Why did some delegation states find it easier than others to abide by the stability and growth pact during EMU's first decade? An explanation of this puzzle that would fit with political institutionalism is that finance ministers in delegation states that breached the pact somehow lack the institutional conditions to make delegation work. Hallerberg et al.'s (2009: 75) survey of budgetary processes in EU member states is the most up-to-date resource for following this line of investigation. This survey measures the 'strength' of finance ministers at three stages of the budget process. During cabinet negotiations, it is assumed that strong finance ministers can set budgetary parameters for spending ministries and negotiate bilaterally with spending ministers, and that cabinet discussions are subject to prior constraint and binding budgetary norms. At the stage of parliamentary negotiations, finance ministers are assumed to be in a strong position if amendments to the government's budget are rare, subject to offsetting and result in the collapse of the government, and if the legislature votes on the total size of the budget before debating specific items contained within. When it comes to the execution of the budget, a strong finance minister, it is argued, will have the power to veto specific expenditures, impose cash limits on spending ministers, block the transfer of funds between budgetary chapters, resist revisions to budget law, and prohibit the carryover of funds to the following year.

Hallerberg et al.'s (2009: 75) index of delegation summarizes the results of this survey, with a score of 1.0 indicating that a finance minister has all of the attributes discussed above (Table 4.4). There is some evidence to suggest that delegation states posting excessive deficits during EMU's first decade had finance ministers in institutionally weak positions but it is not conclusive. Ireland, one of the more prudent delegation states during this period, has a

Table 4.4. Delegation index, 2000 and 2004

	2000	2004
Ireland	0.77	0.77
France	0.81	0.77
Greece	0.75	0.75
Italy	0.73	0.69
Germany	0.62	0.62
Austria	0.62	0.62
Portugal	0.54	0.60
Spain	0.58	0.58
Average	*0.68*	*0.68*

Note: Index ranges from 1.00 when finance minister has a very high degree of control over the budget process to 0.00 when he/she has none.

Source: Hallerberg et al. (2009: 74).

Table 4.5. Delegation index (cabinet negotiations only), 2000 and 2004

	2000	2004
Spain	0.94	0.94
Austria	0.88	0.88
Greece	0.88	0.88
France	1.00	0.88
Ireland	0.88	0.88
Italy	1.00	0.88
Portugal	0.75	0.75
Germany	0.69	0.69
Average	*0.88*	*0.84*

Note: Index ranges from 1.00 when finance minister has a very high degree of control over the budget process to 0.00 when he/she has none.

Source: Hallerberg et al. (2009: 61).

finance minister with a comparatively high degree of autonomy, while the opposite holds true of three member states that fell foul of EMU's fiscal rules, France, Greece, and Italy. Spain and Austria, meanwhile, are shown to have finance ministers with a fairly weak grip on the budgetary process in spite of these member states' strong track record of compliance with the pact.

Focusing on the role of finance ministers during cabinet negotiations only highlights a slightly different pattern (Table 4.5). Spain, Ireland, and Austria emerge with finance ministers who are stronger on average than in most delegation states. Portugal and Germany, in contrast, have comparatively weak finance ministers. This result resonates with earlier empirical work by Hallerberg et al. (2001), which found that the finance ministers of Germany and Portugal had considerably less autonomy over the formulation stages of the budget than their counterparts in other delegation states. It is also consistent with the wider political economy literature on fiscal policymaking in these countries.

That Portugal's finance minister has a precarious grip on the budget process is well documented. A succession of minority governments in the late 1990s led the Portuguese Prime Minister to intervene in budgetary affairs on a number of occasions, thus undermining the institutional position of the finance minister (Hallerberg 2004: 184). This state of affairs was apparent, for example, in 1996 when Prime Minister António Guterres supported a plan by the economy minister, Augusto Mateus, to bail out financially impaired firms, in spite of public opposition from Finance Minister António de Sousa Franco (Stock and Magone 1997: 479). Similarly, in 1999, the finance minister was unable to prevent the prime minister from offering 'a cheese factory, a fishing port, and a health care centre' to the constituency of a member of parliament in return for not voting against the budget (Hallerberg 2004: 185). Perhaps the most serious infringement, however, came when the prime minister assumed control of the civil service in 1996, leaving the finance minister powerless to object to the hiring of 50,000 additional public sector workers between 1996 and 1999, a decision that triggered an annual 8 per cent increase in the public wage bill (Hallerberg 2004: 185).

An additional political economy explanation for Portugal's predicament is that previous attempts to consolidate the position of the finance minister in cabinet have been largely unsuccessful. In a cabinet reshuffle in September 1999, the Ministries of Economics and Finance were brought together under the control of Joaquim Pina Moura in an attempt to promote greater fiscal discipline (Braga de Macedo 2002: 12). Yet, as Hallerberg (2004: 185) records, when fuel prices rose sharply in 2000 this created a paradoxical situation in which '[a]s Economy Minister he [Moura] was expected to uphold his party's pledge to subsidize fuel prices, while as Finance Minister he was to hold down spending'. The experiment lasted less than a year, after which time the separate status of the Ministries was restored. The government of José Manuel Barroso preserved this arrangement when it took office in 2002, although Barroso did strengthen the role of the Finance Minister, Manuela Ferreira Leite, by upgrading her status from Secretary of State to Minister of State, with the latter being equivalent to the office of deputy prime minister (Braga de Macedo 2002: 12).

The institutional position of Portugal's finance minister has also been undermined by a lack of accountability over local government finances. A principal problem here is a new local finance law, which gives local government greater control over expenditure without devolving powers to generate revenue. This creates a problem as the finance minister can neither cap annual net borrowing for investment spending by local government nor impose sanctions if a local government overshoots the debt-servicing ceiling. As Bronchi (2003: 12) observes, this has created a deficit bias in local government finance, as evidenced by the surge in borrowing in advance of the December 2001 municipal elections. Correia da Cunha and Silva (2002: 55) estimate that the local finance law has added between 0.2 and 0.3 per cent of GDP to the total general government budget deficit and, by implication, made it more difficult for the finance minister to keep within the bounds of the stability and growth pact.

In the case of Germany, a different set of political economy factors would appear to account for the institutionally weak position of the finance minister. As Zohlnhöfer (1999: 148) succinctly puts it, 'Germany's polity is characterized by a large number of veto players. The co-operative federalism with its necessity of joint-decision making, the Bundesrat as a powerful quasi-second Chamber, the electoral system compelling parties to build coalition governments, the fragmentation of the policy-making process with the importance of ministries, the Constitutional Court with its broad influence on public policy and the independence of the Bundesbank – they all tend to limit the leeway for reform'.

Hallerberg (2004) argues that these factors have created a system of 'checked' delegation in which the German Finance Minister's authority over budgetary matters is constrained. The obstacles to economic reform in Germany are well documented. In an influential study, Scharpf (1987), as recalled in Zohlnhöfer (1999), noted that the Schmidt administration was frustrated in the mid-1970s in its efforts to implement counter-cyclical fiscal policies by, *inter alia*, the fiscal supremacy of the Länder, opposition from liberal coalition partners, and the dominance of opposition parties in the Bundesrat. Zohlnhöfer (1999: 156) attributes the failure of the Kohl administration to implement 'far-reaching reforms' to the fact that the coalition 'lacked programmatic cohesion and a common understanding of what ought to be changed in the relationship between the state and the market'.

The Schröder administration also encountered difficulties in implementing economic reform when it lost control of the Bundesrat after the Land election in Hesse in February 1999. In budgetary terms, this was significant because Article 105(3) of Germany's Basic Law states that '[f]ederal laws relating to taxes the revenue from which accrues wholly or in part to the Länder or to municipalities (associations of municipalities) shall require the consent of the Bundesrat'. In effect, this meant that the opposition Christian Democrats had a veto over revenue decisions in Germany during the early years of EMU (Hallerberg 2004: 89).

The deleterious impact of this veto on public finances became apparent when, in an effort to win the support of the business lobby and several key Länder, the Schröder administration's draft tax reforms in 1999 were revised to include a reduction in the overall tax burden, rather than (as had originally been envisaged) a mere redistribution of the existing burden (Margerum Harlen 2002: 71). Moreover, when it came to efforts at fiscal consolidation, the loss of the Bundesrat shifted the emphasis from the revenue side to the expenditure side of the budget. As von Hagen and Strauch (2001: 28) note, this proved to be problematic because the finance minister's power to cut expenditure was restrained by rapid increases in predetermined federal spending on social insurance, interest repayments, and public sector wages.

If the large number of veto players in Germany's polity contributed towards a system of checked delegation, then so too, it appears, did the accession of the German Democratic Republic to the Federal Republic of Germany in 1990. For von Hagen and Strauch (2001: 29–31), German unification led to a twofold erosion in the power of the finance minister. Firstly, the use of special 'off-budget' funds to finance unification meant that a significant share of government expenditure was subject to neither the usual checks and balances of parliamentary scrutiny nor the supervision of the finance minister. As von Hagen et al. (2001: 49) record, 'while the federal government's debt rose by a mere 3 per cent of GDP from 1989 to 1997, the combined debt of off-budget entities amounted to 12 per cent of GDP in 1997, half the size of federal government debt'. Secondly, the lead role of the Chancellor's Office in the negotiations preceding German unification undermined the finance minister's authority over budgetary matters. As von Hagen and Strauch (2001: 31) note, when it came to decisions relating to public guarantees for the private debts of firms from the new Länder, for example, the talks were chaired by the Chancellor's Office and the finance ministry was largely excluded. Although it remains a moot point as to whether the finance minister would have taken a more hawkish attitude towards the costs of unification – it appears in retrospect that such costs were widely underestimated (Sinn 2000) – the involvement of the Chancellor's Office in budgetary affairs set a dangerous precedent by loosening the finance minister's grip on the public finances (von Hagen and Strauch 2001).

The federal elections of September 2005 created the potential for further fiscal fragmentation in Germany by producing a grand coalition between the Christian Democratic Union/Christian Socialist Union and the Social Democratic Party for the first time since 1969. The result was an increase in the ideological space within government on tax and expenditure issues from 1.7 to 5.1 (Benoit and Laver 2006), which accounts for Hallerberg and von Hagen's (2005) call for a 'fiscal contract' between the governing parties. Whether the coalition agreement adopted in November 2005 went far enough for these authors is unclear, but it did include a package of expenditure cuts and revenue-raising measures worth €35 billion designed to bring budgetary policy in line with the stability and growth pact. In any case, the coalition agreement played a part in bringing government borrowing below 3 per cent of GDP in 2006, prompting Ecofin to close the excessive deficit procedure against Germany in June 2007 (Council of the European Union 2007*b*).

In summary, the evidence explored in this section sheds some light on delegation states' mixed track record of compliance vis-à-vis EMU's fiscal rules. In member states that complied with the stability and growth pact during the period 1998–2007, Ireland, Spain, and Austria, finance ministers found themselves in an institutionally strong position, according to some measures at least. Two countries that broke the rules, Germany and Portugal, stand out as having finance ministers with a comparatively weak grip on the budgetary process for a variety of political-economy reasons. France, Greece, and Italy do not fit this explanation, however, since they posted excessive budget deficits in spite of their institutionally strong finance ministers.

4.3 Fiscal rules in delegation states

An alternative explanation for the puzzle at the heart of this chapter is that those delegation states that complied with the stability and growth pact had more stringent fiscal rules. This hypothesis contradicts Hallerberg et al.'s (2009: 202) conclusion that fiscal rules are 'neither necessary nor sufficient to maintain fiscal discipline' in delegation states. It does, however, chime with the authors' earlier empirical finding that fiscal targets had a strongly significant effect on government debt in EU delegation states in the period 1985–2001 (Hallerberg et al. 2004) and a 'marginally significant' effect when this exercise was rerun for the period 1985–2004.

Hallerberg et al.'s (2009: 75) survey of budgetary processes in EU member states, once again, allows this hypothesis to be put to the test. An ideal fiscal rule, the authors argue, will be underpinned by a multiannual target covering the full size of the budget and backed by a time horizon of five years and economic forecasts based on a reliable macroeconomic model. They also assume that such a rule will be backed by strong political commitment and by procedures that allow finance ministers to block spending changes during implementation and the transfer of funds between government departments. As with the delegation index, the fiscal rules index awards a score of 1.0 in cases where all of these characteristics are met and a score of 0.0 when none apply.

The fiscal contracts index offers limited evidence, overall, to support the view that fiscally profligate delegation states had less stringent fiscal rules (Table 4.6). Portugal and Italy, two member states that posted excessive deficits during EMU's first decade, have fiscal rules that are less stringent than the average for delegation states, but the same is true of a delegation state that ran large budget surpluses, Spain. Greece and France, on the other hand, have fairly stringent fiscal rules in spite of their well-publicized problems with the stability and growth pact.

Austria, the index shows, dramatically increased the strength of its fiscal rules during the early years of EMU. The catalyst for reform in Austria was the fact that the budget deficit for 1999 reached 2.5 per cent of GDP, creating the possibility that it would become the first euro area member to breach the

Table 4.6. Fiscal rules index, 2000 and 2004

	2000	2004
Austria	0.59	0.91
France	0.46	0.78
Greece	0.49	0.75
Ireland	0.58	0.75
Germany	0.77	0.73
Portugal	0.19	0.69
Italy	0.34	0.66
Spain	0.23	0.53
Average	*0.46*	*0.73*

Note: Index ranges from 1.00 when rules are highly stringent and 0.00 when they are insignificant.

Source: Hallerberg et al. (2009: 61).

excessive deficit ceiling. The government responded by introducing an administrative expenditure freeze, accompanied by reforms that included plans to shed 11,000 public sector jobs (Fallend 2001: 249). Although the Organisation for Economic Cooperation and Development (OECD 2003) criticized Austria's rule for its inflexibility and for its impact on labour force participation, its targets were nevertheless achieved. The Commission (2003*a*: 181), for its part, finds that Austria's fiscal rules helped to restore discipline to its public finances during the initial years of EMU.

Austria also launched a domestic stability pact at this time to assign budgetary targets to provincial governments and local authorities (Commission 2003*a*: 151). Under the terms of the pact, the provinces agreed to 'contribute' to an average budget surplus of 0.75 per cent of GDP over the period 2000–4. The pact allowed individual provinces to temporarily undershoot this target by up to 0.15 per cent on condition that the average budget surplus was not below the 0.75 per cent threshold. The local authorities, meanwhile, committed themselves to achieve balanced budgets by 2004. Temporary provisions were made in the pact for individual authorities to undershoot the target by 0.1 per cent of GDP on condition that the average budget was in balance. The pact was enforced through financial sanctions modelled on those of the excessive deficit procedure (Huber 2003: 7). In the event of a breach, a maximum fine of 8 per cent of the negotiated budgetary target plus 15 per cent of the shortfall was envisaged, providing there is a unanimous vote from all signatories (OECD 2003: 132). There was a degree of flexibility in the domestic stability pact, with sanctions suspended in the event of a serious economic slowdown or (as was witnessed after the floods of 2002) a natural disaster (Commission 2003*a*: 182).

The Commission's index of fiscal rules offers an alternative perspective on this topic. This index, which is based on surveys of national fiscal policy conducted in 2005 and again in 2008, assesses the quality of a fiscal rule according to its stringency and coverage (Commission 2006, 2009). A very stringent rule will, the survey assumes, have a clearly defined legal basis, be monitored by an independent, non-partisan body, trigger disciplinary measures in the event of non-compliance, and attract widespread media attention. A rule with complete coverage, meanwhile, will apply to the sum total of general government finances rather than a fraction thereof. Having scored national fiscal rules according to these criteria, the index is standardized such that the average rule is equal to '0' and has a standard deviation equal to '1'.

Econometric analysis finds a positive correlation between the fiscal rules index and cyclically adjusted primary balances over the period 1990–2008 (Commission 2006). This suggests, in short, that member states with well-defined fiscal rules are, ceteris paribus, more likely to keep government borrowing under control. This result notwithstanding, the index offers limited

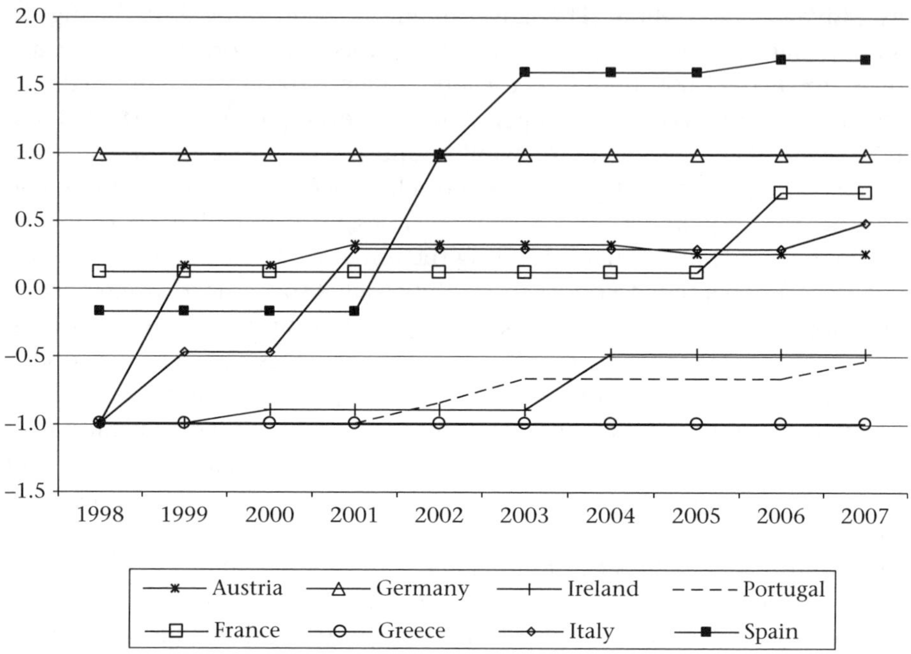

Figure 4.3. Standardized fiscal rules index, 1998–2007

Note: Higher values indicate a more stringent role, with scores standardized such that the average rule over the period 1990–2008 is equal to '0' and has a standard deviation equal to '1'.

Source: DG Economic and Financial Affairs fiscal governance database.

evidence to support claims that fiscal rules were less stringent in those delegation states that posted excessive deficits during EMU's first decade (Figure 4.3). The use of numerical fiscal targets was, the index suggests, equally underdeveloped in Ireland and Portugal in spite of their contrasting fortunes in relation to the stability and growth pact prior to the financial crisis. A more striking finding is that Greece, a serial offender under the pact, employed no fiscal rules whatsoever during the sample period according to the criteria used by the Commission.[2]

Spain stands out in the Commission's index as the delegation state with the most well-developed set of fiscal rules. Under the budgetary stability laws introduced in 2001 and revised in 2006, the general government can borrow up to 1.5 per cent of GDP. This target is disaggregated between the different

[2] The fact that Greece has fairly strong fiscal rules in Hallerberg, Strauch, and von Hagen's survey but none in the Commission's database is due, it would seem, to the fact that the former counts the medium-term budgetary plans set out in Greece's stability programme as a fiscal rule of sorts (see Hallerberg et al. 2001: 8).

levels of government, with the central government allowed to contribute no more than 0.2 percentage points to the country's deficit, with the contributions of the autonomous communities and local entities limited to 0.75 and 0.05 percentage points respectively. Additional deficit spending on investment is also permitted, with central government, autonomous communities, and local entities allowed to borrow a combined 0.5 per cent of GDP for this purpose.

The public audit office monitors the implementation of these provisions. In the event of non-compliance, the central government can issue a non-binding warning to autonomous communities that are putting a strain on the country's finances. These sanctions are still stronger in the event that the country posts an excessive deficit, with any fines imposed by Ecofin passed on to those levels of government that are responsible for this situation. The budgetary stability laws also provide for a contingency fund of up to 2 per cent of total non-financial expenditure to cover government expenditure in the event of unforeseen economic circumstances.

A sign that other delegation states might be following suit is suggested by Germany's decision to incorporate a new fiscal rule into its constitution in 2009. Germany is no stranger to fiscal rules, having prohibited net borrowing by the federal government in excess of (gross) public investment under Article 115 of the Basic Law in 1969. Compliance with this modified golden rule was patchy, however, with net government borrowing respecting this limit less than half of the time between 1970 and 2006, according to Baumann and Kastrop (2007). Under the new rule introduced in 2009, the federal government will be required to run a structural budget of no more than 0.35 per cent of GDP from 2016. The Länder, meanwhile, will be prohibited from issuing new debt from 2020. The debt brake will be enforced by a new stability council, which will include economic and financial officials from the federal and regional governments. In the event of non-compliance with the debt brake, as the new fiscal rules are known, the stability council will be empowered to adopt a restructuring programme for the administrative authority concerned.

In summary, this section has shed further light on delegation states' patchy performance under the stability and growth pact during the period 1998–2007. Two of the euro area's better fiscal students, Austria and Spain, employed a fairly sophisticated set of fiscal rules in spite of their reliance on strong finance ministers to enforce fiscal discipline. In contrast, one of the euro area's worst fiscal performers, Greece, employed no fiscal rules whatsoever, at least according to the criteria used in the Commission's survey of fiscal governance. France, Portugal, Germany, and Italy do not fit this pattern, however, having a set of fiscal rules that seem to have been reasonably well defined.

4.4 Conclusions

The stability and growth pact's reputation as a rule more honoured in the breach than the observance has given rise to a plethora of reform proposals. A puzzle that this reform literature largely puts to one side is why some member states breached the pact's prohibitions on government borrowing during EMU's first decade while others observed them. Political institutionalism offers the most systematic attempt at an explanation, suggesting that the stability and growth pact provides a better fit for member states that rely on contracts to enforce fiscal discipline than those that depend on delegation to strong finance ministers.

The evidence reviewed in this chapter finds that the link between electoral rules and budgetary institutions in euro area members is consistent with the central tenets of political institutionalism, but it challenges its take on the stability and growth pact. Contract states, it was conceded, had a better track record of compliance in relation to EMU's first rules compared to delegation states a whole. The experience of delegation states was found to be far from uniform, however, with France, Germany, Greece, Italy, and Portugal posting excessive deficits, while Austria, Ireland, and Spain kept government borrowing under control.

Differences in the institutional strength of finance ministers among delegation states might account for some of this variation. Whereas the Irish Finance Minister wields considerable influence over the implementation stages of the budget, the same cannot be said of the Finance Ministers of Portugal and Germany. In the former, prime ministerial involvement in expenditure decisions and a lack of control over local government finances are among the factors that have, historically, undermined the autonomy of the finance minister. In the latter, parliamentary involvement in tax policy and the expenditure demands of the Länder are among several factors that have hindered attempts by the finance minister to keep government borrowing under control.

A variation in the use of fiscal rules among delegation states could also account for their divergent experiences in relation to the stability and growth pact. Austria, it was noted, imposed strict limits on administrative expenditure in its attempt to get government borrowing under control in the early years of EMU. Spain, meanwhile, set limits on borrowing by central government, the autonomous communities, and local entities and threatened to pass on fines incurred in the event of an excessive deficit to profligate parts of the public sector. In Greece, in contrast, fiscal rules played no significant role during the first ten years of the single currency, according to the Commission's database on fiscal governance at any rate.

Well-defined fiscal institutions may be essential for fiscal discipline but they cannot, of course, provide a cast iron guarantee of compliance with the stability and growth pact. Few euro area members have fiscal rules that are better suited to their electoral regime than The Netherlands, a contract state that has employed an increasingly sophisticated set of real expenditure targets, real income reference levels, cautious macroeconomic forecasting, and rules for distributing windfall revenue gains since the fiscal crisis that struck in the late 1970s and early 1980s (Heeringa and Lindh 2001: 488). These rules were not sufficient, however, to prevent The Netherlands from posting an excessive deficit in 2005 after a steep economic downturn and a sharp correction in house prices brought a marked rise in government borrowing. Among the delegation states surveyed in this chapter, France and Italy stand out as anomalous cases insofar as they posted excessive budget deficits during EMU's first decade in spite of their seemingly strong finance ministers and fairly well-defined fiscal rules.

Further research is also required to understand the role played by fiscal institutions during the global financial crisis. Perhaps the most pressing puzzle in this regard is how Ireland and Spain with their well-defined fiscal institutions and impeccable track record of compliance with the stability and growth pact in EMU's first decade found themselves at the centre of a sovereign debt crisis in 2010. A related question is what role fiscal institutions will play in the process of fiscal consolidation that is underway in these and other euro area members. Early indications suggest that several delegation states, specifically Austria, France, Germany, Italy, and Portugal, have used the financial crisis as an opportunity to adopt a more stringent set of numerical fiscal rules (Ayuso-i-Casals 2010). Though Greece, another delegation state, is not numbered among this group, a commitment 'to strengthen the fiscal policy framework and fiscal institutions' was included in the memorandum of understanding signed by Greek authorities with the EU and IMF in May 2010 (Commission 2010*b*: 41).

The findings presented in this chapter take issue with political institutionalism's critique of the stability and growth pact, but they concur with its more fundamental insight about the limits of EU economic policy coordination in the absence of well-defined rules and institutions at the national level. This point has not been lost on EU policymakers, who encouraged member states to reinforce the rules and procedures governing national budgetary processes in the March 2005 reform of the stability and growth pact. The Commission's proposals in September 2010 for additional reforms to the pact go further by calling for a regulation on budgetary frameworks in member states that would include, *inter alia*, minimum standards on the use of numerical fiscal rules at the national level (see Chapter 8).

EU policymakers have been more circumspect about exploring the link between national institutions and other aspects of policy coordination (Hodson and Simoni 2009). In the area of structural reform, for example, there has been surprisingly little public debate about whether the specific measures championed by EU policymakers are well suited to the institutional complementarities that characterize different varieties of capitalism (Hall and Soskice 2001; Hancké et al. 2007). A case in point is the Commission's (2010*c*) end of term evaluation of the Lisbon Strategy, which stated that it had 'focused on the right structural reforms' without really seeking to substantiate this claim. This goes against the spirit of the open method of coordination, which consciously rejected a one-size-fits-all approach to economic policy in favour of policies tailor-made to the specificities of national product, labour, and capital markets (Hodson and Maher 2001).

Another serious omission is the lack of attention paid by euro area authorities to differences between national approaches to wage setting. Though the BEPGs pay lip service to the role of the social partners, their calls for the flexible adjustment of prices and wages to market conditions bring to mind a competitive system of wage setting rather than the coordinated approach that prevails in many euro area members. It is also at odds with the Cologne Process, which established a biannual macroeconomic dialogue between EU authorities and the social partners in 1999 to discuss the interaction between monetary and fiscal policies and wage developments.

Though the macroeconomic dialogue continues to meet, its effectiveness as a forum for discussing the wider policy mix has been hindered by a number of factors. For one thing, the parties involved devote around 17 hours per year to discussions at both the technical and political level, which is barely enough to scratch the surface of its mandate (Watt 2005). More serious still is the macroeconomic dialogue's confusing composition. That the EU side is represented by the Ecofin troika of past, present, and future presidencies and the Eurogroup President can make it difficult to address issues specifically related to EMU. On the side of the social partners, the European Trade Union Confederation, the European Centre of Enterprises with Public Participation and of Enterprises of General Economic Interest, and Business Europe speak with authority on a great many issues of relevance to European workers, employers, and firms, but wage setting is not one of them.

Drawing on the experience of the stability and growth pact, a more fruitful approach would be to link discussions of wage developments at the euro area level to the institutions of wage setting at the national level. One such option, suggested by Hancké and Soskice (2003), would be to establish a low inflation pact between wage setters in a small group of large member states, say Germany, France, and Italy. The actors involved in the preparation of such a pact, the authors note, would vary according to national traditions. In France, the government is indirectly involved in collective bargaining with large companies. In Italy, bargaining over cost-of-living increases and competitiveness takes place nationally, with deals on productivity struck at the company level. In Germany, wage bargaining in the engineering sector establishes norms for other industry-level bargains.

5

Why the BEPGs Failed to Bite

In all things, we should only be judged by our peers.

Honoré de Balzac

The exercise of peer pressure through non-binding recommendations is another key characteristic of euro area governance. A case in point is the Broad Economic Policy Guidelines (BEPGs), a set of overarching objectives for the economic policies of member states and the European Union (EU) as a whole adopted by the Economic and Financial Affairs Council (Ecofin) on the basis of a recommendation from the European Commission and with the endorsement of the European Council (Article 121 Treaty on the Functioning of European Union (TFEU)). Though they are, first and foremost, an instrument for fostering consensus on EU economic priorities, the BEPGs also rely on peer pressure to encourage compliance. Member states are bound to conduct their economic policies 'within the context' of these guidelines (Article 120 TFEU) and to inform the Commission about 'important measures taken in the field of their economic policy' (Article 121 TFEU). In the event that national economic policies are found to be inconsistent with these guidelines or a risk to the smooth functioning of Economic and Monetary Union (EMU), Ecofin may, at the instigation of the Commission, issue a non-binding recommendation for corrective action to the member state in question (Article 121 TFEU).

When it comes to issuing guidelines under Article 121(2), EU policymakers have been enthusiastic to the point of overzealous. The first BEPGs, which were adopted in December 1993, contained three general guidelines, covering policies to promote price stability, sound public finances, and employment creation (Commission 1993). Within a decade, the BEPGs had swollen to twenty-three general guidelines, ninety-four country-specific recommendations, and four recommendations addressed specifically to euro area members, covering macroeconomic policies and a host of structural reform priorities under the Lisbon Strategy (Commission 2003*b*). EU policymakers responded by launching the integrated guidelines for growth and jobs in March 2005, bringing together the BEPGs and the EU employment guidelines (Article 148 TFEU) into a single document containing fifteen general guidelines on macro-economic, microeconomic, and employment policies (Commission 2005*a*). The Europe 2020 Strategy, the successor to Lisbon launched in July 2010, continued this trend by cutting the total number of integrated guidelines to ten (Council of the European Union 2010*c*).

When it comes to issuing non-binding recommendations under Article 121(4), EU policymakers have been altogether more reluctant, with only two member states reprimanded for breaching the BEPGs between 1993 and 2010. The first ever Article 121(4) recommendation was addressed to Ireland in February 2001 after plans for tax cuts and expenditure increases in the Irish budget for 2001 were deemed to be inconsistent with the 2000 update of the BEPGs, which had called on Irish authorities to use budgetary policy 'to ensure economic stability given the extent of overheating in the economy' (Council of the European Union 2001*b*). The second Article 121(4) recommendation was addressed to Greece in February 2010 on the grounds that its economic policies had failed to comply with calls in the 2009 update of the BEPGs 'to address macro-economic imbalances and structural weaknesses' and that they risked jeopardizing the smooth functioning of EMU (Council of the European Union 2010*d*).

This chapter seeks to explain why the BEPGs have been used so sparingly as an instrument of peer pressure. Its central argument is that Article 121(4) recommendations can be understood as a sanction that suffers from serious structural shortcomings. Firstly, the BEPGs lack a credible sanctioning institution, insofar as EU policymakers have been reluctant to issue Article 121(4) recommendations for fear of triggering a political backlash. Secondly, the BEPGs lack precise sanctioning criteria, insomuch as there is considerable uncertainty about the conditions under which an Article 121(4) recommendation is likely to be issued. Thirdly, the BEPGs have limited currency in domestic political arenas, reducing the deterrent effects of Article 121(4) recommendations. These findings speak to wider debates about the problems of peer pressure and participation in relation to the open method of coordination launched by EU leaders at Lisbon in March 2000.

The remainder of this chapter is divided into four parts. The first section explores the limitations of Ecofin and the Commission as sanctioning institutions. The second section discusses the sanctioning criteria underpinning the BEPGs, drawing comparisons with the more rigorous standards for enforcing the stability and growth pact. The third section explores EU policymakers' frustrated attempts to involve stakeholders in the formulation and surveillance of the BEPGs. The final section concludes by considering the wider implications of these findings for debates about new governance.

5.1 Sanctioning institutions

To understand the channels through which the BEPGs could exert peer pressure, it is useful to think of Article 121(4) recommendations as a type of sanction. Since the default setting for these recommendations sees them delivered behind closed doors, they can be understood as an attempt by EU finance ministers, backed by the Commission, to bring 'moral pressure' to bear on colleagues who have deviated from commonly agreed principles of economic policy (Deroose et al. 2008). Insofar as Ecofin can, on a proposal from the Commission, vote to make these recommendations public, they can also be an attempt to trigger 'public opinion pressure' by encouraging an open debate on the appropriateness of errant member states' economic policies (Tabellini and Wyplosz 2006: 105).

Gauging the effectiveness of sanctions is problematic for a variety of reasons (see Eaton and Sykes 2000). When sanctions are imposed, it is difficult to know how the target country would have acted if left to its own devices. When sanctions are not imposed, this may be because the threat of sanctions is enough to elicit compliance from the target country or because the sanctioning institution does not expect sanctions to work. These problems are compounded in the case of peer pressure by the nebulous character of non-binding recommendations compared to more traditional, tangible sanctions such as import duties. One approach to such challenges is to think about the institutional conditions under which sanctions in general are likely to take hold before asking whether such conditions are fulfilled in the particular case of peer pressure.

Perhaps the most important condition for effective sanctions is to have a credible sanctioning institution, where credibility refers to the belief that the institution in question is both willing and able to act decisively when the sanctioning criteria are breached. For Martin (1992), credibility in this context will depend, in part, on the costs to the sanctioning institution of imposing disciplinary measures. Where such costs are high, there will be doubts as to the willingness of the sanctioning institution to fulfil its responsibilities. Applied to the case of the BEPGs, the consequences for the Commission and Ecofin of issuing non-binding recommendations become of central importance in understanding the scope and limits of peer pressure as a sanction mechanism.

It was not until the euro had been launched that EU policymakers seriously considered activating Article 121(4). A report on economic policy coordination in Stage 3 of EMU, prepared by Ecofin and adopted by the European Council in Helsinki in December 1999, agreed to step up surveillance of the BEPGs and called on member states 'to give and take open and frank advice, to accept peer pressure and to make the necessary adjustments in order to fulfill commitments that have been undertaken' (Council of the European Union 1999). To this end, it was agreed that the Council would 'stand ready' to endorse Article 121(4) recommendations, while accepting that 'a balance needed to be struck in relation to the frequency' with which this instrument was used (Council of the European Union 1999). The heads of state or government also agreed that Article 121(4) would be used to issue an early warning from Ecofin to member states in need of policy adjustments in the light of major changes to their stability and convergence programmes.

Procedurally, at least, the decisions taken at Helsinki explain the Commission's reasons for initiating an Article 121(4) recommendation against Ireland in February 2001 (Council of the European Union 2001*b*). This move was made in conjunction with Ecofin's opinion on Ireland's updated stability programme, which criticized the Irish budget for pushing through indirect and direct tax cuts and current and capital expenditure increases that were unwarranted by the benign economic outlook foreseen in the previous update. Economically, there was a case to be made at this time for countercyclical fiscal tightening, with such logic looking all the more compelling in the light of the imbalances that built up within the Irish economy in the years leading up to the global financial crisis. Politically, the decision to use Ireland as a test case for enforcing the BEPGs is harder to understand. Chastising the euro area's strongest growth performer – Ireland's real GDP grew by an annual average rate of 9.6 per cent between 1996 and 2000 (Commission 2010*d*: 188) – was always going to be a political hard sell. So too was convincing a country with a large budget surplus to save more at a time when other, larger member states were recording rising budget deficits.

The political backlash that followed Ecofin's recommendation against Ireland brought home to EU policymakers the costs of applying peer pressure through the BEPGs. Irish Finance Minister Charlie McCreevy led the charge against 'Brussels', telling EU finance ministers that their decision was neither proportionate nor even-handed and expressing 'deep concern' about the Commission's decision to make its draft recommendation public (Department of Finance 2001). McCreevy also took aim at Ecofin, questioning EU finance ministers' willingness to take larger member states to task, and insisting that taxation decisions went 'to the core of the democratic principle of the nation state'. These remarks followed a veiled warning by the Tánaiste (Deputy Prime Minister) Mary Harney that the Commission's draft recommendation could deflect from the more important goal of ratifying the Nice Treaty (Harney 2001).

Shrill though some of these criticisms were, they struck a chord at home and abroad. Roughly, 51 per cent of respondents in an *Irish Times*/Ulster Bank poll of business people conducted in February 2001 sided with the Irish Finance Minister in his standoff against Ecofin (O'Sullivan 2001). EU policymakers also faced a backlash in the international arena. Media reaction to the recommendation was unfavourable (see *Economist* 2001; *Wall Street Journal* 2001), with Arthur Laffer (2001) among several prominent economists who came to the Celtic tiger's defence. McCreevy's position was also enhanced by the reluctance of both the Organization for Economic Cooperation and Development (OECD 2001) and the International Monetary Fund (IMF 2001) to criticize Irish fiscal policy at this time.

Having borne the brunt of the criticism following Ecofin's recommendation against Ireland (Dyson 2002: 339), the Commission was ready to throw in the towel by late 2001. Economically, the decision to downgrade Ireland's real GDP growth forecast for 2002 from 7.1 to 3.3 per cent (Commission 2001*b*: 61) made it easier for Irish officials to justify tax cuts and expenditure increases. Politically, a more conciliatory approach to Ireland was critical as preparations for a second referendum on the Nice Treaty got underway. The official line from Ecofin was that the 'implementation of the budget in 2001 reflected some of the concerns underlying the recommendation' (Council of the European Union 2001*c*). Informally, Commissioner David Byrne declared the dispute with his country a 'closed chapter' and let it be known that lessons had been 'learned all round' (Staunton 2001).

Ireland may have paid little heed to the Article 121(4) recommendation, but the experience left a lasting impression on EU policymakers, whose willingness to take member states to task for breaching the BEPGs all but evaporated thereafter. An early indication of this fact occurred in January 2002, when the Commission responded to concerns over rising government borrowing in Portugal and Germany by calling for an 'early warning' under Regulation 1466/97 of the stability and growth pact rather than Article 121(4) (Commission 2002*a*, 2002*b*). Ecofin proved no more willing to play the role of executioner, however, and voted against the early warnings on the grounds that the member states in question had 'effectively responded to the concerns expressed in the Commission's recommendation' (Council of the European Union 2002).

As Hancké (2003) rightly points out, Germany's situation at this time was very different to that of Ireland. After several decades of economic underperformance, Ireland was going through a period of rapid economic catch up that by 2000 had brought double-digit growth and mounting inflationary pressures. Germany, meanwhile, faced the continuing effects of unification on growth, unemployment, and competitiveness and a risk of deflation following the 2001 economic slowdown. This contrast was, as Hancké (2003: 9) argues, duly recognized by EU finance ministers, who 'concluded that a sanction, however symbolic, was premature and unnecessary'.

This fact notwithstanding, Ecofin's actions during this period raised doubts over its willingness to bring moral force to bear on errant member states. Firstly, the fact that Germany escaped censure in the year of a general election created the impression that EU finance ministers had granted a political reprieve to one of their own colleagues. Secondly, the fact that Portugal escaped sanction at this time led to accusations that it had 'piggy-backed' on Germany's predicament (Buti and Guidice 2002: 841). Thirdly, although the conclusions of Ecofin's meeting reveal no indication that a vote took place, unofficial reports indicate that a number of smaller member states, The Netherlands, Belgium, Austria, and Finland, favoured disciplinary measures, but were overruled by the larger member states (Staunton 2002). Although these occurrences merely foreshadowed the legal wrangling over the stability and growth pact in November 2003, they nonetheless provided an early indication of Ecofin's lack of credibility as a sanctioning institution (House of Lords Select Committee on the EU 2003: 18).

EU policymakers' reluctance to apply peer pressure was also evident in the relaunch of the Lisbon Strategy in March 2005. Though the high-level group on the future of Lisbon led by former Dutch Prime Minister Wim Kok explicitly called for greater efforts to 'name and shame' reform laggards (Kok 2004), the Commission agreed only to 'draw attention to underlying difficulties' in the implementation of member states' national reform programmes (Commission 2005*b*). The European Council sided with the Commission, making no reference to the application of peer pressure in general or the use of non-binding recommendations in particular in measures for improving governance adopted in March 2005 (Council of the European Union 2005*a*). Pisani-Ferry and Sapir (2006) were sharply critical of EU policymakers for ignoring the Kok report's recommendations on peer pressure, which they attributed to resistance from large EU member states. Be that as it may, there were inconsistencies between the Kok Group's advocacy of peer pressure and its plea for member states to take ownership of economic reforms (Deroose et al. 2008).

Viewed against this backdrop, the Commission's decision to push for an Article 121(4) recommendation against Greece in February 2010 came out of the blue. According to this reprimand, which EU finance ministers endorsed without delay, Greece failed to address 'macro-economic imbalances and structural weaknesses' as recommended in the June 2009 update of the BEPGs (Council of the European Union 2010*d*). While the warning issued to Ireland in February 2001 was fairly general, Ecofin called on Greece to implement a specific set of structural reforms relating to 'wages, pension reforms, healthcare reforms, public administration, the product market, the business environment, productivity, and employment growth' (Council of the European Union 2010*d*). Another difference with the Irish case is that the Article 121(4) recommendation against Greece was accompanied by a decision to give notice to Greece under Article 126(9) to undertake specific measures to eliminate its excessive deficit by 2012.

Why EU policymakers rediscovered their appetite for peer pressure at this point is not entirely clear. One interpretation is that the costs of inaction in the face of Greece's mounting fiscal crisis outweighed the costs of a political backlash against 'interference' from Brussels. The risks of such a backlash were, in the short term at any rate, quite low. The draft Article 121(4) recommendation followed a technical mission to Athens by officials of the Commission, the European Central Bank, and the IMF during which agreement was reached with Greek authorities on measures to restore confidence in the country's public finances. Public opinion was also conducive to a recommendation at this time. Though overall levels of trust in the EU among Greek respondents to the Eurobarometer fell by 19 per cent between November 2009 and May 2010, levels of trust in the EU's ability to take effective action in response to the financial crisis were considerably higher than levels of confidence in national authorities (Eurobarometer 2010).

5.2 Sanctioning criteria

'The threat of a sanction', as Eaton and Engers (1992: 901) note, 'can be effective only to the extent that the target believes that the sender will stick to its stated policy'. The criteria under which sanctions are imposed are, therefore, of central importance. Where such criteria are imprecise, this will fuel uncertainty about when or whether sanctions will be used, especially if there are doubts as to the credibility of the sanctioning institution. There are also questions of fairness at stake here. While a degree of discretion may be desirable to ensure that sanctions are applied in an appropriate manner, consistency in the treatment of similar cases is key. Imprecise sanctioning criteria will also create uncertainty over the obligations placed on target countries and make it easier for them to contest claims of non-compliance. For this reason and others, Chan and Drury (2000:11) argue, sanctions to support broad aims 'like democracy and human rights' have a comparatively poor track record.

Compared to the excessive deficit procedure (Article 126 TFEU) – the precision of which as a sanction mechanism has been criticized (Hodson and Maher 2004) – the sanctioning criteria underpinning the BEPGs are opaque. As with key stages of the excessive deficit procedure, Article 121(4) recommendations are put to a qualified majority vote in Ecofin, creating the risk that EU finance ministers will show leniency to their peers in the expectation that they will be treated leniently themselves. EU finance ministers are not bound to apply peer pressure to a member state that breaches the BEPGs. Whereas Article 126(7) states that Ecofin 'shall adopt, without undue delay . . . recommendations . . . with a view to bringing that situation to an end within a given period', Article 121(4) states only that the

Council 'may address the necessary recommendations' to member states pursuing economic policies that are inconsistent with the BEPGs or risk jeopardizing the smooth functioning of EMU.

The failure to codify the meaning of inconsistency or jeopardy in this context in the Treaty or secondary legislation adds to the imprecision of Article 121(4). Compliance with the stability and growth pact, in contrast, is governed by Protocol 12(1) TFEU, which prohibits member states from posting budget deficits in excess of 3 per cent of GDP. Council Regulation 1056/2005, it is true, identifies a range of sometimes vague factors to be taken into account when assessing whether breaches of these reference values are exceptional, temporary, and, thus, permissible, but this has not prevented the Commission from initiating disciplinary action against euro area members with budget deficits in excess of 3 per cent of GDP, even at the height of the global financial crisis (Hodson 2010). Article 121(6) allows the Council to adopt 'detailed rules for the multilateral surveillance procedure' referred to in Article 121(4), but it did not do so during the euro's first decade. Calls by the Commission in February 2001 for 'rules of conduct' relating to budgetary policy and structural reforms that would serve as a 'reference framework' for the BEPGs (Commission 2001*c*) are among several initiatives so intended that have sunk without trace.

These problems of assessing compliance with the BEPGs are compounded in the case of guidelines on microeconomic and employment matters by the difficulties of measuring structural reforms. While the excessive deficit procedure has been plagued by well-publicized shortcomings in public finance statistics (see Savage 2005), the BEPGs have come up against the more fundamental problem that economists know more about structural reforms in theory than they do in practice. Moves by the EU Monetary Committee to improve the quality of macroeconomic statistics in the light of EMU began, in earnest, in November 1998, but it was not until December 2005 that the Commission launched LABREF, an annual database on labour-market reforms. Efforts by the EU Economic Policy Committee's Lisbon Methodology group to produce economically robust methods for measuring the implementation and impact of structural reform are ongoing, with the launch in February 2009 of MACMIC, a database that measures the macroeconomic effects of microeconomic reforms, a small but significant step forward in this regard.

A lack of precision concerning Ireland's obligations under the BEPGs certainly made it easier for Irish authorities to contest Ecofin's Article 121(4) recommendation. The fact that the June 2000 update of the BEPGs addressed no less than eight country-specific recommendations to Ireland created uncertainty over what exactly was being asked of the Irish government. Charlie McCreevy exploited this ambiguity to the full, insisting that tax cuts and expenditure increases contained in the Irish budget for 2001 were essential for maintaining the national wage agreement and removing tax-benefit disincentives to labour-participation, as recommended by Ecofin (Department of Finance 2001). Tendentious though these claims were, it was difficult for EU policymakers to refute them in the absence of a commonly agreed methodology for assessing compliance with the BEPGs.

Ecofin's Article 121(4) recommendation against Greece in February 2010 was no more precise. Officially, the country was reprimanded because its economic policies were not in line with the country-specific recommendation set out in the June 2009 update of the BEPGs. EU policymakers offered no evidence, however, to support this claim, referring only to the fact that this update had underlined the need 'to intensify efforts to address the macroeconomic imbalances and structural weaknesses of the Greek economy' (Council of the European Union 2010*d*). That this phrase was used in the preamble to the country-specific recommendations rather than the recommendations themselves (Council of the European Union 2010*d*) only added to the ambiguity surrounding this charge. So too did the fact that the Article 121(4) recommendation called on Greece to 'remove the risk of jeopardising the proper functioning of Economic and Monetary Union' without identifying the nature of the risk or the means to alleviate it (Council of the European Union 2010*d*).

The Lisbon Treaty has introduced a number of changes to the sanctioning criteria underpinning the BEPGs. The fact that member states facing an Article 121(4) recommendation are no longer allowed to vote on their own fate may have made it slightly easier to apply peer pressure to larger member states. More significant still is the provision that disregards the voting rights of non-euro area countries when it comes to Council decisions on whether to issue an Article 121(4) recommendation to a euro area member (Article 139 TFEU). As discussed in Chapter 3, this has given the Eurogroup a greater say in the enforcement of the BEPGs; a point that has not gone unnoticed by the Eurogroup President (Juncker 2010).

The fact that the Commission can now issue a direct warning to member states that breach the BEPGs or risk jeopardizing the smooth functioning of EMU (Article 121(4) TFEU) could make it easier for the EU executive to apply pressure. Such a course of action could leave the Commission even more vulnerable to a backlash, however. That euro area finance ministers would not be altogether adverse to this arrangement is indicated by Juncker's (2010) suggestion that the Commission should not hesitate to make use of direct warnings under Article 121(4) followed by a frank, and presumably informal, discussion with Eurogroup members. The Commission can, it should be recalled, issue direct 'policy advice' to member states that deviate from the adjustment path to meet their medium-term budgetary objectives, but it has done so only on rare occasions.

5.3 The domestic context

As Wallensteen (2000) argues, the effectiveness of international sanctions will depend on the 'double-grip' of international and domestic pressure. By this he implies that even when a sanctioning institution enjoys credibility and the underlying sanctioning criteria are transparent, sanctions are unlikely to work unless they trigger domestic opposition against the government's policies. When this opposition is absent, there is a risk that national governments will use the sanction as an opportunity (to be seen) to defend the national interest against foreign interference (Galtung 1967). Under such circumstances, the target country might actually exhibit a stronger preference for the sanction than the sanctioning institution itself (Drezner 2000: 215).

Media coverage in Ireland of the Article 121(4) recommendation was considerable (see Meyer 2004 for a systematic account). Such was the interest in the reprimand, indeed, that the country's journal of record, the *Irish Times*, took the unusual step of printing the full text of Charlie McCreevy's intervention at the Ecofin Council meeting on 12 February 2001 (*Irish Times* 2001). This newspaper even covered the Commission's supposedly confidential inter-service consultation on the draft recommendation, claiming that calls to cancel €508 million worth of tax cuts in the Irish budget for 2001 had been removed before the issue was discussed in the College of Commissioners (Suiter 2001). High-profile commentators on EU and economic affairs also weighed in with op-ed pieces on the recommendation, with several calling for EU policymakers' advice to be given a fair hearing (Laffan 2001; O'Leary 2001).

Irish politicians were slower on the uptake. Charlie McCreevy was called to account by the lower house of Ireland's parliament, the Oireachtas, on the day after Ecofin's recommendation was issued, but the main thrust of this debate was why the Irish government had failed to block the measure rather than the Council's criticisms of Irish economic policy (Dáil Éireann 2001). This was, moreover, the first time that the BEPGs had been discussed at length in the Oireachtas, meaning that parliamentarians showed limited knowledge of the context in which the recommendation took place. An Oireachtas committee eventually looked at this issue in closer detail – Commissioner for Economic and Financial Affairs Pedro Solbes and Commission President Romano Prodi were among those who gave evidence – but not until June 2001, by which time the debate had lost much of its heat.

In the final analysis, however, the Irish government appears to have paid a limited price at home for breaching the BEPGs. In an *Irish Times*/MRBI poll conducted in January 2001, as news of a possible recommendation from Brussels was beginning to break, some 71 per cent of respondents agreed that the budget was good for the country, with the government's approval ratings rising fifteen points since September 2000 (Coghlan 2001). There was no further polling on the 2001 budget thereafter, but the government's approval rating rose by one point in the *Irish Times*/MRBI poll published in May 2001, suggesting that EU peer pressure had made a limited impact in the intervening period (Brennock 2001*a*).

The effect of the recommendation on Charlie McCreevy's political position is a matter of interpretation. The Irish Finance Minister's trenchant criticisms of the EU, which only hardened after Ireland's 'no' vote to the Nice Treaty in June 2001 (Brennock 2001*b*), were reportedly one of several issues that contributed to tensions with cabinet colleagues. These tensions lingered on until the decision was taken in July 2004 to nominate McCreevy to become Ireland's next member of the Commission. That McCreevy secured the prized portfolio for internal market and services was not without a hint of irony, since it owed something to his high profile on the EU stage following Ireland's stand-off with Brussels over the BEPGs.

The political backlash that followed the EU's reprimand of Greece in February 2010 was altogether more serious. Two days after the Greek government announced a public sector wage freeze and one day after the Commission adopted its draft recommendations under Articles 121(4) and 126(9), Greek customs and tax officials launched a 48-hour strike. This was followed, within a matter of weeks, by the first in a series of general strikes against the government's planned austerity measures. Industrial action was soon accompanied by civil unrest that resulted in the death of three people in a firebomb attack on a bank in Athens in May 2010. The country's sovereign debt crisis took an instant toll on the Papandreou administration's reputation, with levels of trust in the government falling by 19 percentage points between November 2009 and May 2010 (Eurobarometer 2010).

Putting the Greek case to one side, the EU's attempts to apply peer pressure via the BEPGs appear, on the whole, to have had a limited impact on domestic politics. In its review of the Lisbon Strategy, the Kok Group (2004) concluded that 'national parliaments and citizens [had] not been sufficiently associated with the process, so that pressure on governments [had] been less than it should and could have been'. Though EU policymakers did not, as noted above, share the Kok Group's passion for peer pressure, the relaunch of the Lisbon Strategy picked up on this point by calling for 'parliaments, regional, and local bodies, social partners, and civil society' to take an active part in the reform process alongside national governments (Council of the European Union 2005*a*). To this end, it was agreed that member states would draw up national reform programmes on the basis of the new integrated guidelines for growth and jobs in consultation 'with all stakeholders at regional and national level, including parliamentary bodies' (Council of the European Union 2005*a*:

13). Each member state also agreed to appoint a Lisbon coordinator to promote internal coherence on reform issues within government.

National governments were slow to implement these reforms. According to Pisani-Ferry and Sapir (2006), nine out of twenty-five member states failed to involve parliamentary committees in the formulation of the first wave of national reform programmes in Autumn 2005, with eighteen out of twenty-five governments giving no indication of follow-up. Lisbon national coordinators were, eventually, appointed in all member states but the seniority of these office holders, as Begg (2007) notes, varied between member states. Finland, for example, appointed its Finance Minister to serve as the point person for the Lisbon Strategy. The United Kingdom, in contrast, entrusted this task to the Director of European and Global Issues in the Cabinet Office, a position occupied by a comparatively junior member of the senior civil service.

Attempts to foster a 'home-grown' debate on EU economic policy coordination appear to have been quietly shelved in the Europe 2020 Strategy. Though EU leaders continue to pay lip service to the involvement of 'national parliaments, social partners, regions and other stakeholders' (Council of the European Union 2010*e*), member states, it would seem, are no longer expected to consult these actors in the formulation of, and follow-up to, their national reform programmes. There is, likewise, no mention of what role, if any, national coordinators will play in the EU's economic reform agenda. The result for EU policymakers is that the exercise of peer pressure through the BEPGs remains a risky business, with no guarantee that an Article 121(4) recommendation will foster peer pressure from the bottom up.

5.4 Conclusion

As an instrument for fostering consensus, the BEPGs have, as discussed by Deroose et al. (2008), shown some value-added. For example, the process by which guidelines are formulated, though it is unwieldy, fosters a useful exchange of views between a host of policymakers at the EU and national level. Furthermore, the overarching character of the guidelines offers an antidote to the stability and growth pact's fixation with fiscal discipline. As an instrument for applying peer pressure, however, the BEPGs have fallen short, with EU policymakers proving reluctant to name and shame member states in spite of widespread problems of compliance. Article 121(4) recommendations have failed to bite, it has been argued in this chapter, because they suffer from serious shortcomings as a sanction mechanism.

As a test case for establishing the credibility of Article 121(4) recommendations, the reprimand issued to Ireland in February 2001 could not have, with the benefit of hindsight, fared much worse. Firstly, the backlash against Brussels led by Irish Finance Minister Charlie McCreevy confirmed the high political costs to EU policymakers of applying peer pressure via the BEPGs. Secondly, the ease with which Irish authorities contested Ecofin's recommendation confirmed that the sanctioning criteria underpinning the BEPGs lacked precision. Finally, the fact that EU policymakers struggled to sway public opinion in Ireland on the government's economic policy was symptomatic of the BEPGs' failure to find a foothold in domestic politics.

The exercise of peer pressure via the BEPGs, it has been noted, was all but abandoned thereafter. Article 121(4) remained dormant for a decade, as EU policymakers grew gradually more reluctant to criticize member states for failing to meet their commitments under the BEPGs. This shift culminated in the relaunch of the Lisbon Strategy in March 2005, with EU policymakers ignoring the Kok Group's pleas for a more aggressive use of naming and shaming in favour of a less confrontational approach. The emphasis on ownership in this relaunch was an attempt to foster a 'home-grown' debate on EU economic policy coordination by encouraging member states to involve national parliaments and other stakeholders in the formulation of, and follow-up to, the new integrated guidelines for growth and jobs. Compliance with this request was patchy and piecemeal, however.

The Commission's decision to push for, and Ecofin's decision to endorse, an Article 121(4) recommendation against Greece in February 2010 came as something of a surprise in the light of these developments. A lack of alternatives for addressing Greece's fiscal crisis was one of the reasons offered in this chapter for why EU policymakers may have resorted to peer pressure at this time. Another was that the risks of a backlash against Brussels were low in the short term and, in any case, lower than the costs of inaction in the face of rising concerns about cross-border contagion from the crisis. Compared to Ecofin's reprimand of Ireland in February 2001, the Article 121(4) recommendation against Greece was no more precise, but it was accompanied by a powerful political response in the domestic arena. What impact this political response will have in the long run on the Greek government's response to its fiscal crisis and the country's relationship with the EU remains to be seen.

Whether Ecofin's reprimand of Greece marks the beginning of a new era of peer pressure is another open question. Member states' ambivalence about using the BEPGs to name and shame errant member states was evident from the non-papers submitted to the Commission in preparation for the launch of the Europe 2020 Strategy, the successor to Lisbon. While the Danish government called for peer pressure to be linked to transfers from the EU budget, the German government argued that recommendations against specific countries should be used sparingly and only then in consensus with the member state in question.[1] Given the lack of agreement on this issue, it was unsurprising that the European Council remained silent on the question of peer pressure when it formally launched the Europe 2020 Strategy in June 2010. EU heads of state or government did, however, agree to make 'better use of the instruments provided by Article 121' (Council of the European Union 2010*e*). An attempt to reactivate Article 121(4) by spelling out more clearly the criteria under which non-binding recommendations should be delivered is at the heart of the Commission's proposals for reforming EU economic governance presented in September 2010 (see Chapter 8).

How do these findings speak to wider debates about EU policymaking? The BEPGs were, as Hodson and Maher (2001) observe, a forerunner to the open method of coordination. It is perhaps not surprising, therefore, that the open method's effectiveness has also been hindered by a lack of precision in the underlying sanctioning criteria and a lack of participation by key stakeholders. Zeitlin (2009: 13), for example, finds that the EU's ability to exert 'external pressure' on national employment and social policies depends 'on domestic conditions, notably the perceived legitimacy, intellectual basis, and procedural fairness of EU objectives, guidelines, targets, recommendations, and rankings, the level of public support for the EU and sensitivity to European criticism, and the national visibility of OMC processes – all of which are often found lacking'.

All of this begs the question of whether the EU should persevere with peer pressure. Arguments against suggest that the benefits of championing closer coordination between member states in the fields of fiscal policy and structural reform may be outweighed by the backlash against the EU for being the bearer of bad tidings. Ecofin's Article 121(4) recommendation against Ireland appears, in the end, to have had little discernable impact on those who voted against the Nice Treaty in June 2001 (Sinnott 2001), but concerns for the EU's perceived neo-liberalism were high on the list of reasons given by French voters for rejecting the Constitutional Treaty in May 2005 (Eurobarometer 2005). Arguments for persevering with peer pressure point to the lack of viable alternatives; financial penalties are more contentious still as a sanction mechanism and are yet to be invoked under the excessive deficit procedure.

If EU policymakers are serious about peer pressure, then further thought must be given to the question of how to boost the effectiveness of non-binding recommendations as a sanction mechanism. The experience of the BEPGs suggests that national governments cannot always be relied on to encourage a home-grown debate on the coordination of economic reforms

[1] Member states' responses to the consultation on the Europe 2020 Strategy are available at: http://ec.europa.eu/dgs/secretariat_general/eu2020/contrib_member_states_en.htm

in the EU. This invites a discussion of whether more might be done at the EU level to encourage participation by social partners and other relevant stakeholders in the open method of coordination. Research by Smismans (2008) on the EU's failure to engage with civil society actors through new modes of governance in the area of EU occupational health and safety gives reason to be sceptical. Research by de la Porte and Pochet (2005) on the EU's comparatively successful efforts to involve non-governmental actors in the open method on social inclusion gives grounds for greater optimism.

The BEPGs, finally, bring bad news not only about the effectiveness of new governance but also about its legitimacy. An important lesson from Ecofin's ill-fated Article 121(4) recommendation against Ireland in February 2001 is that the EU is vulnerable to accusations of competence creep even in areas where it has bent over backwards to respect member states' sovereignty. This conclusion chimes with Hodson and Maher's (2001) warning that new governance's pragmatic approach to legitimacy could fall short if member states choose to play the sovereignty card in the face of criticisms from EU policymakers. It also recalls Mashaw's argument (2005), cited by Maher (2007), that accountability in general hinges not only on who is held accountable according to what standards but also on whom the individual or entity in question is held accountable to. Charlie McCreevy's criticisms of Ecofin's even-handedness in February 2001 stung precisely because they spoke to concerns about the risk of collusion between powerbrokers in Ecofin, concerns that were, as noted above, borne out by the leniency shown to Germany and Portugal one year later. It is against this backdrop that the Commission's proposals on strengthening economic governance and the recommendations of the Van Rompuy Taskforce looked at ways of increasing the credibility and legitimacy of sanctioning institutions in relation to both the BEPGs and the stability and growth pact (see Chapter 8).

Part III

New Modes of Economic Diplomacy

6

Ensemble Acting in the G20 and the IMF

And one man in his time plays many parts.
William Shakespeare

The delegation of plenipotentiary powers to supranational institutions is a hallmark of the Community method. Nowhere is this more evident than in relation to European Union (EU) external trade policy, where the Commission has the authority to initiate and conduct negotiations with third countries and international organizations (Article 207 Treaty on the Functioning of the European Union (TFEU)). No such provision exists in relation to the external aspects of EU macroeconomic policy. The Treaty, it is true, allows the Council of Ministers to establish a unified representation in 'international financial institutions and conferences' (Article 138 TFEU), but the Commission's attempts to make use of this provision have thus far been rebuffed. Instead, member states have adopted ad hoc and informal measures to coordinate EU involvement in the International Monetary Fund (IMF), the World Bank, the Organisation for Economic Co-operation and Development (OECD), the Group of 7 (G7), the Group of 8 (G8), and the Group of 20 (G20) (see van den Noord et al. 2008; Chang 2009 for an overview of these measures).

The EU's fragmented presence in multilateral settings has been roundly booed by students of International Political Economy. For McNamara and Meunier (2002: 850), the 'cacophony' of European voices in multilateral settings means that 'the pre-eminence of the United States in international monetary matters, as in other realms, is likely to remain unchallenged'. This point is echoed by Cohen (2008*a*), who criticizes the Treaty for failing to spell out who is in charge of Economic and Monetary Union's (EMU) external representation. Current arrangements for coordination, he insists, are 'bound to lack impact' in the absence of a 'strategic commitment to achieve and defend common positions . . . backed by genuine political commitment' (Cohen 2008*a*: 51).

Calls for a centralized system of external representation are commonplace. McNamara and Meunier (2002: 860) suggest that giving the Eurogroup primary responsibility for 'coordination and communication between the national economic policy realm and the international political and financial community' would help 'to transform the EU into a truly global actor'. Aherne and Eichengreen (2007: 142) sound a similar note, arguing that 'consolidating Europe's representation would . . . enhance the continent's influence' and, to this end, the authors advocate the creation of single seats for euro area members and all other EU member states on the IMF Executive Board and in the G7 and G20. Bini Smaghi (2009: 77) adds to this chorus by arguing that a single EU constituency 'would enable EU member states to have a strong impact on IMF policies, potentially as strong as that of the United States'.

Plausible though these arguments might be, evidence that the euro area's coordinated approach to external representation has led to a lack of international influence is scant. McNamara and Meunier (2002: 851) recall that EU member states failed to reach a consensus on IMF lending to Russia and Turkey, but they do not say what, if anything, a single EU representative at the Fund could have done to overcome such differences. Bini Smaghi (2009) offers a more striking example of how the EU's influence has been undermined by its fragmented presence in the Fund. All EU member states, he observes, supported plans for an IMF crisis resolution mechanism when the issue was raised in April 2003, but the Executive Director from Spain was forced to vote against this proposal because its voice was drowned out by some of the Latin American countries in its constituency.

One reason why more is not known about the euro area's role in multilateral settings is that international economic policy coordination is a scarce commodity, especially during periods of apparent economic calm. McNamara and Meunier (2002: 859) tacitly acknowledge this point when they argue that a failure by euro area members to reach consensus on international issues would be more costly during a financial crisis, since it is under such circumstances that 'delays can be damaging'. This chimes with Cohen (2008*a*: 40) who argues that 'European states seem remarkably unprepared to cope with any wider instability that might erupt in international finance'. The global financial crisis that began in 2007 thus provides an unprecedented opportunity to gauge the euro area's ability to speak with one voice during a period in which the international community had more than usual to say.

This chapter reviews the role played by the EU at the height of the financial crisis in two key multilateral fora: the G20 and the IMF. In the case of the former, it finds that EU member states were at the forefront of efforts to forge an international consensus on policy responses to the crisis and that they secured key concessions at the landmark G20 leaders' summits in 2008 and 2009. In the case of the latter, it finds that EU member states exercised considerable collective influence within the IMF when it came to the provision of financial support for Hungary, Latvia, and Romania. The EU was more circumspect about seeking financial assistance for Greece and other euro area countries, but such delays were rooted in deep-seated differences between EU member states rather than a lack of coordination between European representatives at the Fund. Viewed in the round, the fact that EU member states were forced to seek financial assistance from the IMF is a blow to Europe's international standing, but the manner in which such funding was secured provides evidence of the EU's influence within the Fund.

These findings point to a paradox in the external representation of EMU: when member states agree on international economic priorities, there is little point in establishing a more unified system of external representation, but when member states fundamentally disagree about what to do on the world stage, there is little hope that a more unified system of external representation could fare any better. As regards the first of these points, the EU, it should be recalled, had a seat at the G20 leaders' summits in Washington, DC, London, and Pittsburgh but it played a supporting role to the collective efforts of France, Germany, and the United Kingdom. With respect to the second, there is little that a single EU chair at the IMF could have done to bring forward financial support for Greece since this decision ultimately required a financial commitment by member states. None of this suggests that EMU's system of external representation should be immune from reform, but it challenges claims that the EU cannot speak with one voice on the international stage because of its coordinated approach to economic diplomacy.

The remainder of this chapter is divided into four sections. The first explores the EU's involvement in the G20 during the global financial crisis. The second section takes stock of the EU's relations with the IMF as concerns over a fiscal crisis in Europe mounted. The third section revisits debates about the need for a single euro area chair in multilateral settings in the light of these findings. The final section draws some general conclusions about what the preceding analysis means for the EU's ambitions to be a global actor.

6.1 The EU in the G20

One of the most striking facets of the financial crisis from a global governance perspective is the extent to which the G20 has eclipsed meetings of finance ministers and central bank governors in the G7 and summits of heads of state or government in the G8. The members of the G7 launched the G20 in December 1999 to encourage a regular exchange of views between finance ministers and central bankers from 'systematically significant economies' in the aftermath of the Asian financial crisis (G7 1999).[1] It was not until the international banking system went into freefall in October 2008 that the heads of state or government of these countries saw fit to meet. The first G20 leaders' summit, which was held in Washington, DC, in November 2008, was followed by high-profile meetings in London in April 2009 and Pittsburg in September 2009. At the Pittsburg summit, it was agreed that the G20 leaders would meet at least once a year, thus confirming the new forum's central role in the global governance architecture.

For Kirton (2000), the emergence of the G20 reflects two structural shifts in the international political economy. From a neorealist perspective, he suggests, the economic rise of developing countries such as India and China shifted the balance of political power away from developed countries and, by implication, the G7 and G8. From a Westphalian perspective, as Kirton calls it, the intensification of globalization required a forum that includes representatives from all regions of the world. If these trends made the G20's rise likely in the long term, then the timing of the first leaders' summit owed something to the international influence of EU member states.

Nicolas Sarkozy, in particular, used his country's presidency of the EU in the second half of 2008 to make the case for a summit of world leaders in response to the financial crisis. In a speech to the UN General Assembly on behalf of the EU in September 2008, Sarkozy argued that the G8 should be enlarged to include emerging economic powers such as Brazil, China, India, Mexico, and South Africa in response to the crisis (Sarkozy 2008), a message that he took to the Asia European Meeting in Beijing and the Francophone Summit in Quebec. The French President returned to the United States in October 2008 armed with a mandate from the European Council and accompanied by Commission President José Manuel Barroso for a meeting with President George W. Bush at Camp David. This mission was significant as it paved the way for the summit of G20 leaders in Washington, DC in November 2008, which in turn laid the groundwork for more substantial summits in London in April 2009 and Pittsburgh in September 2009 (Kirton and Guebert 2010).

As with the domestic aspects of euro area policy coordination (see Chapter 3), the growing influence of EU heads of state or government on international economic issues occurred at the expense of finance ministers in general and the Eurogroup in particular. Jean-Claude Juncker was conspicuous by his absence from the EU's diplomatic mission to the United States in October 2008 and from the G20 leaders' summits that stemmed from this meeting. The official reason for Juncker's non-attendance at the G20 was that the EU is usually

[1] The founding countries of the G20 are Argentina, Australia, Brazil, Canada, China, France, Germany, India, Indonesia, Italy, Japan, Mexico, Russia, Saudi Arabia, South Africa, Republic of Korea, Turkey, the United Kingdom, and the United States. The EU occupies the twentieth seat.

represented by the President of the Economic and Financial Affairs Council (Ecofin) in the case of ministerial meetings and the President of the European Council in the case of leaders' summits. However, such protocol did not prevent Sarkozy from allowing Spanish Prime Minister José Luis Rodríguez Zapatero and Dutch Prime Minister Jan Pieter Balkenende to stow away in the EU delegation to the Washington summit in November 2008.

Why the EU has its own seat on the G20 while the euro area does not is a matter of debate. At the Vienna European Council in December 1998, EU leaders agreed that the Eurogroup President could attend meetings of the G7 finance ministers (Council of the European Union 1998). This announcement came after several months of talks with those EU member states not intent on joining the euro area and was followed by several months of negotiations to win the support of Japan, Canada, and the United States. That euro area members had exhausted their political capital in securing a seat for the Eurogroup President at the G7 is one explanation for why the EU did not push for a euro area presence in the first meeting of the G20 in December 1999. Indeed, the fact that the EU was offered full membership at the G20 seems to have been due to efforts by non-European G7 deputies to exclude smaller EU member states from the new grouping rather than diplomatic efforts by the Europeans (G20 2008*a*: 21).

That the Eurogroup President is on the cast list for the G7 but not the G20 encapsulates the EU's protean presence in multilateral fora, but it should not be mistaken for a lack of collective action among member states. In fact, EU member states maintained a remarkably united front in the G20 at the height of the financial crisis. One such display of unity was the decision by EU leaders to make public an agreement on 'principles and approaches' in advance of the G20 leaders' summit in Washington in November 2008 (Council of the European Union 2008*b*). This document, though it papered over differences between the United Kingdom on one side and France and Germany on the other concerning the need for a coordinated fiscal stimulus, identified a range of issues on which EU member states sought progress.

The G20 leaders' summit in Washington, DC, fell well short of promises by Brown and Sarkozy to build a 'new Bretton woods' (Hall and Eaglesham 2008), but it showed no shortage of EU influence. The summit's timid language on regulatory reform may have been a blow to the EU, which had called for 'no market, no territory and no financial institution' to escape regulation or oversight (Council of the European Union 2008*b*), but the Europeans won concessions in other areas. For example, EU member states sought and secured: (*a*) an immediate review of the resources made available to the IMF and the role of the Financial Services Forum; (*b*) stronger oversight of credit rating agencies; and (*c*) a commitment to review and align global accounting standards (G20 2008*b*). EU member states also achieved their demand for a follow-up summit of G20 leaders within 100 days, thus helping to maintain the momentum for international cooperation in the face of continued financial uncertainty.

The run-up to the G20 in London in April 2009, once again, witnessed intense behind-the-scenes cooperation between EU member states. The four EU members of the G20, France, Germany, Italy, and the United Kingdom, took the lead on these discussions, but the adoption of 'agreed language with a view to the G20 summit in London' by the European Council (Council of the European Union 2009*a*) ensured a degree of buy-in from all heads of state or government (Nasra et al. 2009: 6). This document was ambiguous in places – its simultaneous support for a continued fiscal stimulus and a planned withdrawal of macroeconomic stimuli is a case in point – but its pledge of €75 billion to enhance the IMF's lending capacity showed that Europeans were serious about giving the Fund a greater role in crisis management.

The London summit was far from being an unqualified success – its silence on global macroeconomic imbalances was among its most serious shortcomings – but the final communiqué respected a number of the EU's red lines (G20 2009*a*). The G20's avoidance of additional fiscal stimulus measures, though it was not necessarily in the interests of the global economy or to the satisfaction of UK Prime Minister Gordon Brown, was a boon for the euro area's fiscal hawks. The trebling of the IMF's financial resources and the establishment of a Financial Stability Board were also consistent with the EU's calls for a reform of the international financial architecture, while the decision to enhance the oversight of systemically important hedge funds and credit rating agencies harkened back to European demands at the Washington, DC, summit (Council of the European Union 2008*b*).

The G20's decision to take immediate action and, if necessary, impose sanctions against tax havens was the issue on which the influence of EU member states was most discernable. The fact that Angela Merkel and Nicolas Sarkozy insisted on this point in their pre-summit press conference was interpreted at the time as a split in the EU camp (Hall 2009), but Gordon Brown had made similar remarks in the run-up to the London meeting (Houlder 2009). The more serious divide at the summit was between EU member states and China, with the latter expressing concerns that the OECD, a body of which it is not a member, would be asked to draw up a list of tax havens. In the end, US President Barack Obama brokered a compromise between Sarkozy and Chinese President Hu Jintao that ensured the G20 would take note of, but not be bound by, OECD blacklists (Luce 2009).

Not all EU member states, it is true, celebrated the G20's decision to clamp down on tax havens. This issue, it should be recalled, had not been included in the 'agreed language' adopted by the European Council in advance of the London summit and it prompted critical remarks from those member states that were eventually cited by the OECD for not being fully compliant with tax cooperation rules (Nasra et al. 2009: 6). The member states in question, Austria, Belgium, and Luxembourg, wasted little time, however, in accepting the EU's position and taking the necessary steps to remove themselves from the OECD's 'grey list'.

After the publicity surrounding the London summit, the follow-up meeting of G20 leaders in Pittsburg was a more prosaic affair, but it saw no shortage of coordination between EU member states. A further sign of the apparent convergence in views between France, Germany, and the United Kingdom on the future of financial capitalism (see Moschella 2010) came in the form of a joint letter from Merkel, Sarkozy, and Brown to Swedish Prime Minister Frederik Reinfeldt, the President in office of the European Council, calling on the EU to send a strong message to the G20 over the need for further reforms to international financial regulation (Brown et al. 2009). The ideas set out in this letter formed the basis for 'agreed language' for the G20 summit in Pittsburgh adopted by the EU heads of state or government at an informal meeting in Brussels on 17 September 2009 (Council of the European Union 2009*c*). This document repeated the EU's by now familiar cry for credible exit strategies from macroeconomic stimulus packages and included a fresh proposal for binding rules on bankers' bonuses.

EU leaders sounded some discordant notes in the run-up to the Pittsburgh summit in September 2009 – an eleventh-hour call for a financial transactions tax by German Finance Minister Peer Steinbrück apparently took other EU member states by surprise (Benoit 2009) – but they stood firm on regulatory issues and achieved a result on bankers' bonuses. The G20's language on compensation policies may have lacked the legal bite that the EU was looking for, but it endorsed the implementation standards agreed by the Financial Stability Board and sent a clear signal to banks about encouraging excessive risk taking (G20 2009*b*). More significant still was the agreement at Pittsburgh that the G20 should become the 'premier forum for . . . economic policy coordination' and that leaders' summits should be held on an annual basis from 2010. This decision, it would seem, makes permanent the power shift from the G7 and G8 to the G20, a shift that owes much to the diplomatic efforts of the EU.

6.2 The EU and the IMF

If the financial crisis altered the G20's place in the global governance architecture, then it was also a game changer for the role of the IMF. Prior to the crisis, as Pisani-Ferry (2008*a*: 1) acknowledges, 'it was widely held . . . that the IMF had lost its relevance in a world of increasingly free capital mobility where the financing needs of more and more developing countries were covered by capital markets'. Beattie (2009) put this point more succinctly when he compared the Fund during the early years of the new century to 'a bored coastguard staring across a calm sea'. Once the financial storm struck, however, the IMF wasted little time in reasserting itself. The Fund's first-hand knowledge of crisis management and the political astuteness of its Managing Director, Dominique Strauss-Kahn, were among the factors that helped to reinvigorate the IMF. The G20's aforementioned decision to treble the IMF's financial resources also put it in a much stronger position to provide financial support to stricken economies.

Among EU member states, only France, Germany, and the United Kingdom have the right to appoint their own Executive Directors to the IMF Executive Board, which runs the Fund on behalf of the Board of Governors. The remaining EU member states belong to the so-called 'mixed constituencies', which elect Executive Directors to speak on their behalf. Constituencies generally include a mix of developed and developing economies (Van Houtven 2002: 20), with the result that smaller EU member states find themselves in groupings that include at least some countries from outside the Union. Ireland, Poland, and Spain are extreme cases in this respect since they vote as part of blocs that include no other EU member state. Whereas Spain takes turns with Mexico and Venezuela to serve as Executive Director, Poland and Ireland belong to constituencies that are permanently chaired by countries that hold a majority of votes; Switzerland in the case of the former and Canada in the case of the latter.

At the Vienna European Council in December 1998, EU leaders granted the European Central Bank (ECB) observer status at the IMF and decided that the Executive Director of the member state holding the presidency of the Eurogroup would speak up on matters specifically related to EMU (Council of the European Union 1998). To this end, it was (eventually) agreed to appoint a Commission official to the office of the Executive Director in question and to strengthen practical coordination between EU members on IMF business in Brussels and Washington, DC. The Economic and Financial Committee's Sub-Committee on the International Monetary Fund (SCIMF) is responsible for coordinating EU policy on IMF business from Brussels. A body known simply as 'EURIMF' facilitates an informal exchange of views in Washington, DC, between IMF Executive Directors and Alternates from EU member states, the ECB's observer to the Fund and an official from the EU Delegation to the United States.

The EU's approach to the Fund may be Byzantine – the SCIMF alone includes over sixty officials and operates on the basis of consensus – but member states still showed themselves capable of coordination during EMU's first decade. The SCIMF produced 'common understandings' between member states on issues ranging from debt relief to IMF quota and voice and took charge of preparing the Ecofin President's speech at meetings of the IMF's

International Monetary and Financial Committee (EURODAD 2006). The EURIMF took a big step forward in 2007 by appointing the Executive Director from Germany, Klaus Stein, as its first 'permanent' President. The EURIMF President's primary function is to present the views of the EU and the euro area to the IMF Executive Board in the form of written statements (Aubrechtová et al. 2010). These statements cover issues such as Article IV reports on the euro area and EU member states and issues of specific relevance to EMU, such as exchange rates and macroeconomic imbalances.[2]

That member states of the EU, not to mention the euro area, would find themselves in IMF programmes seemed like a remote possibility before the financial crisis. EU countries have traditionally been among the IMF's most creditworthy constituents. Indeed, such was the belief in the EU's overriding economic stability that Mahieu et al. (2005) warned that switching to a single euro area chair could trigger tensions within the IMF Executive Board by creating a powerful creditor constituency. Viewed in the light of this claim, the fact that Hungary, Latvia, Romania, and, most worrying of all from the point of view of EMU, Greece and Ireland were forced to seek financial assistance from the IMF dealt a serious blow to the EU's international standing. Whether this loss of face was accompanied by a loss of international influence is a more complex matter, however.

When it came to member states whose currency is not the euro, the EU acted decisively and in a way that was revealing of its influence in the international arena. In October 2008, the EU joined forces with the IMF and World Bank to provide a €25.1 billion rescue package to Hungary, which was among the European countries worst hit by the crisis as a result of its burgeoning budget and current account deficits. The €6.5 billion that the EU contributed to this scheme was more than just a show of solidarity to a stricken member state. It was an unexpected display of financial force by the EU; this was, after all, the first time that Ecofin-activated Article 143 TFEU, which provides for mutual assistance to euro outsiders facing balance of payments difficulties.

The EU's support for Hungary allowed it to draw on the financial resources of the IMF while retaining a say over the conditions attached to the overall package and the assessments of its implementation. A statement released by the Ecofin Presidency on 14 October 2008 made it clear that EU officials were 'in close consultations with the Hungarian authorities and the Fund to ensure that any conditionality attached to possible IMF financing [was] consistent and mutually reinforcing with EU policy advice under the Treaty framework' (Ecofin Presidency and the Commission 2008). The Commission was a big

[2] Article IV reports are prepared in the light of IMF missions to members and form the basis for Executive Board discussions of economic policies and developments in the economy in question.

winner on the EU side. Although Ecofin retains final say on whether to grant balance of payments assistance under Article 143 TFEU, it falls to the Commission to initiate such action and to raise the necessary funds. The Commission's influence in the Hungarian case was evident from the fact that Commissioner for Monetary Affairs Joaquín Almunia signed the Memorandum of Understanding with Hungary on behalf of the Community and from the fact that officials from DG Economic and Financial Affairs joined their counterparts from the IMF in missions to Hungary to review progress made (Commission 2008*b*).

The EU also moved quickly during the financial crisis to join international efforts to support Latvia and Romania. In the case of Latvia, the EU contributed €3.1 billion in balance of payments support compared with €1.7 billion from the IMF.[3] In the case of Romania, the EU stumped up €5 billion, compared with €13 billion from the IMF.[4] The EU's influence was most evident on the conditions attached to the first of these packages, which included support for the lat's peg to the euro. With memories of Argentina's ill-fated link with the dollar looming large among Fund staff, it is debatable whether the IMF would have chosen this course of action if left to its own devices (Economist 2009). EU officials undoubtedly had more to lose in this situation since a devaluation of the lat would have jeopardized Latvia's plans to join the euro area and could have triggered a crisis of confidence in the Exchange Rate Mechanism (ERM II).

To underline the EU's determination to speak with one voice concerning Latvia, EURIMF took the unusual step of submitting a 'common gray' to the IMF Executive Board. This was procedurally important, as a 'common gray' is a more binding instrument of coordination than a 'presidency gray'. In the case of the latter, each EU Executive Director issues a 'national gray' that merely 'associates' itself with the written statement by the EURIMF President. In the case of the former, the 'common gray' is the sole statement issued by EU member states to the IMF Executive Board. The significance of this distinction was not lost on IMF watchers, who warned that the Fund was in danger of being captured by EU interests (Beattie 2010).

When it came to the fiscal effects of the financial crisis in euro area members, the EU was altogether more hesitant about what role the IMF should play. Initially, the EU sought to go it alone, with Peer Steinbrück's statement in February 2009 that 'other states would have to rescue those running into difficulty' interpreted as an implicit guarantee that the EU would act to

[3] The Latvian package also included contributions of €1.8 billion from a consortium of Nordic countries, €400 million from the World Bank, €200 million from the Czech Republic, and €100 million each from Estonia, Poland, and the European Bank for Reconstruction and Development.

[4] The package included an additional €1 billion in support from the World Bank, the European Bank for Reconstruction and Development, and other lenders.

prevent any euro area member state from defaulting on its sovereign debt (Benoit and Barber 2009). Steinbrück's remark helped to calm financial market fears about Ireland's perilous public finances in the short term but concerns over a fiscal crisis in the euro area resurfaced in October 2009 after the true state of Greece's public finances came to light. Initially, EU finance ministers sought to reassure markets by giving notice to Greece to implement budgetary cuts under Article 104(9) TFEU. By the beginning of February 2010, however, it was clear that such measures would not be sufficient to return Greek debt to a sustainable path and that financial assistance in some shape or form was inevitable.

Whereas the EU moved within a matter of days to provide balance of payments support for Hungary, Latvia, and Romania, it took three long months of haggling between member states before the terms of a rescue package for Greece were finally hammered out. A statement issued by EU heads of state or government on 11 February 2010 promised to draw on the 'expertise' of the IMF (Heads of State or Government of the European Union 2010), but widening interest rate differentials between Greek and German government bonds suggested that markets remained unconvinced about the EU's ability to do without the Fund's financial resources. By the middle of March 2010, several euro area members including Finland, The Netherlands, and Italy were warming to the idea of IMF involvement in a rescue package (Barber 2010). Angela Merkel came to the same view on the eve of the European Council meeting in Brussels on 25–26 March 2010 (Wiesmann and Peel 2010) and convinced other euro area heads of state or government to sign up to 'a package involving substantial International Monetary Fund financing and a majority of European financing' (Council of the European Union 2010*b*).

Financial markets at first welcomed this deal, but fears over Greece's fate soon resurfaced. Ambiguity in the fine print of the European Council's agreement was partly to blame here. For one thing, EU leaders' insistence that EU financial support should be 'ultima ratio' raised concerns that support for Greece would arrive too late. Furthermore, the fact that the disbursement of bilateral loans would be decided by unanimity meant that EU leaders had agreed to give financial support to Greece in principle but not yet in practice. Worst of all, the European Council's insistence that these loans be offered at 'non-concessional' interest rates put Greece in the paradoxical position of being offered money at market rates only after market rates became unbearable (Münchau 2010). It also raised questions about why Greece should borrow from the EU at punitive rates rather than turning in the first instance to an IMF stand-by facility charged at a preferential interest rate. Euro area finance ministers brokered a deal on this last point in mid-April 2010, whereby IMF and EU funding would be disbursed simultaneously with the latter bearing an interest rate that was below the market rate but above the rate being offered by the Fund.

Although this decision arguably penalized Greece for being a member of the euro area, Greek Prime Minister George Papandreou had little choice but to issue a request on 15 April 2010 for talks with the Commission, the ECB, and the IMF concerning the modalities of financial assistance. These talks concluded a little over two weeks later with a technical agreement over a joint euro area/IMF financial package worth €110 billion over three years. The conditions attached to this loan were multifarious and included public sector wage cuts, pension reforms, and other fiscal consolidation measures designed to reduce government borrowing below 3 per cent of GDP by 2014 (Commission 2010*b*).

The manner in which this deal was reached shone a spotlight on the balance of power between the EU and the IMF as the euro area's fiscal crisis intensified. To all appearances, the relationship was one of equals, with the Commission, the ECB, and the IMF conducting a joint mission to Athens and the Commissioner for Economic and Monetary Affairs Olli Rehn and the IMF Managing Director Dominique Strauss-Kahn issuing a joint statement on the conclusions of the talks. The EU's prevarication over the Greek fiscal crisis nonetheless weakened the former's bargaining position in relation to the Fund and left the Commission and the ECB with little alternative but to implement some fairly significant policy changes in the days after the rescue package for Greece was unveiled. On 4 May 2010, the Commission revised the Article 126(9) recommendation issued against Greece earlier in the year to accommodate the timetable and budgetary adjustment path agreed under the EU–IMF financial rescue package. On 3 May 2010, the ECB announced that it would henceforth accept Greek bonds as collateral in credit operations irrespective of the country's sovereign credit rating, a move that the Bank had hitherto resisted.

This is not to suggest that the IMF did not have to make some concessions to the EU over Greece. Some Fund staff reportedly wanted to discuss the possibility of debt restructuring, but this idea was resisted at this stage by EU policymakers (Sakoui and Hope 2010). Despite noises off from some IMF Executive Directors that the Fund had been too lenient towards Greece (Brown et al. 2010), the Executive Board approved the financial rescue package on 9 May 2010. The EURIMF helped to expedite this decision by adopting a 'common gray', which expressed the support of all euro area Executive Directors for this package. The signature of the UK Executive Director was noticeably absent from this statement, but this reflected a reluctance to give formal support to a decision of this magnitude while discussions over the formation of a coalition government were taking place in London; the fact that the UK Executive Director made an oral statement to the Executive Board in favour of financial assistance for Greece reinforced this point.

Differences within EU member states still remained, however, with Angela Merkel facing a closely run vote in the Bundestag and a preliminary ruling by the Constitutional Court in Karlsruhe before the government could authorize the disbursement of its contributions to the Greek rescue package. This paved the way for a euro area summit on 8 May 2010 at which the heads of state or government of the member states sharing the euro area authorized the provision of €80 billion in bilateral loans to Greece in line with the EU–IMF rescue package (Council of the European Union 2010*b*). Greece received the first tranche of these loans on 18 May 2010, some four months after euro area leaders had promised 'to take determined and coordinated action . . . to safeguard financial stability in the euro area as a whole' (Heads of State or Government of the European Union 2010) and some four weeks after the rating agency, Standard and Poor's, downgraded Greek debt to junk bond status.

A further twist in this tale occurred on 10 May 2010, with the announcement of a joint EU–IMF initiative to provide €720 billion in loans and credit guarantees for euro area member states facing the same fate as Greece (Council of the European Union 2010*f*). This agreement put the ad hoc cooperation between the EU and IMF forged at the height of the Greek fiscal crisis on a more permanent footing, with the Fund agreeing to contribute up to €220 billion in financial support and the EU covering the remaining €500 billion through two new financial instruments. The first, the European financial stabilization mechanism (ESFM), put aside €60 billion in support under a seldom-seen provision of the Treaty that allows the Council of Ministers, acting on a proposal from the Commission, to grant financial assistance to a member state facing 'exceptional occurrences beyond its control' (Article 122 TFEU). The second, the European financial stability facility (ESFS), promised up to €440 billion in additional loans through a special purpose vehicle to which all euro area members (bar Greece) agreed to contribute on a pro rata basis corresponding to their shares in the capital of the ECB. Ireland was the first member state to make use of these arrangements, concluding an €85 billion financial support package with the EU and IMF in November 2010, which included €22.5 billion in contributions from the ESFM and €17.7 billion from the EFSF, with the remainder coming from the Fund, bilateral loans from Denmark, Sweden, and the United Kingdom, and contributions from the Irish government's own pension reserves (Eurogroup and Ecofin Ministers 2010).

6.3 The paradox of external representation

Though the final curtain has yet to fall on the financial crisis, the events recounted in the two preceding sections reveal a great deal about the EU's character as an international actor. In the first act of the crisis, which was dominated by international summitry, the EU showed a surprising degree of influence, with Nicolas Sarkozy and, to a lesser extent, José Manuel Barroso instrumental in convincing George W. Bush to convene a G20 leaders' summit in Washington, DC, in November 2008. The EU, it was noted, maintained a surprisingly coherent stance at this summit and at follow-up meetings in London and Pittsburgh through the adoption of agreed language in the European Council. Though the EU was forced to give ground on some of its desiderata, it secured a number of concessions at these summits, including commitments to clamp down on tax havens and revise the rules on bankers' bonuses. Whether the G20's efforts went far enough or even in the right direction is a matter of debate, but the EU's influence in this forum was nonetheless plain to see.

The second act of the financial crisis was dominated by concerns over sovereign debt in Europe and political debate over what role the IMF should play in financial rescue efforts. That EU member states were forced to seek assistance from the Fund, an unthinkable thought before the financial crisis, dealt a serious blow to EMU's international standing. Yet amid this turmoil, the EU's international influence was manifest in its efforts to secure the IMF's financial resources while giving the Union a say over the surveillance of member states' economic policies. The EU's support for Latvia was the most striking example in this regard since it helped to avoid a devaluation of the lat against the euro that would have undermined the credibility of ERM II. Procrastination over the fiscal crisis in the euro area, it was suggested, may have weakened the EU's hand in relation to the IMF, but EU policymakers still secured a central role in formulating, and monitoring compliance with, the conditions attached to the financial rescue package for Greece and in the wider deal reached on the creation of the EFSM and EFSF.

What difference, if any, would a unified system of external representation have made to the EU's involvement in the G20 at the height of the financial crisis? The EU, it should be recalled, is already a full member of this body, meaning that the EU presidency had a seat at the G20 leaders' summits in Washington, DC, London, and Pittsburgh. There is little evidence, however, to suggest that the EU delegation played a decisive role at these meetings. Such was the importance of the EU's G20 seat to Nicolas Sarkozy that he offered it to Spanish Prime Minister José Luis Rodríguez Zapatero and Dutch Prime Minister Jan Pieter Balkenende, neither of whom played a prominent, public role in Washington, DC. The head of the EU's delegation to the London summit, Mirek Topolánek, did hit the headlines in March 2009 by warning that certain aspects of the US fiscal stimulus package could lead to 'the road to hell', but this comment ensured that the Czech Prime Minister had a largely nonspeaking role at the summit itself (Topolánek 2009). Swedish Prime

Minister Fredrik Reinfeldt, who led the EU's delegation at Pittsburgh, at most played a behind-the-scenes role, while the same could be said of Commission President José Manuel Barroso, who attended all three summits.

De facto responsibility for representing the EU at the landmark G20 summits in 2008 and 2009 fell to the leaders of the three largest EU economies: France, Germany, and the United Kingdom. Gordon Brown, Angela Merkel, and Nicolas Sarkozy, as noted above, maintained a fairly coherent line at these meetings, with the French President and German Chancellor, in particular, closely calibrating their diplomatic efforts. Tensions between national leaders did arise from time to time (e.g. over the focus on global imbalances at Pittsburgh), but there is little reason to believe that a sole EU representative would have secured a better deal for Europe, particularly as he or she would have been unable to make the kinds of policy commitments on macroeconomic and regulatory issues that Brown, Merkel, and Sarkozy could. Juncker's inclusion in the EU delegation to G20 leaders' summits is, for the same reason, unlikely to have made much difference, although his omission made little sense given the presence of finance ministers in other national delegations.

A recurring reason against giving the Eurogroup President a seat at G20 leaders' summits is that the EU's delegation to such meetings is already overcrowded. If this argument holds, then the representative of euro area finance ministers surely has a more legitimate claim to join the delegation than the Prime Ministers of Spain and The Netherlands. The fact that President Herman Van Rompuy led the EU's delegation to the G20 leaders' summit in Toronto in June 2010 suggests, however, that the European Council will continue to overshadow the Eurogroup in this setting for some time to come. An interim step would be to give the Eurogroup President a place in the EU's delegation to meetings of the G20 finance ministers and central bank governors. In so doing, it would also make sense to invite the Commissioner for Economic and Monetary Affairs to participate fully in this particular forum.

As with the heads of state or government's hands-on involvement in euro area governance (see Chapter 3), the question arises as to whether the willingness of large EU member states to put up a united front at the G20 will outlast the financial crisis. Gordon Brown's defeat in the UK general election of June 2010 certainly robbed the European Council of one of its more enthusiastic proponents of global governance, but early signs suggest that his successor, David Cameron, is prepared to work in his own way with his European colleagues on shared international priorities. The informal bilateral talks between Cameron and Merkel in advance of the G20 leaders' summit in Seoul in November 2010 were an encouraging step in this regard.

Turning to the IMF, it is far from evident that a more unified system of external representation would have made much difference at the height of the financial crisis. The EURIMF and SCIMF might involve an inordinate number of officials in the preparation of common positions on IMF business, but this did not prevent EU member states from acting swiftly and decisively to provide support to Hungary, Latvia, and Romania. The EU could certainly have played its hand differently in relation to the Greek fiscal crisis, but financial support would probably not have come any sooner if there had been a single EU or euro area seat at the IMF. Within the Fund, there is not much more that a single European representative could realistically have done to expedite agreement in the Executive Board over Greece that the EURIMF did not do. Within the EU, there is little that the occupant of a single chair could have done to overcome deep-seated differences between member states that went right to the highest levels of government and which were resolved only after eleventh-hour talks in the European Council. This speaks to Frieden's (2004) point, echoed by Cohen (2008*a*: 52), that heterogeneous preferences between national governments on international issues will make it more difficult for the EU to speak with one voice whether it has a single chair on the IMF Executive Board or not.

This is not to suggest that the process of coordination between EU member states at the Fund could not be strengthened. There are, in particular, reasons to doubt whether the SCIMF gives the EURIMF a sufficient steer on IMF business. Firstly, the SCIMF meets on a monthly basis, whereas the EURIMF meets as many as three times per week when there are urgent matters to discuss. Secondly, the SCIMF devotes most of its attention to horizontal policy issues such as the development of common views on exchange rate policy and the international economic situation, whereas the EURIMF spends most of its time trying to reach a common view on country-specific issues in the context of IMF Article IV consultations. Thirdly, the SCIMF is hindered by its composition, which includes too many officials, some of whom are too junior to speak with authority on sensitive policy issues. In overcoming these and other shortcomings, the SCIMF might learn a thing or two from the EU Trade Committee (previously known as the Article 133 committee), which closely monitors the Commission's involvement in international trade talks through weekly meetings at the level of deputies and monthly meetings at the level of full members (see Pollack 2003: 278–9).

The financial crisis has also revealed the rather anomalous position of the Commission in relation to the Fund. Although it found itself working closely with Fund staff on rescue packages, the Commission was all but invisible to the IMF Executive Board. The decision taken by EU leaders at the Vienna European Council in December 1998 to appoint a representative of the Commission to the office of the Executive Director has only been partially implemented to date. An official from the Directorate General for Economic and Financial Affairs was appointed to this post but she serves as an advisor to the EURIMF President and does not represent the Commission as such on the EURIMF. This particular role falls instead to a Commission official based at the EU delegation in Washington, DC. Whether the Commission would wield more influence within the Fund by being given the same kind of observer status on the IMF Executive Board as the ECB enjoys is unclear. On one hand, observer status would allow the Commission to address the IMF Executive Board and give it greater access to internal Fund briefings and documentation. On the other hand, ECB observers at the Fund are shut out of decision-making and can be viewed with a degree of distrust by Executive Directors. A more radical alternative would be to allow the Commission to serve as an Alternate Executive Director in the constituency chaired by the EURIMF Presidency. For historical reasons, this seat is reserved for a Bundesbank official, which seems somewhat anachronistic given the central bank's diminished policymaking role since the launch of the euro.

A final lesson from the financial crisis for the external representation of the euro area is that there seems to be a serious gap in multilateral settings between EU economic diplomacy and wider foreign policy imperatives. The EU's reluctance to provide financial assistance to Ukraine in October 2008 in spite of the two sides' commitment to 'privileged political links, and deeper economic integration' at the EU–Ukraine summit a little over a year earlier is the most striking example in this regard (Council of the European Union 2007*c*). This left Ukraine with little option but to turn to the IMF, which later pulled the plug on its $16.5 billion payments facility after a perceived lack of budgetary consolidation. Ecofin's offer of €500 million in macro-financial assistance to Ukraine in October 2009 was too little too late, coming as it did just five months before Viktor Yanukovych narrowly defeated Prime Minister Yulia Tymoshenko in the country's presidential elections. Though Yanukovych has spoken of the need for closer ties with the EU, his decision to renew the Russian Navy's lease on the port of Sevastopol and his openness to a merger of Ukraine's oil and gas company, Naftogaz, with its Russian counterpart, Gazprom, are just two indications that Ukraine has an eastern partnership of its own in mind.

6.4 Conclusion

'In spite of my great admiration for individual splendid talents, I do not accept the star system. Collective creative effort... requires ensemble acting and whoever mars that ensemble is committing a crime not only against his comrades but also against the very art of which he is the servant', thus wrote Constantin Stanislavski, the father of modern acting. Stanislavski's system might shed some light on debates about the EU's presence as an international actor, which have tended to focus on the search for a single star to speak for

Europe rather than first seeking evidence of what the ensemble of EU institutions and member states can and cannot achieve on the world stage.

One reason why the literature on EU external representation has tended to focus on either describing existing institutional arrangements or designing new ones is that the opportunities for international policy coordination are rare during periods of economic normalcy. The global financial crisis thus provided an unprecedented opportunity to observe how the EU responded to the biggest challenge to face the global economy since the Great Depression. The analysis presented in this chapter suggests that EU member states showed a surprising capacity for collective action during the crisis, thus challenging claims by McNamara and Meunier (2002) among others that EMU is bound to lack influence on the international stage because of its fragmented system of external representation.

In the case of the G20, the EU can rightly claim to have shown leadership at the landmark summits of heads of state or government in 2009 and 2010. The idea of a leaders' summit was not new, but Nicolas Sarkozy and José Manuel Barroso can claim some credit for driving an international response to the crisis that went beyond the limits of the G8. Even more impressive was EU member states' coordinated approach to these summits based on agreed language adopted by the heads of state or government. The EU delegation to these summits seems to have played a limited role in its own right and the Eurogroup was excluded altogether, but the fact remains that the leaders of the three largest EU economies, France, Germany, and the United Kingdom, forged a united front at these meetings that few would have thought possible before the crisis.

Calling in the Fund can only have hurt the EU's international standing, but what came next demonstrated Europe's influence within the Fund. Although much has been made of the EU's excessively bureaucratic efforts to coordinate positions at the IMF through the SCIMF and the EURIMF, these committees did not stop the EU from acting swiftly and decisively in response to unfolding fiscal developments in Hungary, Latvia, and Romania. Though the EU acted much less decisively when the fiscal crisis first struck the euro area, this owed more to political differences between member states than the absence of a single EU or euro area seat on the IMF Executive Board. In any case, member states eventually agreed to a joint EU–IMF financial rescue package for Greece and committed to make similar arrangements available to other member states. It remains to be seen precisely how much say EU officials will have over the implementation of the programmes attached to these loans, but the signs thus far suggest that it could be considerable.

What are the wider implications of these findings for the study of the EU as a global actor? On the one hand, the financial crisis shows that the EU can, however imperfectly, work towards an international order based on effective multilateralism, which is one of the core objectives of the European Security Strategy adopted by the European Council in 2003. On the other hand, the financial crisis showed the limits of what supranational actors can realistically achieve without the right diplomatic levers. The limited international role played by the Commission and the Eurogroup President at the height of the financial turmoil, in particular, does not bode well for what the High Representative of the Union for Foreign Affairs and Security Policy and the new full-time President of the European Council could achieve in a comparable political crisis.

Put less pessimistically, the common purpose shown by France, Germany, and the United Kingdom during the financial crisis serves as a reminder that member states play many parts and that they are sometimes the most credible ambassadors for the EU. The United Kingdom and France's failure to agree on a (second) United Nations Security Council Resolution on the use of military force against Iraq in March 2003 serves as a stark reminder that such agreement is not always obtainable (Peterson 2004). The concerted efforts by the foreign ministers of France, Germany, and the United Kingdom to address international concerns over Iran's nuclear programme show that it is sometimes possible (Denza 2003).

7

Bilateral Diplomacy in Beijing and Beyond

If a man continually blusters, if he lacks civility, a big stick will not save him from trouble, and neither will speaking softly avail.

Theodore Roosevelt

Empowering a single actor to speak on behalf of the European Union (EU) in negotiations with third countries is an important characteristic of the Community method. In the area of EU external trade policy, the European Commission is responsible for negotiating bilateral trade agreements (Article 207 Treaty on the Functioning of the European Union (TFEU)). For bilateral agreements in other areas, the Council of Ministers can, on a recommendation from the Commission or, in some cases, the High Representative of the Union for Foreign Affairs and Security Policy, nominate a single EU negotiator or a head of an EU negotiating team (Article 218 TFEU). This provision could, in principle, be used for a bilateral agreement on (certain) macroeconomic issues, but it never has been. Neither has the provision allowing the Council, acting on a recommendation from the Commission or the European Central Bank (ECB), to enter the euro area into an exchange rate system with a third country (Article 219 TFEU).

Though these legal provisions lie dormant, there has been a surge in the number of informal, bilateral dialogues with third countries on macroeconomic issues in recent years. Prior to 2005, the EU's only dialogue of this kind was with Japan. Since this time, the EU has opened annual dialogues devoted wholly or partly to macroeconomic issues with Brazil, China, India, and Russia. Plans to create similar arrangements with Mexico and South Africa are in the pipeline. Macroeconomic dialogues typically take place at the level of officials and involve a delegation from the EU rather than the euro area (Commission 2008*a*: 145). The exception to this rule concerns the Eurogroup's decision to send the Eurogroup President, the ECB President, and the Commissioner for Economic and Monetary Affairs to Beijing in November 2007 for the first in a series of meetings with Chinese authorities on exchange rate issues.

Scholars have so far given little thought to the EU's macroeconomic dialogues – one exception is a short discussion in van den Noord et al. (2008) – preferring instead to focus on the Union's presence in multilateral settings (see Chapter 6). This omission is surprising since bilateralism, which ranges from informal contacts between economic policymakers and formal treaties, is the oldest, and still the most popular, mode of economic diplomacy (Woolcock 2007: 144). Bilateralism can, furthermore, occasionally reach places that multilateralism cannot, especially when it comes to negotiations among actors with strong bargaining positions seeking international agreements that are comparatively easy to reach, monitor, and, if necessary, withdraw from (Bayne 2007).

This chapter seeks to explain the factors driving the EU's macroeconomic dialogues and asks what this trend towards bilateralism means for the euro area's ability to exert influence on the international stage. Its central findings are threefold. Firstly, macroeconomic dialogues, by and large, reflect the EU's wider foreign policy concerns rather than the economic priorities of the euro area, although in some cases the two objectives cohere. Secondly, the euro area's response to China's exchange rate policy might have fallen short of expectations, but it was closer to US efforts at bilateral diplomacy towards China than some commentators have suggested. Thirdly, the EU's willingness to establish bilateral macroeconomic dialogues suggests that the benefits of speaking with a single voice are greater in bilateral settings than in multilateral ones.

The remainder of this chapter is divided into four sections. The first explores the geographical orientation of the EU's macroeconomic dialogues. The second charts the euro area's response to concerns over China's exchange rate policy and compares it to the diplomatic efforts of the United States. The third section contrasts external representation in bilateral and multilateral settings. The final section revisits debates about the EU's global role in the light of this analysis.

7.1 Explaining the EU's bilateral macroeconomic dialogues

Why has the EU opened macroeconomic dialogues with some countries but not with others? The International Political Economy literature points towards two principal avenues of inquiry. The first, which follows Cooper (1968), asks whether the dialogues are a form of policy cooperation driven by economic interdependence between the EU and third countries. The second, which follows Baldwin (1985), considers whether the dialogues are a form of economic statecraft that reflects the EU's wider foreign policy concerns. If the first of these approaches echoes the liberal tradition in international relations, with its emphasis on the primacy of economic considerations, then the second chimes with mercantilism, which sees sovereignty as paramount.

Economic interdependence, at best, offers only a partial explanation for the EU's decision to initiate bilateral dialogues with Brazil, China, India, Japan, Mexico, Russia, and South Africa. The intensity of the trade relationship between the euro area and these countries over the period 1999–2008 varied considerably (see Figure 7.1). The most dramatic contrast is between China, which saw its share of total euro area external trade rise from 3.3 to 7.9 per cent, and Japan, which saw its trade share fall from 5.2 to 2.9 per cent. Russia's importance as a trading partner for the EU rose during this period, but Brazil, India, Mexico, and South Africa saw their share of EU trade remain below 2.0 per cent. Countries without EU macroeconomic dialogues but with an equal or higher share of euro area external trade on average over the period 1999–2008 include Switzerland (5.5 per cent), Norway (2.1 per cent), South Korea (1.6 per cent), and Canada (1.3 per cent).

More puzzling still from this perspective is the absence of an EU macroeconomic dialogue with the United States, which accounted for 13.4 per cent of euro area external trade on average over the period 1999–2008. Macroeconomic issues, it is true, are aired from time to time in the EU–US financial markets regulatory dialogue, which brings together officials from the Commission's Directorate General for the Internal Market, the US Treasury, the US Securities and Exchange Commission (SEC), and the US Federal Reserve Board, but this body is primarily concerned with microeconomic issues (see Posner 2009). The same is true of the Transatlantic Economic Council (see Peterson and Steffenson 2009). This gathering of officials from the Commission and

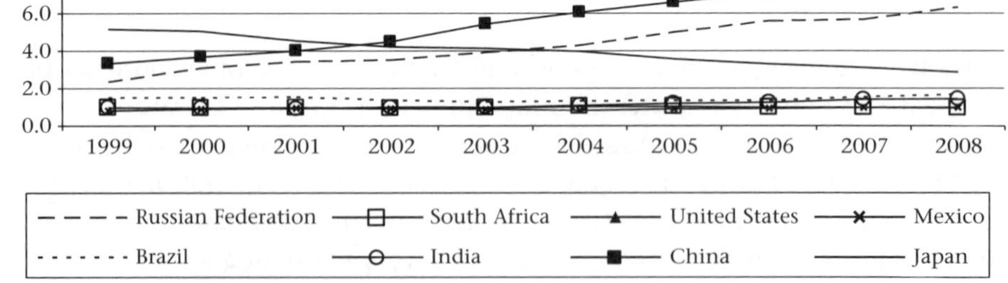

Figure 7.1. Euro area trade shares with selected countries, 1999–2008

Note: The trade share measures the sum of imports and exports with a country as a percentage of total euro area imports and exports.

Source: Eurostat.

the White House plays a key role in the preparation of EU–US summits but it has had little to say about macroeconomic issues, even at the height of the global financial crisis.

Facilitating balance of payments adjustment is, according to Cooper (1968), a key reason for policy coordination between countries. This explanation may fit the EU's macroeconomic dialogue with China, as discussed in the next section, but the same cannot be said of its other bilateral partners (see Figure 7.2). While the euro area's trade balance with China rose from €21.6 billion in 1999 to €119.7 billion in 2008, it remained close to balance or in surplus with Mexico, India, and South Africa. The euro area's trade deficit with Russia and, to a lesser extent, Brazil grew steadily in this period, but it fell in relation to Japan. The fact that the euro area's trade surplus with the United States rose from €20.9 billion in 1999 to a high of €74.3 billion in 2006 may explain European reluctance to open a transatlantic dialogue on macroeconomic matters. French Finance Minister Hervé Gaymard hinted as much in January 2005 when he insisted, somewhat ironically given the euro area's subsequent stance on the renminbi, that the US government must face up to imbalances within its own economy and that 'adjustment for America's deficits should not be made through foreign exchange markets' (Atkins and Thornhill 2005).

The link between the EU's macroeconomic dialogues and its wider foreign policy concerns is difficult to quantify but discernable nonetheless. A commitment to strengthening bilateral relations with third countries was central to the European Security Strategy, a report prepared by the EU's High

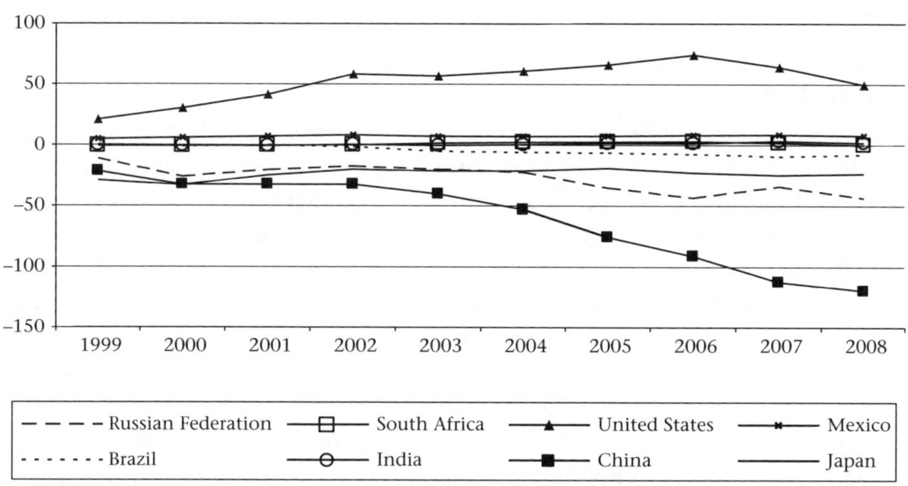

Figure 7.2. Euro area trade balance with selected countries, 1999–2008 (€ billion)

Note: The trade balance measures the difference between total exports and imports.

Source: Eurostat.

Representative for the Common Foreign and Security Policy, Javier Solana, adopted by the European Council in December 2003 (Council of the European Union 2003*a*), and described by one commentator as an 'innovative conceptual framework for the whole of EU external action' (Biscop 2005: 15). To this end, the report called on the EU to develop 'strategic partnerships' with Canada, China, India, Japan, Russia, and other countries that share and support the EU's goals and values (Council of the European Union 2003*a*: 14). Though no mention was made in this context of macroeconomic dialogues – the European Security Strategy contained only paltry references to economic issues – the decision to create these fora can, in most cases, be situated within wider efforts to realize strategic partnerships with third countries.

A case in point is the EU–Russia dialogue on macroeconomic and financial issues, which held its first full meeting in Brussels in October 2007. This dialogue was one of nearly twenty EU–Russia bodies created at this time on issues ranging from agriculture, energy, and the environment to transport and the regulation of industrial products. These dialogues formed part of the EU's efforts to strengthen its strategic partnership with Russia by creating 'common spaces' in (*a*) economics; (*b*) research, education, and culture; (*c*) freedom, security, and justice; and (*d*) external security. Though the original agreement on these common spaces, signed in St Petersberg in May 2003, did not explicitly refer to macroeconomics (Council of the European Union 2003*b*), a roadmap for a common economic space adopted in Moscow in May 2005 specifically called for a dialogue to 'exchange... information on economic issues and policies' (Council of the European Union 2005*b*: 8). Preliminary talks on these issues were held in June and November 2006, paving the way for the adoption of terms of reference for the EU–Russia dialogue on macro economic and financial issues in February 2007(Council of the European Union 2008*c*).

The EU–India Macroeconomic Dialogue, which was launched in New Delhi in July 2007, can also be viewed through the lens of economic statecraft. Though EU–India relations predate the European Security Strategy by several decades – the two sides signed a commercial cooperation agreement in 1972 – they moved up a gear in November 2004 with the establishment of an EU–India strategic partnership (see Hodson and Rahman 2007). This accord, which built on the 1994 EU–India cooperation agreement, called for collaboration on a host of issues, including human rights, security, science and technology, and bilateral trade and investment flows. A joint action plan adopted in September 2005 set out plans for cooperation in these and other areas and included a proposal for a macroeconomic dialogue 'on matters of common interest' (Council of the European Union 2005*c*: 11).

Among the common interests cited in this plan was the need for both sides to have 'a strong and growing presence in international financial discussions'

(Council of the European Union 2005*c*: 11). This speaks to de Vasconcelos's (2008) point that strategic partnerships reflect the EU's attempts to make sense of a world where multilateralism matters and power is multipolar. By this he means that the EU must work with a wider range of countries than ever before to address cross-border challenges that it cannot hope to meet alone. The G20 leaders' summit, which necessitated cooperation with rising powers such as India and China as well as with established powers such as the United States, exemplifies this point (see Chapter 6). There are numerous other examples of this trend in the EU–India strategic partnership, including a pledge to work together for a post-2012 framework on climate change, support for the United Nations' efforts to combat international terrorism, and a commitment to cooperate in the World Trade Organization (WTO) to ensure the successful conclusion of the Doha Round.

India's rise to global prominence over the last twenty years is second only to that of China. A higher rate of population increases means that economic growth in the former could outpace economic growth in the latter over the next four decades (Wilson and Purushothaman 2003: 10), but China is already a first-tier player in the international system. In economic terms, China's annual GDP (measured in current prices) overtook that of France in 2005, the United Kingdom in 2006, Germany in 2007, and Japan in 2010, leaving it behind only the euro area and the United States for the time being.[1] In political terms, China is a central figure in some of the most important international challenges of the age: it produced 8.1 billion tonnes of carbon dioxide in 2009, more than any other country (Olivier and Peters 2010: 5–6); it holds a permanent seat on the UN Security Council and is a lead player in six-party talks over North Korea's nuclear programme; it has been a full member of the WTO since 2001; and it has been an influential voice for developing countries in the Doha Round.

For these and other reasons, the EU has arguably invested more time and energy in its relationship with China over the last three decades than with any other country. A trade and economic cooperation agreement, which was signed in September 1985 and continues to provide the legal basis for EU–China relations, included a most favoured nation clause covering a host of trade issues and a commitment to strengthen cooperation in agriculture, science and technology, energy, transport and communication, and environmental protection (European Economic Community and China 1985). A political dialogue was launched in 1994, followed by one on human rights in 1995. The former was progressively upgraded to include a regular exchange of views among officials and ministers and annual summits at the level of

[1] *Source*: International Monetary Fund (IMF) World Economic Outlook database.

heads of state or government. The decision to develop a strategic partnership at the EU–China summit in October 2003 (Council of the European Union 2003*c*: 5) was not accompanied by a new framework agreement – negotiations on a new partnership and cooperation agreement were eventually launched in January 2007 – but it did lead to plans for new sectoral dialogues on competition, intellectual property, health, employment, and education.

The EU–China summit in October 2003 also unveiled plans for a dialogue on 'macroeconomic questions' (Council of the European Union 2003*c*: 5). This paved the way for the first meeting of the EU–China dialogue on macroeconomic policy and financial regulation in Brussels in February 2005. The EU delegation was led by the Commission's Directors General for Economic and Financial Affairs and the Internal Market and Services and included a representative of the ECB. China's delegation included officials from the ministries of finance, foreign affairs, and commerce and representatives of regulatory agencies responsible for banking, securities, and insurance. A parallel macroeconomic dialogue between the Commission's Directorate General for Economic and Financial Affairs and China's National Development and Reform Commission was launched in March 2006.

The EU's most recent macroeconomic dialogues all stem from strategic partnerships with rising global powers. The EU–Brazil strategic partnership, unveiled at Lisbon in July 2007, for example, called for a dialogue on macroeconomic and financial issues (Council of the European Union 2007*d*: 5), an idea endorsed by representatives of European and Brazilian business (EU-Brazil Business Summit 2007: 3). This paved the way for the first High Level EU–Brazil Macroeconomic Dialogue, which held its first meeting in Brasilia in July 2009. Strategic partnerships signed with South Africa in October 2007 and Mexico in July 2008 look set to run along similar lines. Macroeconomic policy was included in a list of 'areas of cooperation to be developed' under the EU–South Africa joint action plan (Council of the European Union 2007*e*: 5). A reference to the need for a 'sectoral dialogue on macroeconomic issues' was included in the conclusions of the EU–Mexico Summit in Comillas in May 2010 (Council of the European Union 2010*g*).

It follows from this line of argument that the EU is less likely to open macroeconomic dialogues with countries that are not also strategic partners. This is certainly the case with respect to the United States, which the EU has tended to treat as a *sui generis* partner rather than a strategic one. The European Security Strategy underlined this point by calling for an 'effective and balanced partnership' with the United States but not listing it as a potential strategic partner (Council of the European Union 2003*a*: 13). This was an odd decision, especially as the list was left open to all countries that share the EU's 'goals and values' (Council of the European Union 2003*a*: 14), but it was consistent with a multipolar worldview in which the United States wields less international influence than it once did. Whether intentional or not, one consequence of the European Security Strategy is that EU–US relations have experienced few of the institutional innovations over the last decade witnessed in EU cooperation with China, India, and Russia. Though the EU and the United States were free to choose a macroeconomic dialogue during this period, the institutional momentum that drove the EU's macroeconomic diplomacy towards other countries was lacking.

Talk of an EU–Canada strategic partnership in the European Security Strategy did not materialize. Instead, there followed a more modest EU–Canada partnership agreement in March 2004, which focused on plans for a new trade and investment enhancement agreement and practical cooperation in fields such as science and technology. The accord made no reference to the need for a macroeconomic dialogue, leaving officials from the EU and Canada to exchange views on economic and financial issues in the margins of other meetings. The idea of an EU–Japan strategic partnership in the European Security Strategy also fizzled out as attention switched to rising powers. To date there has been no attempt to establish an EU–Japan strategic partnership. This leaves the EU–Japan action plan agreed in Brussels in 2001 as the template for cooperation between the two sides. It also leaves unchanged the macroeconomic dialogues established in 1979 and 1985. The first involves regular meetings on macroeconomic and financial matters between the Commission's Director General for Economic and Financial Affairs and Japan's Vice Minister for International Finance. The second involves a dialogue on macroeconomic and structural issues between officials from the Commission's Directorate General for Economic and Financial Affairs and Japan's Cabinet Office.

The EU has, in summary, initiated macroeconomic dialogues with some countries but not with others for reasons that have more to do with economic statecraft than economic interdependence. The fact that trade shares and trade balances with the EU's macroeconomic partners vary considerably provides the surest indication that its choice of partners is motivated by more than economic concerns. That decisions to create macroeconomic dialogues stemmed in all cases but one from efforts to develop strategic partnerships with third countries suggests that this motivation lies in the area of foreign policy.

Explaining the geographical orientation of the EU's macroeconomic dialogues is one thing. Assessing their ability to project EU influence abroad is another matter. For the most part, the dialogues have involved little more than information sharing on technical issues. The EU–India macroeconomic dialogue, for example, typically involves an exchange of views on the economic outlook, a review of key policy developments, and an in-depth discussion on issues such as fiscal consolidation or raising productivity growth. A recurring theme in this macroeconomic dialogue and others is the need for closer cooperation on multilateral issues. The EU–India macroeconomic dialogue in New Delhi in October 2009, for example, spoke of developing common strategies vis-à-vis the G20, even if it offered little indication of what they might be (DG Economic and Financial Affairs 2009*a*).

There are signs that some macroeconomic dialogues have been more constructive than others. A case in point is the High Level EU–Brazil Macroeconomic Dialogue, which produced agreement on a number of shared priorities to take to the G20 summit in Pittsburgh, including the need to make derivative products more transparent and executive compensation more closely linked to risk (DG Economic and Financial Affairs 2009*b*). This exercise was not dissimilar to the European Council's adoption of 'agreed language' in advance of Pittsburgh (see Chapter 6) and offers a rare practical example of the EU using a strategic partnership to further its interest in the international arena. Perhaps the most striking example of macroeconomic dialogue in action concerns the EU's efforts to promote greater exchange rate flexibility in China. It is to this topic that the next section turns.

7.2 The euro area and the renminbi question

Few issues have dominated debates on international economic policy over the last decade more than the problem of global imbalances (see Eichengreen 2006). Simply put, this complex problem refers to the accumulation of large current account surpluses in Asian and oil-exporting countries since the late 1990s, which have been mirrored by the largest current account deficit in the history of the United States. Opinion is divided on the causes of these imbalances, with explanations focusing on, *inter alia*, foreign investors' appetite for US assets, the combination of low public savings in the United States, weak domestic demand in Europe and high precautionary savings in Asian countries, the effects of rising oil prices, and the decision of several surplus countries to peg their currencies to a depreciating dollar (see Obstfeld and Rogoff 2009).

Of all the factors that may have contributed to global imbalances, China's exchange rate policy has received most – and, it could be argued, disproportionate – attention. Starting in mid-1995, the Chinese authorities pegged the renminbi to the US dollar as part of a wider package of reforms to establish a functioning market for foreign exchange in which the pursuit of stability was paramount. This policy produced a sharp appreciation of China's real effective exchange rate in the second half of the 1990s, but this trend was abruptly reversed in 2002 as the dollar began to fall against other currencies. This change brought about a surge in the competitiveness of China's already-competitive economy, which saw its current account surplus rise from $44 billion in 2002 to $134.1 billion in 2005 (Figure 7.3).

These developments were a twofold source of concern for euro area policymakers at this time. Firstly, although the euro area's overall current account was in surplus, its trade deficit with China was, as already indicated in Figure 7.2, rising apace in this period. Secondly, the fact that China pegged itself to a depreciating dollar raised questions about whether the euro area was carrying a disproportionate burden in the adjustment of the dollar to the US current account deficit (see Ahearne and von Hagen 2006). China's switch from a dollar peg to a managed float against an undisclosed basket of international currencies in July 2005 offered temporary respite to the United States, but it only added to the euro area's worries. Specifically, the fact that the renminbi rose by 8.2 per cent against the dollar between November 2005 and November 2007 but fell by 14.4 per cent against the euro raised the possibility that China was deliberately making its exports to Europe cheaper to compensate for its loss in competitiveness vis-à-vis the United States (Figure 7.4).

For these reasons, the euro area's response to China's exchange rate policy was a critical test of the former's ability to exert influence on macroeconomic issues in bilateral settings. Henning (2007: 790), for one, is critical of Europe's performance, arguing that euro area policymakers 'did not form any particularly clear or coherent policy toward the Chinese currency during 2003–2005'. Pisani-Ferry (2008*b*: 268) goes further, criticizing the ECB and euro area

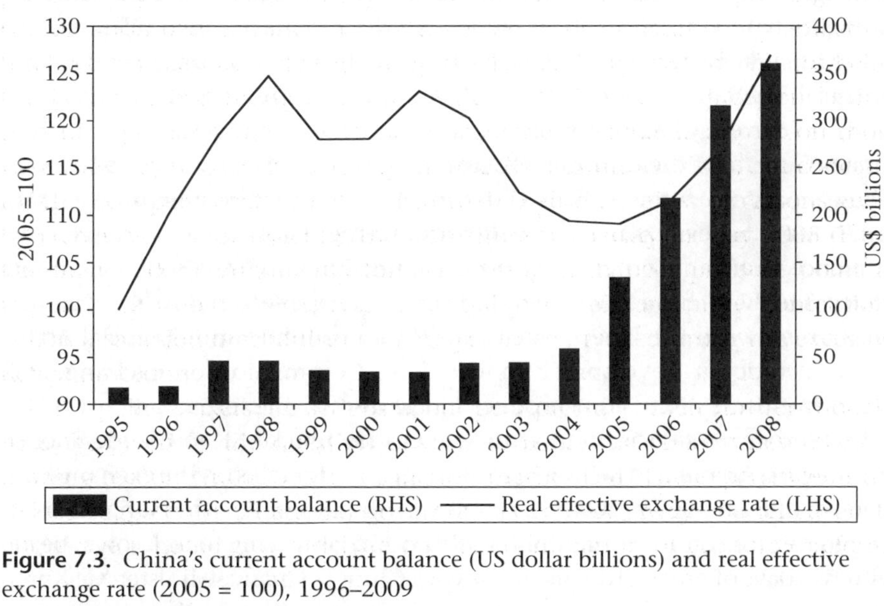

Figure 7.3. China's current account balance (US dollar billions) and real effective exchange rate (2005 = 100), 1996–2009

Note: The real effective exchange is measured in terms of relative consumer prices.

Source: IMF International Financial Statistics.

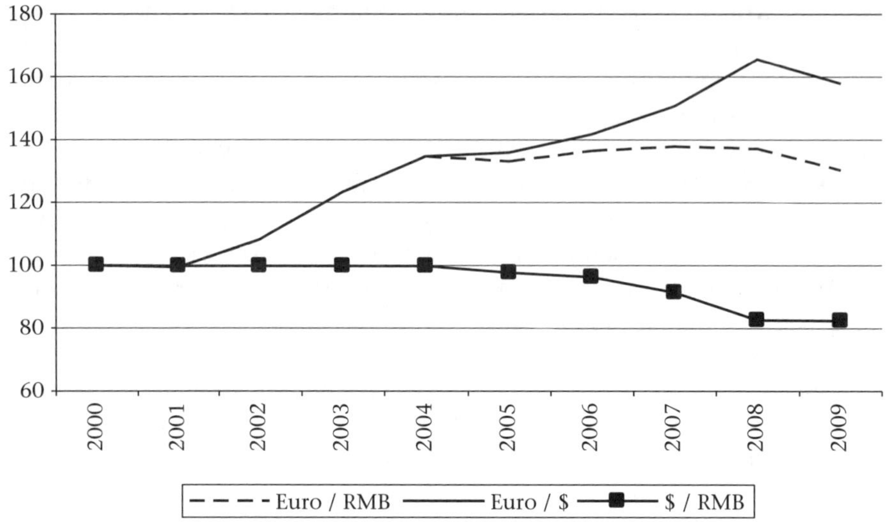

Figure 7.4. Renminbi in relation to the euro and dollar, 2000–9 (nominal exchange rate, August 2000 = 100)
Source: European Central Bank.

finance ministers for paying too little attention to the renminbi question and for effectively free riding on US diplomatic efforts to encourage exchange rate flexibility. Though this commentary glosses over the EU's macroeconomic dialogues with China, such fora, in truth, failed to make much difference on this particular issue. The EU–China dialogue on macroeconomic policy and financial regulation issues proved ill-suited to facilitating an exchange of views on currency issues, containing as it did representatives from two Directorates General of the Commission and six institutions with responsibility for China's economic policy. This gathering also excluded representatives from the National Development and Reform Commission, which exerts more influence than any other body on the direction of China's exchange rate policy. The EU–China macroeconomic dialogue opened channels of communication between the Directorate General for Economic and Financial Affairs and the National Development and Reform Commission on exchange rate issues, but these discussions produced little discernable impact.

The Eurogroup's decision to send Jean-Claude Juncker, Jean-Claude Trichet, and Joaquín Almunia to Beijing in November 2007 for talks on the exchange rate marked, as Pisani-Ferry (2008*b*: 277) puts it, 'the end of Europe's long-standing benign neglect toward the renminbi'. The troika, as it came to be known, began with two days of preparatory meetings with Chinese Finance Minister Xie Xuren and the Governor of the People's Bank of China Governor, Zhou Xiaochuan, followed by high-level discussions with Chinese Premier Wen Jiabao in the margins of the EU–China summit. The summit's communiqué took note of these discussions and acknowledged the determination of both sides 'to make concerted efforts to adopt comprehensive measures, intensify structural adjustment, and avoid drastic movement of exchange rates, so as to make due contribution to the orderly adjustment of global imbalances' (Council of the European Union 2007*f*). The precise content of these measures remained vague, although the summit did unveil a new working group on exchange rate issues between the People's Bank of China and the ECB and a new High Level Economic and Trade Dialogue between the Commission and the State Council of the People's Republic of China to discuss 'issues affecting the trade imbalance' (Council of the European Union 2007*f*: 12).

Whether the euro area's bilateral diplomacy exerted influence on China's exchange rate policy is difficult to say. The troika can, at a stretch, claim some credit for the renminbi's eventual appreciation against the euro – the Chinese currency rose 21 per cent against the single currency between April 2008 and February 2009 – but a host of international and domestic factors are likely to have had a bearing on this change. One area in which the troika did fall short was in its efforts to establish a permanent high-level dialogue with China on macroeconomic issues. Prior to the crisis, the Eurogroup President placed particular emphasis on the need for 'a regular, structured macroeconomic dialogue with China' (Watson 2007). The conclusions of the EU–China summit in November 2007 'agreed to enhance their cooperation in macroeconomic policy', but made no reference to the creation of a more permanent dialogue (Council of the European Union 2007*f*: 12).

The troika's failure to win a concession on this last point did not prevent the euro area from engaging in further acts of bilateral diplomacy towards China over the renminbi question. In November 2009, euro area finance ministers sent Juncker, Trichet, and Almunia on a second troika mission to Nanjing to make the case for a renewed appreciation of the renminbi, which had fallen by 16.5 per cent against the euro since February of that year. The representatives of the euro area met once again with Chinese Premier Wen Jiabao and his senior economic officials in the margins of the EU–China summit, although there were few tangible outputs on this occasion; the summit conclusions welcomed these discussions but said little more (Council of the European Union 2009*d*). This was followed in October 2010 by meetings between Wen Jiabao and the troika in the margins of the EU–China summit in Brussels. The euro area's sovereign debt crisis dominated discussions at this meeting, but the summit communiqué did call 'for flexible responses to the evolution of economic fundamentals' (Council of the European Union 2010*h*). A less coded reference to exchange rate issues occurred in the speeches delivered to the concurrent EU–Business China Summit in Brussels, with José Manuel Barroso (2010) calling for a 'broad based appreciation of the Chinese currency exchange rate', and

Wen Jiabao (2010) pushing back with a plea to European political and business leaders not to 'join the "chorus" to pressure China to appreciate the yuan'.

The Eurogroup may have been behind the curve in initiating high-level discussions with China over its exchange rate policy – US Treasury Secretary John Snow travelled to Beijing in September 2003 to make the case for exchange rate flexibility – but the euro area's eventual efforts at bilateral diplomacy towards China were, when all is said and done, not too dissimilar from those employed by the United States. The US Treasury Secretary is empowered to name and shame countries participating in 'currency manipulation' under the Omnibus Trade and Competitiveness Act of 1988, but this instrument has not been used against China since 1992 or, indeed, against any country since 1994. Instead, US Treasury Secretaries have tended to rely on a strategy of 'quiet bilateral diplomacy' (Goldstein and Lardy 2008: 53) and methods of 'moral suasion' (Henning 2008). The emphasis on consensus building over coercion was enshrined in the Strategic Economic Dialogue, a forum established in September 2006 to facilitate an exchange of views between the United States and China on currency developments and other aspects of macroeconomic policy and later subsumed under the US–China Strategic and Economic Dialogue launched in July 2009.

Although some commentators have heralded the Strategic and Economic Dialogue as a powerful new G2 that could sideline the EU on questions of international importance (see Garrett 2010), the new body's treatment of macroeconomic issues is not necessarily superior to that of the euro area troika. A clear advantage is that the Strategic and Economic Dialogue is held on an annual rather than an ad hoc basis, bringing greater continuity to discussions of the dollar/renminbi exchange rate than is the case in relation to the euro. A potential disadvantage is that discussions of macroeconomic issues in the US–China Strategic and Economic Dialogue are held at a slightly lower level than the euro area troika missions. Whereas the former is centred on an exchange of views at cabinet level (i.e. between the Treasury Secretary on the US side and a vice premier on the Chinese side), the 2007 and 2009 troikas, as noted above, culminated in discussions between the euro area delegation and Chinese Premier Wen Jiabao.

The most important difference between EU and US engagement with China on macroeconomic issues, as Henning (2007) notes, concerns the role of the legislative branch. Whereas the European Parliament has paid little attention to the euro/renminbi exchange rate, the US Congress has consistently used its authority over trade matters to put pressure on China to allow greater exchange rate flexibility. The Schumer-Graham Bill (S. 295), which threatened to impose an import duty of 27.5 per cent on all imports from China in the absence of, *inter alia*, 'a substantial upward revaluation' of the renminbi, is among the most notorious examples in this respect, but it is far from being the only one. Hufbauer and Brunel (2008), indeed, counted thirty-six draft Congressional bills threatening similar sanctions against China in the period 2005–8 alone.

The European Parliament's disinterest in the renminbi question is unsurprising given its limited involvement in the oversight of euro area macroeconomic policy or, prior to the entry into force of the Lisbon Treaty, EU trade policy. The point stands, however, that EU policymakers with responsibility for external trade, the Commission included, were reluctant to threaten China with trade sanctions over its exchange rate policies. While Jean-Claude Juncker delivered the blunt message in Beijing in November 2007 that the weak renminbi was fuelling China's trade surplus and surpluses could produce a 'protectionist reaction' from Europe (Sanderson 2007), Peter Mandelson's line on this issue at the time was altogether more nuanced. Though he dutifully called for a stronger renminbi at this time, the Commissioner for External Trade was equally insistent that 're-balancing the trade relationship [was] not a question of reducing Chinese exports to Europe' (Mandelson 2007).

Whether the threat of trade sanctions has made the United States a more credible interlocturer with China is debatable. For one thing, none of the Congressional bills promising a protectionist backlash over the renminbi have become law, with even Senators Charles Schumer and Lindsey Graham admitting that their effort in 2003 was intended as a 'wake-up call' over China's currency rather than a realistic attempt to rewrite US trade law. This wake-up call and others like it were, it should be added, aimed less at Chinese authorities than the US Treasury. The principal role of Congress in US exchange rate policy, Henning (2008) explains, is to hold the executive branch of government to account when fluctuations in the exchange rate contradict explicit or implicit economic policy goals. The absence of an equivalent mechanism in the EU may explain the euro area's sluggish response to the renminbi question, but it does not necessarily mean that Chinese authorities took the US Treasury more seriously as a result.

In the final analysis, neither softly spoken words from the Eurogroup and the US Treasury nor 'big stick' economic diplomacy from the US Congress have thus far produced a lasting shift in China's exchange rate policy. Though the switch to a managed float in July 2005 allowed the renminbi to appreciate against the dollar and the euro, such adjustment was short-lived. In July 2008, China reinstated its dollar peg in response to rising inflationary pressures at home and uncertainty over the global financial crisis, a measure that remained in place until June 2010. China's stop–start exchange rate reforms, it would seem, have had a negligible impact on its current account deficit, which continued its rapid rise in the second half of the 2000s until the real effects of the financial crisis took their toll on demand for Chinese imports.

7.3 Bilateralism vs. multilateralism

McNamara and Meunier (2002) argued that the Eurogroup should assume responsibility for the external representation of the euro area by delegating authority to a single actor, who would work in close collaboration with the ECB President and the Commissioner for Economic and Monetary Affairs. Though the authors had in mind a more permanent arrangement modelled on the post of High Representative of the Union for Foreign & Security Policy, the euro area's high-level dialogue with China over the euro/renminbi exchange rate described in the preceding section comes close to this ideal type of external representation. This approach has not yet been replicated in the euro area's relations with third countries, but the EU has, as discussed in the first section of this chapter, shown itself to be capable of establishing lower level macroeconomic dialogues with a growing list of strategic partners.

Chapter 6 pointed to a paradox in the external representation of the euro area insofar as a unified representation in multilateral settings seems unnecessary when member states agree on international priorities and impotent when they do not. How can this claim be squared with the EU's apparent willingness to allow the Commissioner for Economic and Monetary Affairs, in the case of lower level dialogues, and the Eurogroup President, in the case of the troika missions, to speak for the EU or euro area in bilateral settings? The answer, it would seem, is that the pay-off from speaking with one voice varies between these settings for three principal reasons.

Firstly, the sovereignty costs of creating bilateral dialogues are, by and large, lower than those associated with a move to a more unified representation in multilateral settings. Establishing a single euro area seat on the IMF Executive Board, for example, would make it harder for EU member states, especially those that appoint their own Executive Director, to exert direct influence over the day-to-day business of the Fund. Opening a dialogue between China and the EU on macroeconomic policy, in contrast, has not required member states to cede bilateral contact with China on this issue. The fact that the euro area troika mission to Beijing in November 2007 coincided with a state visit by the French President illustrates this point. Though macroeconomic issues were not high on the agenda of the France–China summit, Nicolas Sarkozy made clear his desire to see an appreciation of the renminbi, following discussions with Chinese President Hu Jintao.

Secondly, EU member states have, under certain conditions, more to gain by sending a fragmented representation to multilateral fora than to bilateral dialogues. The fact that there are many seats available in multilateral settings means that EU member states can maximize their influence by occupying as many places at the table as possible, providing these countries put their weight behind a common cause and do not provoke too big a backlash from other countries in the process. The collective influence of France, Germany, and the United Kingdom at the G20 leaders' summits in 2008 and 2009, described in Chapter 6, provides a case in point. That there is effectively only one seat available to the EU in bilateral settings implies that EU member states risk diminishing their influence by overloading delegations to third countries. From this perspective, the decision to allow the Commission to lead on the EU's macroeconomic dialogues and the Eurogroup President to lead the troika missions to China seems like a pragmatic choice.

Finally, bilateralism, as Oye (1985) notes, can be a second-best solution for tackling collective action problems in the international economic system when multilateralism fails. By the time the decision was taken to send the troika mission to Beijing in November 2007, the Eurogroup had good reason to doubt the effectiveness of multilateral efforts to encourage greater exchange rate flexibility in China and a solution to the problem of global imbalances more generally. On the first point, internal tensions over the renminbi question meant that there had been no meaningful discussion of Chinese economic policy in the IMF Executive Board since September 2006. On the second point, the IMF's multilateral consultations on global imbalances, in which the Eurogroup was represented alongside economic officials from China, Japan, Saudi Arabia, and the United States, concluded in April 2007 with an agreement in principle on what needed to be done, but offered little in the way of binding policy commitments.

7.4 Conclusion

The euro area's piecemeal progress in establishing a unified representation in multilateral fora since 1999 stands in stark contrast to the proliferation of bilateral dialogues with third countries. The analysis presented in this chapter links these macroeconomic dialogues to a wider strategy of EU economic statecraft aimed at establishing strategic partnerships with rising powers rather than an attempt to foster policy cooperation among interdependent economies. This explains the EU's decisions to establish macroeconomic dialogues with developing economies such as Brazil, China, India, Russia, and, more recently, Mexico and South Africa.

China's exchange rate policy may have received disproportionate attention in debates on the international economy, but it nonetheless provided an important test of the euro area's ability to exert influence in bilateral settings, especially after the IMF's efforts to break the deadlock over the renminbi question and the wider problem of global imbalances fell short. The Commission responded by initiating low-level bilateral dialogues with

China on macroeconomic and financial issues in 2005, followed by a parallel dialogue on macroeconomic policy in 2006. The Eurogroup took the lead thereafter, sending a high-level troika mission to Beijing in 2007 for the first in a series of talks with senior economic officials and the Chinese premier.

That the euro area waited over five years to respond to the renminbi's marked depreciation against the euro after 2002 is true. That the euro area troika missions extracted some concessions but failed, in the final analysis, to produce a decisive shift in Chinese exchange rate policy is also a fair assessment. That the diplomatic approaches employed towards China by the United States and the Treasury were fundamentally different is not. The US Congress was more vocal in its criticisms of China than either the European Parliament or the Commission, but talk of US trade sanctions over China's exchange rate policy has thus far remained just that. This has left *de facto* responsibility for this matter in the hands of the US Treasury, which has resisted pressure from Congress to cite China for currency manipulation, relying instead on the same powers of peer pressure and persuasion as the Eurogroup. The fact that the United States too has little to show for its engagement with China is a reminder that limited influence in the international arena is not germane to the euro area.

What are the wider implications of this finding for the themes of this book? The way in which the EU's macroeconomic dialogues with third countries have sprung from its wider strategic partnerships indicates a degree of coherence between EU economic diplomacy and foreign policy that was found wanting in the EU's policy on IMF lending at the height of the financial crisis (see Chapter 6). Instances of misalignment between the EU as a global actor and the euro as a global currency were noted, however. Questions were raised as to whether the EU's decision to develop strategic partnerships with rising powers may have unintended consequences for its relations with those powers that have already arrived. The EU's failure to initiate a macroeconomic dialogue with the United States, the most strategically important economy for the euro area, or with any other developed country bar Japan, suggests that it might.

8

Conclusion: Tender Union

Surely some revelation is at hand.

W.B. Yeats

Aside from the freedom to travel, work, and study abroad, the single currency is what most people mention when asked by pollsters what the European Union (EU) means to them (Eurobarometer 2010: 17). If this answer illustrates the symbolic power of the euro then it also betrays an irony, insofar as Economic and Monetary Union (EMU) is strikingly different to traditional conceptions of how the EU works. Under the so-called Community method, the Commission proposes policy and legislation, shares responsibility for policy execution with national authorities, and represents the EU in international negotiations. The Council and Parliament, meanwhile, adopt legislative and budgetary acts and the Court of Justice ensures respect for the rule of law. Under EMU, in contrast, the European Central Bank (ECB) has sole responsibility for monetary policy and member states retain final say over the formulation and implementation of their economic policies. It falls to the Council, with input from the Commission, to foster policy coordination through measures that are, by and large, legally non-binding and to decide on matters relating to the external representation of the euro area on a case-by-case basis. The Parliament and the Court of Justice, for the most part, play a minor role in the governance of the euro area.

EMU's break with the Community method is relevant for three overarching debates about policymaking in the euro area and the EU. Firstly, it chimes with controversies about the sustainability of the single currency without a centralization of economic policies to take account of cross-country spillover and ensure coherence in the monetary and fiscal policy mix. Secondly, EMU is a trial balloon for the wider application of new modes of policymaking, relying as it does on delegation to specialist agencies and decentralized and deliberative approaches to policy coordination. Thirdly, EMU's fragmented system of external representation raises questions about the euro's place in a rapidly changing international monetary order and, by implication, the credibility of the EU's claims to be a global actor in its own right.

This book has explored how EMU fared in the absence of the Community method from the launch of the euro in 1999 to the onset of the euro area's sovereign debt crisis in 2010. It began by focusing on two institutions that were tailor-made for the euro, the ECB and the Eurogroup, before examining the evolution of the Broad Economic Policy Guidelines (BEPGs) and the stability and growth pact as instruments of economic policy coordination. This was followed by an exploration of the euro area's international influence in multilateral and bilateral settings. This chapter summarizes the key findings of this investigation and discusses their wider significance. It ends by speculating about the fate of new modes of policymaking in the EU at large before asking whether reforms to euro area governance in the light of the global financial crisis and its after-effects might pave the way for the reinvigoration of the Community method.

8.1 Summary of findings

8.1.1 The sustainability of EMU without a centralized economic policy

Policymaking in the euro area is far from having been a success. The Eurogroup has, in spite of its early promise, disappointed as a forum for fostering an exchange of views between finance ministers and the ECB. Member states have a mixed track record of compliance with the stability and growth pact, which must shoulder some of the blame for the perilous state of public finances in the euro area in the wake of the global financial crisis. The BEPGs have shown some value-added as an overarching instrument for fostering consensus on the EU's economic objectives, but they have failed to bite as an instrument of peer pressure. This book makes no bones about these and other areas where the governance of EMU has fallen short, but it challenges attempts to reduce these shortcomings to the absence alone of a centralized, hierarchical approach to euro area economic policy.

The Eurogroup's deficiencies, it was argued in Chapter 3, lie not in its informal working methods but rather in its gradual emergence as a formal body with a permanent secretariat, a semi-permanent president, and *de facto* decision-making powers. This formalization allowed euro area finance ministers to exert collective influence within the Economic and Financial Affairs Council (Ecofin), for example on the reform of the stability and growth pact in March 2005, and on the international stage, with the troika missions to China in 2007 and 2009 a case in point, but it also sowed the seeds of the Eurogroup's downfall in two key respects. Firstly, it politicized the Eurogroup's monetary dialogue with the ECB, with the semi-permanent president coming under pressure from some member states to get tough with Frankfurt in advance of his reappointment in September 2006. Secondly, the Eurogroup's growing influence over fiscal policy fuelled tensions with some heads of state or government, leading the European Council to seize the initiative during the global financial crisis over economic policy coordination in the EU and euro area. Thus far, there is little sign that the European Council will relinquish this position once economic normalcy returns, with the new full-time President of the European Council, Herman Van Rompuy, seeking an active role in relation to euro area governance.

These findings challenge claims by Jacquet and Pisani-Ferry (2001: 11) that the Eurogroup's informality is a barrier to policy coordination and speak to Puetter's (2006) point that deliberation is difficult to achieve inside the hard bargaining environment of the Council. The need for informal channels of communication between monetary and fiscal authorities, it was recalled in Chapter 2, is not unique to EMU. In the United States, as Meyer (2000) notes, the Chairman of the Federal Reserve and the Treasury Secretary hold regular one-on-one meetings behind closed doors. Comparable arrangements existed in euro area member states prior to the launch of the single currency (Bini Smaghi and Casini 2000: 379).

The stability and growth pact, it was suggested in Chapter 4, must shoulder some of the blame for the euro area's sovereign debt crisis, but it should not serve as a scapegoat. Fiscal crises tend to follow financial turmoil (Reinhart and Rogoff 2009: 224) and the euro area was not alone among industrialized economies in experiencing a sharp rise in government deficits and debt in the wake of the global financial crisis. That said, the stability and growth pact fell short in several respects, not least in Ecofin's decision to end the excessive deficit procedure against Greece in June 2007 (Council of the European Union 2007*g*).

The case of Ireland is more complex. Though it fell foul of the BEPGs in February 2001, Ireland was a more or less model student in relation to the stability and growth pact until the end of its housing boom, a sharp economic slowdown, and pandemonium in its banking sector placed an unforeseen and ultimately unsustainable burden on the country's public finances. Whether stricter fiscal rules could have spared Ireland the ignominy of turning to the EU and International Monetary Fund (IMF) for financial support is debatable, with serious shortcomings in financial supervision and a failure to address the build up of unsustainable macroeconomic imbalances in the preceding decade more plausible suspects in this regard.

Member states' mixed track record of compliance with the stability and growth pact has led a legion of scholars to propose procedural and substantive changes to EMU's fiscal rules over the years. Less attention has been paid to the reasons why some countries found it easier than others to keep government borrowing under control during EMU's first decade. A notable exception is political institutionalism, a pioneering approach to the comparative political economy of public finances that stresses a link between electoral regimes and fiscal institutions (Hallerberg et al. 2001, 2009; Hallerberg 2004).

The evidence explored in Chapter 4 is consistent with the central tenets of political institutionalism; during EMU's first decade, euro area members electing single-party majority governments or ideologically convergent coalitions typically delegated control over the budgetary process to strong finance ministers, while those electing ideologically diverse coalitions tended to rely on fiscal contracts. It challenges political institutionalist claims, however, that countries in the first of these groupings ('delegation states') were ill-suited to the rule-based approach of the stability and growth pact. Fiscal discipline in delegation states, it was noted, varied during the period 1998–2007, with France, Germany, Greece, Italy, and Portugal posting excessive deficits, while Austria, Ireland, and Spain kept government borrowing within seemingly acceptable limits. The reasons behind this puzzle are not entirely clear, but the comparatively weak institutional position of finance ministers in Germany and Portugal and the total absence of numerical fiscal rules in Greece suggests that the fault may rest with national fiscal institutions rather than EMU's fiscal rules alone.

The BEPGs failed to bite, it was argued in Chapter 5, because they suffered from three serious shortcomings as a sanction mechanism. Firstly, they lacked credible sanctioning institutions, with both the Commission and Ecofin reluctant to issue non-binding recommendations against errant member states under Article 121(4) of the Treaty on the Functioning of the European Union (TFEU). Secondly, they lacked precise sanctioning criteria, meaning that EU policymakers were under no obligation to enforce the BEPGs and making it easier for errant member states to contest claims of non-compliance. Thirdly, the BEPGs failed to find a foothold in domestic political arenas, with the result that the costs to member states of breaching the guidelines were as trivial as the risks of a backlash against the EU were significant. All three factors were in play in Ecofin's ill-fated Article 121(4) recommendation against Ireland in February 2001, a move that provoked widespread criticism of Brussels for interfering in Irish economic policy and, in so doing, all but eroded EU policymakers' willingness to apply peer pressure.

8.1.2 EMU and new modes of EU policymaking

A key finding of this book for students of EU policymaking is that the ECB is an atypical supranational agent that challenges conventional assumptions about what EU institutions want. From a rational choice institutionalist perspective, supranational agents like the Commission and the Court of Justice tend to have more intensive preferences for European integration than their principals, the member states, creating the potential for agency loss (Pollack 2003). The ECB's preferences for further integration, it was argued in Chapter 2, are subordinate to its preferences for price stability. In cases where the ECB saw further integration as compatible with price stability, such as coordinated approaches to fiscal discipline, flexible markets, and, above all, financial supervision, Frankfurt was a willing champion of more Europe. In cases where it saw a threat to price stability, as was true of efforts to strengthen EU anti-fraud policy, coordinate macroeconomic policies, and clarify the ECB's status in the Treaty, the Bank firmly opposed further integration. This conclusion challenges claims by Heisenberg and Richmond (2002) that the ECB is an EU institution like any other. It also invites discussion as to whether EU member states might exercise closer control over the pace of European integration by delegating decision-making powers to function-specific agencies with well-defined policy preferences.

The analysis presented in this book also speaks to students of EU policymaking about the scope and limits of new governance. As discussed in Chapter 2, the Eurogroup's initial achievements as an informal, deliberative forum did not go unnoticed in other fields of EU policymaking. In the area of justice and home affairs, for example, the practice of inviting the US Secretary for Homeland Security to informal Council meetings has become central to transatlantic consensus building over post-9/11 security issues. Informal meetings in the margins of the European Council have also taken on an added significance in recent years as was evident during the global financial crisis. A key development in this regard was the emergence of informal summits between euro area heads of state or government as part of efforts to reach agreement on a coordinated bank rescue plan and a financial support package for Greece. Whether informal methods of this kind are sustainable is open to question. The Eurogroup's value-added as a deliberative body, it was noted, declined as its growing influence brought *de facto* decision-making responsibilities in relation to the stability and growth pact and other aspects of economic policy coordination.

Chapter 4's findings on the stability and growth pact have wider implications for economic policy coordination in the EU. While there is a growing awareness among EU policymakers about the importance of national fiscal institutions for compliance with the stability and growth pact (see discussion of minimum standards for fiscal frameworks below), this interest in comparative political economy does not extend to other types of policy coordination. There has, for example, been next to no public discussion about whether structural reforms under the Lisbon Strategy and, its successor, Europe 2020 are well suited to the institutional complementarities underpinning different varieties of capitalism (see Hall and Soskice 2001; Hancké et al. 2007). Scant attention has also been paid to national approaches to wage setting in the euro area in spite of well-documented problems of cross-country wage adjustment during EMU's first decade (Hancké and Soskice 2003). These shortcomings go against the spirit of the open method of coordination, which is supposed to be sensitive to the specificities of national labour markets.

The failure of the BEPGs to bite is a blow not only for the effectiveness of new modes of governance but also for their legitimacy. That the Commission waited until the euro area faced a full-blown fiscal crisis before issuing its second ever Article 121(4) recommendation, it was suggested in Chapter 5, reveals not only the limits of peer pressure but also the EU's contested involvement in this domain in spite of its curtailed competence. This chimes with concerns raised in Hodson and Maher (2001) that new governance's pragmatic approach to the problem of legitimacy might not suffice if recalcitrant states choose to play the legitimacy card. The Irish government's decision to do so in February 2001 may have had little bearing on the country's 'no' vote to the Nice Treaty in the end, but the EU paid a high price for its perceived interference in economic matters in France's ill-fated referendum on the Constitutional Treaty in May 2005 (Schmidt 2009).

8.1.3 The euro area and EU in the international system

Perhaps the most controversial conclusion of this book from an International Political Economy perspective is that the euro area has been an influential international actor in spite of its fragmented system of external representation. A key finding of Chapter 6 is that the EU was a principal player on the world stage during the global financial crisis. Nicolas Sarkozy, in his capacity as President in office of the European Council, and Commission President José Manuel Barroso, it was argued, can claim some credit for convening the first ever summit of the heads of state or government of the Group of 20 (G20) in Washington, DC, in November 2008. In the G20 leaders' summits that followed, EU member states showed a surprising capacity for coordination, pushing for, and securing, several key concessions. A similar conclusion is reached with respect to European involvement in the IMF. That member states of the EU and, worse still, the euro area were forced to turn to the Fund for financial support is a blow to EMU's international standing, but this does not take away from the fact that member states exerted considerable collective influence in Washington, DC, during the financial crisis. Informal coordination between IMF Executive Directors and Alternates from EU member states in the EURIMF was pivotal in this regard, helping as it did to produce a common European line on the terms and conditions of financial support for Hungary, Latvia, Romania, and Greece.

These findings challenge calls by Aherne and Eichengreen (2007), Bini Smaghi (2009), and others for a single EU or euro area chair in international organizations. In the case of the G20, the EU presidency was a full participant in the landmark leaders' summits of 2008 and 2009, but it was the leaders of the large member states, Gordon Brown, Angela Merkel, and Nicolas Sarkozy, who did most to push the EU line on issues such as the reform of international financial regulation. The Eurogroup President was a noticeable absentee from these summits, but it seems unlikely that his inclusion in an already overcrowded EU delegation, which included the Presidents of the European Council and European Commission and, bizarrely, the Prime Ministers of Spain and The Netherlands, would have made much difference.

In the case of the IMF, there is little that a single chair could have done that the EURIMF did not do to expedite financial support for EU or euro area member states. With respect to Greece, it was disagreement between, and within, national capitals rather than a lack of coordination that explained the long months of delay before agreement was reached on a joint EU–IMF rescue package. These findings point to a paradox in the euro area's external representation: when member states see eye to eye on international priorities, there is little need to establish a more unified system of external representation, but when member states fundamentally disagree on such matters, there is little hope that a unified system of external representation could fare much better.

The EU's unexpected influence in the international monetary order is also evident in its efforts at bilateral diplomacy. Recent years have, as discussed in Chapter 7, witnessed a proliferation of informal, macroeconomic dialogues between the EU and third countries. Prior to 2005, the Commission engaged in bilateral diplomacy of this sort with Japan only. Since 2005, the EU has opened channels of communication with macroeconomic authorities in Brazil, China, India, Russia, Mexico, and South Africa. These dialogues have, for the most part, involved little more than information exchange, although the common language agreed by the High Level EU–Brazil Macroeconomic Dialogue in advance of the G20 summit in Pittsburgh in September 2009 gives an indication of what can be achieved by these informal fora.

An instance of bilateral diplomacy that is more significant still is the euro area's engagement with China over the renminbi question. In November 2007, and again in November 2009, euro area finance ministers dispatched a troika mission, led by the Eurogroup President and including the ECB President and the Commissioner for Economic and Monetary Affairs, for talks with Chinese Premier Wen Jiabao amid mounting concerns about the renminbi's marked depreciation against the euro. Though scholars such as Henning (2007) and Pisani-Ferry (2008*b*) have drawn unfavourable comparisons between euro and dollar diplomacy over China's exchange rate policy, the two approaches were not, in the end, so far apart. Much has been made of the Omnibus Trade and Competitiveness Act (1988), which allows the United States Treasury to cite countries for currency manipulation, but successive Treasury Secretaries have been at pains to avoid using it, preferring instead the same powers of persuasion employed by the euro area troika. A significant difference between the two sides concerned the role of legislatures and the macroeconomic-trade nexus. While members of the US Congress have threatened trade sanctions over China's exchange rate policy on countless occasions, neither the European Parliament nor successive EU Trade Commissioners have had much to say about the renminbi question. Whether such sabre rattling by the US legislature was seen as a credible threat by Chinese authorities is far from clear. What is more certain is that neither euro nor dollar diplomacy has much to show for its efforts, with domestic considerations still dominating China's stop–start approach to exchange rate reform.

These findings both bode well and ill for the EU's ambitions to be a global actor. On the one hand, the global financial crisis is a rare example of an international emergency in which the EU's claims to international leadership were matched, more or less, by its capabilities. Though international finance and foreign policy may seem like strange bedfellows, it should be recalled that the EU's role as joint supervisor of the world economy was identified by Hill (1993) in his seminal article on the capabilities–expectations gap in the common foreign and security policy. On the other hand, the global financial crisis has laid bare the limited influence of the Commission and the President in office of the European Council in multilateral fora compared to the collective endeavours of large EU member states. When applied to the EU's wider international relations, this begs the question of what, if anything, the new full-time President of the European Council and High Representative of the Union for Foreign Affairs and Security Policy can do that member states acting in concert cannot.

One answer to this question offered by this book is that a unified approach to EU external representation might fare better in bilateral settings. The aforementioned proliferation of macroeconomic dialogues between the EU and third countries suggests that member states are more willing to speak with one voice to third parties than they are in international financial institutions and fora. Three explanations of this puzzle were offered in Chapter 7. Firstly, the sovereignty costs of creating a bilateral dialogue are comparatively low because it does not require member states to close channels of communications with the country in question. Creating a single EU chair in international organizations, in contrast, requires some or all member states to give up their seat at the table. Secondly, the pay-off from collective diplomacy varies between bilateral and multilateral settings. In multilateral fora, it pays for EU member states to turn up in large numbers, providing they can act in concert.

In bilateral fora, EU member states have learned the hard way that showing up on masse for talks with an individual country can backfire. Thirdly, bilateralism can be the last refuge when multilateralism fails to deliver. The Eurogroup, for example, had few options but to send a high-level delegation to China for talks on the euro/renminbi exchange rate once confidence in the IMF's efforts to broker a solution to the wider problem of global imbalances faded.

8.2 The future of new modes of EU policymaking

'At the very moment that academics started using the concept . . . the practice had already peaked', wrote Schmitter and Grote (1997: 1) about the neo-corporatist turn in comparative political economy in the mid-1970s. Could the current governance turn in EU studies (Kohler-Koch and Rittberger 2006) face a similar fate, with scholars' interest in decentralized and non-hierarchical modes of policymaking waxing as their use by EU policymaking wanes?

The practice of creating function-specific EU agencies, for one, has continued apace in recent years. Prior to the mid-1990s, there were only three bodies of this kind: the Euratom Supply Agency in Luxembourg, the European Centre for the Development of Vocational Training in Thessalonica, and the European Foundation for the Improvement of Living and Working Conditions in Dublin. Since this time, some twenty-three EU agencies have opened their doors for business, including the European Fundamental Rights Agency in Vienna, the European Maritime Safety Agency in Lisbon, and the European Food Safety Authority in Parma. The reforms to EU financial supervision agreed in the aftermath of the global financial crisis will have added to this list, with the official launch in January 2011 of the London-based European Banking Authority, the Frankfurt-based European Insurance and Occupational Pensions Authority, and the Paris-based European Securities and Markets Authority.

In spite of EU agencies' inexorable rise, a recentralization of decision-making in the EU could yet be on the cards. According to the Court of Auditors (2009: 223), agencies and other decentralized bodies of the EU spend approximately €1.5 billion per year on administration and other costs. Though a few of these bodies are self-funding, most receive some form of subsidy from the EU budget. Whether these subsidies are well spent is a matter of debate. A recent evaluation of EU agencies carried out on behalf of the Commission concluded that the location of many of these bodies was a source of significant inefficiency. A case in point is the European Food Safety Authority, which reportedly spends €1 million per year on airport transfers for visitors and staff (Ramboll Management Consulting 2009). Such wastefulness is economically indefensible at any time, but it is politically tone deaf during a period in which EU member states face swingeing budget cuts. If national trends are anything to go by – the UK government announced plans in October 2010 to abolish 192 quasi-non-governmental organizations (Cabinet Office 2010) – the fate of some EU agencies might hang in the balance in negotiations over the financial perspectives for the period 2012–21.

New governance, likewise, continues to occupy a pivotal place in EU policy-making. Nowhere is this clearer than in relation to Europe 2020. For all the talk of a stronger governance architecture (Commission 2010*d*), the EU's new-look reform agenda relies on the same modes of new governance as its predecessor, the Lisbon Strategy (Armstrong 2010: 274). Under Europe 2020, the Council continues to adopt Integrated Guidelines on macroeconomic, micro-economic, and employment policies on the basis of which member states will draw up national reform programmes. Though these programmes are now submitted at the same time as the stability and convergence programmes, this makes little practical difference to surveillance and enforcement procedures. The Commission continues to monitor the design and delivery of national reform programmes in an annual report to the European Council, and the Council of Ministers continues to issue non-binding country-specific recommendations on the advice of the Commission.

In spite of this continuity, EU policymakers have become less effusive in their support for new governance than was once the case. While the open method of coordination was given pride of place in the Lisbon Strategy's launch in March 2000, the Commission's communication on Europe 2020 in March 2010 made just one reference to the open method and only then to call for its transformation in the area of social exclusion and social protection into a more effective platform for cooperation (Commission 2010*e*: 18). The need to strengthen existing instruments of coordination was a recurring theme in this document. That the instruments in question should be located in the Treaty was made clear at the European Council in March 2010, which agreed that the Europe 2020 strategy required EU policymakers to make better use of Articles 121 and 136 TFEU to promote economic policy coordination in the EU and euro area respectively (Council of the European Union 2010*e*).

One reading of Europe 2020's silence on the open method is that the Commission and the European Council were at pains to promote only treaty-based instruments of coordination given the metaphorical blood and treasure expended over the ratification of the Lisbon Treaty. From this perspective, the new Treaty's failure to give the open method a clear constitutional status – a desiderata of some members of the European Convention – may serve as a brake on those aspects of new governance that are entirely without legal basis. For de Witte (2008: 103), the Lisbon Treaty leaves the open method with a 'twilight existence' by incorporating this approach to policy-making in all but name in areas such as public health, industry, and research while remaining vague about its current status in areas such as education or its future use in fields such as migration.

New governance's potential loss, of course, is not necessarily the Community method's gain. The Lisbon Treaty is equally equivocal about the EU's traditional modus operandi. Though it extends the Community method into areas such as policing and judicial cooperation on criminal matters and strengthens the role of the European Parliament in agriculture and external trade, the new Treaty leaves a whole host of policy areas more or less dependent on the pre-existing policy framework (Wallace et al. 2010: 497). That this is the case is ironic. The Lisbon Treaty is, after all, the culmination of nearly a decade of institutional introspection that began with the Commission's call in its 2001 White Paper on European Governance to reinvigorate the Community method to address the 'widening gulf between the European Union and the people it serves' (Commission 2001*a*: 7).

8.3 The fate of EMU

A well-worn cliché among the EU commentariat is that crises are a catalyst for change. The adoption of the internal market programme, it is oftentimes said, was a response to the EEC's economic malaise in the early 1980s, just as the launch of the single currency is frequently portrayed as a reaction to the exchange rate instability that periodically gripped member states since the 1970s. It comes as little surprise, therefore, that EU watchers have asked whether the global financial crisis might herald a new era of European integration (Barber 2008; Persaud 2008). Euro area heads of state or government did little to dampen such speculation when they decided, in March 2010, to create a taskforce to consider 'all options to reinforce the legal framework' surrounding EU economic governance (Council of the European Union 2010*b*). The taskforce, it was agreed, would be convened by the President of the European Council, Herman Van Rompuy, in cooperation with the Commission and include representatives of the member states, the ECB, and, in a sign that decision-making under the Lisbon Treaty is less streamlined than some had hoped for, the rotating presidency of the EU.

The Van Rompuy Taskforce went about its work slowly and secretively, taking almost two months to hold its first meeting and giving little away in public until it published its final report five months later. The Commission, in contrast, wasted little time in initiating a public debate on the future of EU economic governance (Commission 2010*e*). In May 2010, the EU executive published a communication that rolled out a number of reform ideas, including the so-called European semester, a change to the coordination calendar that would allow the Commission and Council to review stability and convergence programmes and national reform programmes under Europe 2020 before budgets have been adopted by member states. EU leaders endorsed the idea of a European semester at the European Council in June 2010, took note of several of the Commission's suggestions, and invited the Commission and the Van Rompuy Taskforce to 'develop . . . and make operational these orientations' (Council of the European Union 2010*i*). While little was heard of the Van Rompuy Taskforce in the months that followed, the Commission waited for two weeks to issue a follow-up communication that further refined its reform ideas and promised legislative proposals (Commission 2010*g*).

In preparing the ground for these reforms, the Commissioner for Economic and Monetary Affairs, Olli Rehn, argued that it was 'high time to reinforce the economic union in the EMU' through measures that 'respect and reinforce the Community method' (Rehn 2010). Procedurally, at least, the Commissioner made good on this promise. The package of legislative proposals tabled by the Commission in September 2010 reflected the EU executive's determination to exercise its right of initiative with regard to the rules underpinning multilateral surveillance (Article 121(6) TFEU), the excessive deficit procedure (Article 126 (13) TFEU), and, in a new provision introduced by the Lisbon Treaty, measures specific to the euro area (Article 136 TFEU). It also sent a message to the President of the European Council about encroaching on the Commission's turf and reached out to those Members of the European Parliament who made clear their desire to see the Community method strengthened in this domain (Pop 2010). That the Parliament's views carried as much weight as they did was also due to the Lisbon Treaty, which extended the ordinary legislative procedure to regulations governing the conduct of multilateral surveillance (Article 121[6]).

Substantively, the draft legislation presented by the Commission in September 2010 includes changes to the preventive and corrective arm of the pact, new legislation on the establishment of an excessive imbalance procedure, and a draft directive establishing minimum standards for national fiscal frameworks (Commission 2010*g*, 2010*h*). Taken as a whole, these changes would:

- Operationalize the Treaty's debt criterion by requiring countries with government debt in excess of the 60 per cent of GDP to reduce this figure at a rate of 0.05 per cent per year over a three-year period;
- Replace medium-term budgetary objectives with a new principle of prudent fiscal policymaking, which would require member states to keep annual government expenditure growth below the medium-term growth rate of GDP;
- Impose financial penalties as soon as a member state is found to be in a state of excessive deficit and allow for fines against countries that breach the prudence principle;

- Step up the surveillance of macroeconomic imbalances, with member states threatening 'the proper functioning of the economy of a Member State or of Economic and Monetary Union, or of the Union as a whole' facing guidelines and recommendations under Article 121 TFEU and the possibility of fines;
- Introduce a principle of reverse voting for disciplinary measures under the excessive deficit procedure and excessive imbalance procedure, whereby Commission recommendations to impose sanctions would be carried unless a qualified majority of finance ministers vote against them; and
- Establish agreed minimum standards for, *inter alia*, public accounting and statistics, forecasts, and numerical fiscal rules.

Though these proposals would significantly extend the scope of economic policy coordination in the euro area, they do not fundamentally depart from EMU's decentralized approach to economic policy. The revisions to the stability and growth pact would strengthen the Commission's agenda-setting powers when it comes to the imposition of disciplinary measures and shift the balance from peer pressure to pecuniary sanctions, but they do not alter the fact that member states retain control over the formulation and implementation of their fiscal policies. The prudence principle could have a direct bearing on member states' expenditure decisions, but the emphasis on medium-term rather than short-term growth rates should provide room for manoeuvre. The proposed excessive imbalance procedure would, likewise, rely for the most part on the same mechanisms of enforcement as the BEPGs, namely non-binding guidelines under Article 121(2) TFEU and non-binding recommendations for corrective action under Article 121(4) TFEU. Though the Commission envisages the use of pecuniary sanctions in the event of excessive imbalances, such measures would, as in the case of the original stability and growth pact, be used only as a last resort.

The Commission's draft directive on budgetary frameworks in member states comes closest, perhaps, to the Community method. Though it leaves unchallenged member states' right to make decisions on fiscal policy, it would impose hard law obligations that could have a significant impact on the institutional context in which these decisions take place. If minimum standards such as these had been enforced prior to the global financial crisis, Greek authorities might have been able to exert a tighter grip on the budgetary process. They would, in any case, have found it harder to conceal the true state of their public finances in the presence of more reliable fiscal data for all tiers of general government updated on a monthly basis.

Predictably, the Van Rompuy Report, which was published in October 2010, rowed back on some of the more ambitious aspects of the Commission's proposals. On the subject of the stability and growth pact, the Taskforce agreed that member states breaching the preventive arm should face the possibility of financial penalties and that pecuniary sanctions should be applied at an earlier stage of the excessive deficit procedure. The Taskforce was more cautious, however, on the issue of reverse voting, insisting that qualified majority voting should continue to apply for the later stages of the excessive deficit procedure. The Van Rompuy Report also endorsed the idea of an excessive imbalance procedure, although it underlined the point that financial penalties should be applied only as a last resort. Finally, it endorsed the need for minimum standards for budgetary frameworks, but shied away from suggesting that such provisions should be enshrined in EU law.

The Van Rompuy Report also contained several ideas that were not in the Commission's proposals for strengthening euro area governance. Among the more interesting ones was a recommendation concerning 'the use or setting up of public institutions or bodies to provide independent analysis, assessments and forecasts on domestic fiscal policy matters' (Taskforce to the European Council 2010: 11). If nothing else, this recommendation suggests an understanding of the limits of imposing peer pressure from Brussels without first having sufficient support in domestic political arenas (see Chapter 5).

By far the most controversial conclusion of the Van Rompuy Taskforce was an acceptance of the need to establish a credible crisis resolution mechanism for the euro area in the medium term. The report was vague on what form this framework should take, beyond emphasizing the need to overcome problems of moral hazard among policymakers and the private sector by offering *ex ante* financial guarantees to stricken member states. It also accepted that such a mechanism 'may imply a need for Treaty changes, depending on its specific features' (Taskforce to the European Council 2010: 12).

This last point was an astonishing admission, coming as it did less than a year after the Lisbon Treaty entered into force. It owed much to German angst about the constitutionality of the ad hoc financial support offered to euro area members during the sovereign debt crisis, with Chancellor Angela Merkel arguing on the eve of the European Council in October 2010 that a change in the Treaty was essential to ensure that a framework for preventing future financial crises is 'legally unchallengeable' (Peel 2010). It also provided an opportunity for Germany to claw back some of the concessions that it had made on EMU's fiscal rules during the negotiation of the Maastricht Treaty and the original stability and growth pact. Plans for a European Monetary Fund, floated by Wolfgang Schäuble in March 2010, insisted that member states must, as a point of principle, be allowed to default on their debt and spoke of the need for strict conditions to be attached to emergency liquidity aid, including stringent sanctions under the excessive deficit procedure imposed on a mandatory basis, the suspension of voting rights in the Council of Ministers on matters related to euro area business, and even expulsion from EMU (Schäuble 2010).

Germany was forced to give ground on several of these issues. The reference to member states exiting monetary union was an early casualty. The idea of mandatory sanctions was replaced with a call for 'more automaticity' in a deal done by Angela Merkel and Nicolas Sarkozy at Deauville on the eve of the European Council in October 2010 (Franco-German Declaration 2010). The issue of voting rights was put to one side at the summit itself, but it was agreed that the President of the European Council would draw up plans for a permanent crisis resolution mechanism with a view to concluding a limited change to the Lisbon Treaty by mid-2013, this coming alongside an agreement to take forward the Commission's proposals on economic governance with a view to making the necessary legislative changes by mid-2011 (Council of the European Union 2010*a*).

The prospect of further treaty change raises a host of economic and political questions, but the most pertinent one with which to conclude this book is whether a permanent crisis resolution mechanism could pave the way for the Community method under EMU. It remains to be seen at the time of writing precisely what form such a mechanism will take and whether treaty changes can be ratified without difficulty. These caveats notwithstanding, two broad avenues of approach are open to EU policymakers (Alexander 2010). A more centralized solution would entail the creation of an EU debt-restructuring agency to facilitate negotiations between a debtor state and its creditors and to provide financial support to the country subject to strict conditionality.[1] A more decentralized solution could involve making greater use of collective action clauses in sovereign bond contracts to facilitate agreement between bond holders over the restructuring of debt, should the need arise.

The first of these choices would lend itself more easily to the Community method. In their proposal for a European Crisis Resolution Mechanism, Gianviti et al. (2010), for example, foresee a central role for both the Court of Justice and the Commission. The Court of Justice, they argue, should be given responsibility for assessing the claims of debtor countries and creditors and for enforcing an agreement on debt restructuring. The Commission, they suggest, could take the lead in deciding by how much debt needs to be reduced to restore solvency in the country in question, which in turn would inform the question of what the settlement between the debtor country and its creditors should be.

[1] Gianviti et al. (2010: 4) define debt restructuring as a 'procedure to initiate and conduct negotiations between a sovereign debtor with unsustainable debt and its creditors leading to, and enforcing, an agreement on how to reduce the present value of the debtor's future obligations in order to re-establish the sustainability of its public finances'.

The prospects for this proposal or any other solution that would significantly strengthen the role of the Commission or the Court of Justice in crisis resolution seem slim in the light of a deal struck at the European Council in December 2010. At this summit, EU leaders agreed to seek changes to Article 136 TFEU, which would allow 'a stability mechanism to be activated if indispensable to safeguard the stability of the euro area as a whole' (Council of the European 2010*j*: 6). Insolvent member states, it was agreed, would be entitled to support under this mechanism but only after the country in question had negotiated a restructuring plan with its creditors. No mention was made of EU institutions playing a role in this arbitration process, with member states agreeing only to include standardized and identical collective action clauses in all new government bonds issued from mid-2013.

The EU's permeable plans for a permanent crisis resolution mechanism notwithstanding, the likelihood of a major shift in EMU's policymaking architecture in the light of the global financial crisis appears remote at the present juncture. For the foreseeable future, therefore, it would seem that the euro area's experimental system of economic governance is here to stay. Uncertainty may surround the fate of the euro, but member states seem in no mood to countenance the Community method or otherwise cede control over their economic policies to the EU. The result is that EMU is set to remain a tender union that is wed, for better or worse, to new modes of EU policymaking.

References

Ahearne, A., and von Hagen, J. (2006), 'European Perspectives on Global Imbalances', Bruegel Working Papers 58.

Aherne, A., and Eichengreen, B. (2007), 'External Monetary and Financial Policy: A Review and a Proposal', in A. Sapir (ed.), *Fragmented Power: Europe and the Global Economy* (Brussels: Bruegel) 128–55.

Alexander, K. (2010), 'Market Impact of Orderly Sovereign Default', in Economic and Monetary Affairs Unit (ed.), *Euro Area Governance – Ideas for Crisis Management Reform* (Brussels: European Parliament) 63–78.

Amable, B. (2009), 'Structural Reforms in Europe and the (In)Coherence of Institutions', *Oxford Review of Economic Policy*, 25/1: 17–39.

Andrews, D. (2003), 'The Committee of Central Bank Governors as a source of rules', *Journal of European Public Policy*, 10/6: 956–73.

—— (ed.) (2006), *International Monetary Power* (Ithaca, NY: Cornell University Press).

Annett, A. (2006), 'Enforcement and the Stability and Growth Pact: How Fiscal Policy Did and Did Not Change Under Europe's Fiscal Framework', IMF Working Paper WP/06/116.

Armstrong, K. (2010), *Governing Social Inclusion: Europeanization Through Policy Coordination* (Oxford: Oxford University Press).

Artis, M.J., and Buti, M. (2000), '"Close to Balance or in Surplus": A Policy-Maker's Guide to the Implementation of the Stability and Growth Pact', *Journal of Common Market Studies*, 38/4: 563–91.

Atkins, R. (2005), 'Ministers Urged to Voice Views to ECB', *Financial Times*, 16 June.

—— Norman, P. (1998), 'Lafontaine Dares to Call for Rates Cut', *Financial Times*, 3 October.

—— Parker, G. (2005*a*), 'Juncker Outlines Terms of Dialogue Over Euro', *Financial Times*, 12 January.

—— —— (2005*b*), 'ECB Under Pressure on Rate Rise', *Financial Times*, 8 November.

—— —— (2006), 'Trichet Snubs Calls to Listen to Politicians', *Financial Times*, 8 June.

—— Thornhill, J. (2005), 'France and Germany Attack US over Dollars Slide', *Financial Times*, 25 January.

—— Daneshkhu, S., and Parker, G. (2005), 'Eurozone Ministers Say Rates Must Stay on Hold', *Financial Times*, 30 November.

Aubrechtová, J., Coussens, W., and Pineau, G. (2010), 'How to Reconcile EU Integration with the Governance of the International Monetary Fund', *Banking Journal*, 18: 5–9.

Ayuso-i-Casals, J. (2010), 'National Fiscal Governance Reforms across EU Member States. Analysis of the Information Contained in the 2009–2010 Stability and Convergence Programmes', European Economy, Occasional Papers, No. 67 (Brussels: European Commission).

Baldwin, D.A. (1985), *Economic Statecraft* (Princeton NJ: Princeton University Press).

Barber, T. (2008), 'Unity in Crisis', *Financial Times*, Brussels Blog, 6 October.

—— (2010), 'Splits Open on Role of IMF in Greece', *Financial Times*, 18 March.

—— Hope, K. (2009), 'Papandreou Says Greece is Corrupt', *Financial Times*, 12 December.

—— Crooks, E., and Norman, P. (2001), 'Blunt IMF Message Tells Europe to Cut Interest Rates', *Financial Times*, 21 April.

—— Graham, R., and Simonian, H. (2001), 'Euro-Zone Interest Rates are Held', *Financial Times*, 12 April.

Barroso, J.M. (2010), 'Speech at the EU–China Business Summit', Brussels, 6 October.

Baumann, E., and Kastrop, C. (2007), 'A New Budget Rule for Germany', in Banca d'Italia (ed.), *Fiscal Policy: Current Issues and Challenges* (Rome: Banca d'Italia) 595–612.

Bayne, N. (2007), 'Bilateral Economic Diplomacy: The United States', in N. Bayne and S. Woolcock (eds.), *The New Economic Diplomacy: Decision-Making and Negotiation in International Economic Relations* (Aldershot: Ashgate) 163–80.

Bean, C. (1998), 'The Interaction of Aggregate-Demand Policies and Labour Market Reform', *Swedish Economic Policy Review*, 5/2: 353–82.

Beattie, A. (2009), 'Doubts Remain on IMF Global Power', *Financial Times*, 3 October.

—— (2010), 'A Reach Regained', *Financial Times*, 22 April.

Beetsma, R., and Bovenberg, A. (1995), 'Does Monetary Unification Lead to Excessive Debt Accumulation?', Centre for Economic Policy Research Discussion Paper No. 1299.

—— Uhlig, H. (1999), 'An Analysis of the Stability and Growth Pact', *Economic Journal*, 109/October: 546–71.

Begg, I. (2007), 'Lisbon II, Two Years On: An Assessment of the Partnership for Growth and Jobs', Special CEPS Report (Brussels: Centre for European Policy Studies).

Benoit, B. (2008), 'Merkel Rejects Eurozone "Summit"', *Financial Times*, 16 January.

—— (2009), 'Steinbrück Calls for Global Finance Tax', *Financial Times*, 12 September.

—— Barber, T. (2009), 'Germany Ready to Take Steps to Support Eurozone', *Financial Times*, 19 February.

Benoit, K., and Laver, M. (2006), *Party Policies in Modern Democracies* (London: Routledge).

Bini Smaghi, L. (2009), 'A Single EU Seat in the International Monetary Fund?', in K.E. Jørgensen (ed.), *The European Union in International Organizations* (London: Routledge) 61–79.

—— Casini, C. (2000), 'Monetary and Fiscal Policy Co-operation: Institutions and Procedures in EMU', *Journal of Common Market Studies*, 38/3: 375–91.

Biscop, S. (2005), *The European Security Strategy: A Global Agenda for Positive Power* (Aldershot: Ashgate).

Blanchard, O., and Giavazzi, F. (2003), 'Improving the SGP Through a Proper Accounting of Public Investment', mimeo (Cambridge, MA: Department of Economics, Massachusetts Institute of Technology).

Borrás, S., and Greve, B. (2004), 'Concluding Remarks: New Method or Just Cheap Talk?', *Journal of European Public Policy*, 11/2: 329–36.

Braga de Macedo, J. (2002), 'Portugal's European Integration: The Good Student with a Bad Fiscal Constitution', mimeo (Paris: Institut d'Études Politiques), http://prof.fe.unl.pt/~jbmacedo/papers/HARVARD.html

Brennock, M. (2001*a*), 'FF, Ahern Maintain Support as Labour Slips 2% Further', *The Irish Times*, 18 May.

—— (2001*b*), 'McCreevy Hails "Anti-Establishment" Statement', *The Irish Times*, 16 June.

Bronchi, C. (2003), 'The Effectiveness of Public Expenditure in Portugal', OECD Economics Department Working Paper No. 349.

Brown, G., Merkel, A., and Sarkozy, N. (2009), 'Letter to the Prime Minister of Sweden', 3 September (London: Downing Street).

Brown, K., Oliver, C., and Johnston, T. (2010), 'Asia Irked by IMF "Leniency"', *Financial Times*, 1 May.

Buiter, W. (1999), 'Alice in Euroland', *Journal of Common Market Studies*, 37/2: 181–209.

Bundesbank (2003), 'Statement by the Executive Board of the Deutsche Bundesbank on the Draft EU Constitution and the Stability and Growth Pact', Frankfurt am Main, 10 December.

Burda, M., and Gerlach, S. (2010), 'Greek Lessons', www.VoxEU.org 11 May.

Buti, M., and Guidice, G. (2002), 'Maastricht's Fiscal Rules at Ten: An Assessment', *Journal of Common Market Studies*, 40/5: 823–48.

—— Roeger, W., and In't Veld, J. (2001), 'Stabilizing Output and Inflation: Policy Conflicts and Co-operation Under a Stability Pact', *Journal of Common Market Studies*, 39/5: 801–28.

—— Eijffinger, S., and Franco, D. (2003), 'Revisiting EMU's Stability Pact: A Pragmatic Way Forward', *Oxford Review of Economic Policy*, 19/1: 100–11.

Cabinet Office (2010), 'Quango Reforms Herald New Age of Accountability in Government', Press Release CAB 167-10, 14 October.

Calmfors, L. (2003), 'Fiscal Policy to Stabilise the Domestic Economy in the EMU: What Can We Learn from Monetary Policy?', *CESifo Economic Studies*, 49/3: 319–53.

Campanella, M. (2000), 'The Battle Between ECOFIN-11 and the European Central Bank: A Strategic Interaction Perspective', in M. Green Cowles and M. Smith (eds.), *The State of the European Union*, Vol. 5 (Oxford: Oxford University Press) 110–26.

Canzoneri, M., Grilli, V., and Mason, P. (eds.) (1992), *Designing a Central Bank for Europe* (Cambridge: Cambridge University Press).

Chalmers, D., and Lodge, M. (2003), 'The Open Method of Coordination and the European Welfare State', ESRC Centre for the Analysis of Risk and Regulation, Discussion Paper No. 11.

Chambraud, C., Leparmentier, A., and Ricard, P. (2008), 'Le président français veut instaurer un gouvernement économique européen', *le Monde*, 23 October.

Chan, S., and Drury, A.C. (2000), *Sanctions as Economic Statecraft: Theory and Practice* (London: Macmillan/St Martin's).

Chang, M. (2009), *Monetary Integration in the European Union* (Basingstoke: Palgrave Macmillan).

Coghlan, D. (2001), 'Opposition May Lose Enthusiasm for Election', *The Irish Times*, 26 January.

Cohen, B. (1971), *The Future of Sterling as an International Currency* (Basingstoke: Macmillan).

—— (1998), *The Geography of Money* (Ithaca, NY: Cornell University Press).

—— (2008*a*), 'The Euro in a Global Context: Challenges and Capacities', in K. Dyson (ed.), *The Euro Area at 10: Europeanization, Power and Convergence* (Oxford: Oxford University Press), 37–53.

—— (2008*b*), 'The International Monetary System: Diffusion and Ambiguity', *International Affairs*, 84/3: 455–70.

Commission (1993), 'The 1993 Broad Economic Policy Guidelines', European Economy, No. 55 (Luxembourg: Office for Official Publications of the European Communities).

—— (2000), 'Public Finances in EMU – 2000', European Economy, No. 3 (Luxembourg: Office for Official Publications of the European Communities).

—— (2001*a*), 'European Governance: A White Paper', COM(2001), 428 final, 25 July.

—— (2001*b*), 'Autumn 2001 Economic Forecasts for 2001–2003', European Economy, Supplement A, Economic trends 10/11 (Luxembourg: Office for Official Publications of the European Communities).

—— (2001*c*), 'Communication From the Commission on Strengthening Economic Policy Co-ordination Within the Euro Area', COM(2001) 0082 final.

—— (2002*a*), 'Commission Assesses Updated Stability Programme of Portugal', Press Release IP/02/165, 30 January.

—— (2002*b*), 'Commission Assesses Updated Stability Programme of Germany', Press Release IP/02/164, 30 January.

—— (2003*a*), 'Public Finances in EMU – 2003', European Economy, No. 3 (Luxembourg: Office for Official Publications of the European Communities).

—— (2003*b*), 'The 2003 Broad Economic Policy Guidelines', European Economy, No. 4 (Luxembourg: Office for Official Publications of the European Communities).

—— (2005*a*), 'The Broad Economic Policy Guidelines for the 2004–08 period', European Economy, No. 4 (Luxembourg: Office for Official Publications of the European Communities).

—— (2005*b*), 'Working Together for Growth and Jobs: A New Start for the Lisbon Strategy', Communication to the Spring European Council, Brussels, COM(2005) 24, 2 February.

—— (2006), 'Public Finances in EMU – 2006', European Economy, No. 3 (Luxembourg: Office for Official Publications of the European Communities).

—— (2008*a*), 'EMU@10: Successes and Challenges after 10 years of Economic and Monetary Union', European Economy 2/2008 (Luxembourg: Office for the Official Publications of the European Communities).

—— (2008*b*), 'Memorandum of Understanding between the European Community and the Republic of Hungary' (Brussels: DG ECFIN).

—— (2009), 'Public Finances in EMU – 2009', European Economy Reports and Studies, No. 3 (Luxembourg: Office for Official Publications of the European Communities).

—— (2010*a*), 'European Economic Forecast – Spring 2010', European Economy, No. 2. (Luxembourg: Office for Official Publications of the European Communities).

—— (2010*b*), 'The Economic Adjustment Programme for Greece. First Review – Summer 2010', European Economy. Occasional Papers, No. 68 (Luxembourg: Office for Official Publications of the European Communities).

—— (2010*c*), 'Lisbon Strategy Evaluation Document', SEC(2010) 114 final, 2 February.

—— (2010*d*), 'Statistical Annex to European Economy – Spring 2010' (Luxembourg: Office for Official Publications of the European Communities).

—— (2010*e*), 'A Strategy for Smart, Sustainable and Inclusive Growth', COM(2010) 2020 final, 3 March.

—— (2010*f*), 'Reinforcing Economic Policy Coordination', COM(2010) 250, 12 May.

—— (2010*g*), 'Enhancing Economic Policy Coordination for Stability, Growth and Jobs – Tools for Stronger EU Economic Governance', COM(2010) 367/2, 30 June.

—— (2010*h*), 'Economic Governance Package (1): Strengthening the Stability and Growth Pact', MEMO/10/455, 29 September.

—— (2010*i*), 'Economic Governance Package (2): Preventing and Correcting Macroeconomic Imbalances', MEMO/10/454, 29 September.

Committee for the Study of Economic and Monetary Union (1989), 'Report on Economic and Monetary Union in the Community' (Brussels: Committee for the Study of Economic and Monetary Union).

Committee on Economic and Monetary Affairs (2001), 'Monetary Dialogue with the President of the European Central Bank', 28 May (Brussels: European Parliament).

Cooper, R. (1968), *The Economics of Interdependence: Economic Policy in the Atlantic Community* (New York: McGraw-Hill).

Correia da Cunha, J., and Silva, P. (2002), 'Local Finance and Fiscal Consolidation in Portugal', Bank of Portugal Economic Bulletin, March: 47–56.

Council of the European Union (1997), 'Presidency Conclusions', SN 400/97, 12–13 December.

—— (1998), 'Presidency Conclusions', Press Release: 00300/1/98 REV, 11–12 December.

—— (1999), 'Report by the ECOFIN Council to the European Council in Helsinki on Economic Policy Coordination: Review of Policy Instruments and Experience in Stage 3 of EMU', Press Release 13123/99, 24 November.

—— (2000), 'Presidency Conclusions', SN 400/1/00, 7–9 December.

—— (2001*a*), 'Presidency Conclusions', SN Nr: 00300/1/0, 14–15 December.

—— (2001*b*), 'The 2329th Economic and Finance Ministers' Council Meeting', Press Release 696/01, 12 February.

—— (2001*c*), 'The 2382nd Economic and Finance Ministers' Council Meeting', Press Release 13474/01, 6 November.

—— (2002), 'The 2407th Economic and Finance Ministers' Council Meeting', Press Release 6108/02, 12 February.

Council of the European Union (2003*a*), 'A Secure Europe in a Better World: The European Security Strategy', Brussels, 12 December.
—— (2003*b*), 'Joint Statement: EU–Russia Summit', Press Release, 31 May.
—— (2003*c*), 'Joint-Press Statement: 6th EU China Summit', Brussels, Press Release 13424/03, Beijing, 30 October.
—— (2004), '2580th Council Meeting', Press Release 9063/04, 11 May.
—— (2005*a*), 'Presidency Conclusions', Press Release 7619/05, 23 March.
—— (2005*b*), 'Roadmap for the Common Economic Space – Building Blocks for Sustained Economic Growth', Press Release, 10 May.
—— (2005*c*), 'The India–EU Strategic Partnership: Joint Action Plan', New Delhi, 7 September.
—— (2007*a*), 'Presidency Conclusions', Nr: 16616/1/07, 13–14 December.
—— (2007*b*), '2804th Economic and Financial Affairs Council meeting' Press: 126 Nr: 10319/07, 5 June.
—— (2007*c*), 'EU–Ukraine Summit', Kiev, Press Release 12927/07, 14 September.
—— (2007*d*), 'Joint Statement: EU–Brazil Summit', Press Release 11531/07, 4 July.
—— (2007*e*), 'The South Africa–European Union Strategic Partnership Joint Action Plan', Press Release 9650/07, 15 May.
—— (2007*f*), 'Joint Statement: 10th China–EU Summit', Press Release 16070/07, 28 November.
—— (2007*g*), 'Council Decision of 5 June 2007 abrogating Decision 2004/917/EC on the existence of an excessive deficit in Greece' (2007/465/EC), *Official Journal of the European Union*, L 176/21, 6 July.
—— (2008*a*), 'Presidency Conclusions', SN 14368/08, 15–16 October.
—— (2008*b*), 'Agreed Language', Informal Meeting of EU Heads of State or Government, Brussels, 7 November.
—— (2008*c*), 'EU–Russia Common Spaces – 2007 Progress Report', Brussels, 7 April.
—— (2009*a*), 'Presidency Conclusions', SN 7880/1/09 REV1, 19–20 March.
—— (2009*b*), 'Presidency Conclusions', SN 11225/2/09, 18–19 June.
—— (2009*c*), 'Agreed Language for the Pittsburgh G20 Summit', Informal Meeting of EU Heads of State or Government, 17 September.
—— (2009*d*), 'Joint Statement of the 12th EU–China Summit', Press Release 16845/09, 30 November.
—— (2010*a*), 'Conclusions', Nr: EUCO 25/1/10 REV 1, 28–29 October.
—— (2010*b*), 'Statement of the Heads of State or Government of the Euro Area', 7 May (Brussels: Council of Ministers of the European Union).
—— (2010*c*), 'Europe 2020 strategy for Jobs and Growth: The Council Adopts Broad Economic Policy Guidelines', Press: 202, Nr: 12082/10, 13 July.
—— (2010*d*), 'Council Gives Notice to Greece to Correct its Government Deficit by 2012, Setting out a Timetable for Corrective Measures', Press Release 6501/10, 16 February.
—— (2010*e*), 'Conclusions', Nr: EUCO 7/10, 25–26 March.
—— (2010*f*), 'Extraordinary Council meeting: Economic and Financial Affairs', Press Release 9596/10, 9–10 May (Brussels: Council of Ministers of the European Union).

—— (2010*g*), 'Joint Statement: 5th EU Mexico Summit', Press Release 9815/10, 16 May (Brussels: Council of Ministers of the European Union).

—— (2010*h*), '13th EU–China Summit – Joint Press Communiqué', 14577/10 PRESSE [267], 6 October.

—— (2010*i*), 'Conclusions', Nr: EUCO 13/10, 17 June.

—— (2010*j*), 'Conclusions', Nr: EUCO 30/10, 17 December.

Court of Auditors (2009), 'Annual Report on the Implementation of the Budget', *Official Journal of the European Union*, 2009/C 269/01, 10 November.

Dáil Éireann (2001), 'Private Notice Questions – Budgetary Policies', Volume 530, 13 February.

Davies, H., and Green, D. (2008), *Global Financial Regulation: The Essential Guide* (London: Polity Press).

de Haan, J., Eijffinger, S., Waller, S. (2005), *The European Central Bank: Credibility, Transparency, and Centralization* (Cambridge, MA: MIT Press Books).

de la Porte, C., and Nanz, P. (2004), 'The OMC – A Deliberative-Democratic Mode of Governance? The Cases of Employment and Pensions', *Journal of European Public Policy*, 11/2: 267–88.

—— Pochet, P. (2005), 'Participation in the Open Method of Coordination: The Cases of Employment and Social Inclusion', in J. Zeitlin, P. Pochet, and L. Magnusson (eds.), *The Open Method of Co-ordination in Action: The European Employment and Social Inclusion Strategies* (Brussels: P.I.E. Peter Lang), 353–89.

de Larosière Group (2009), *The High Level Group on Financial Supervision in the EU* (Brussels: European Commission).

Denza, E. (2003), 'Non-Proliferation of Nuclear Weapons; The EU and Iran', *European Foreign Affairs Review*, 10: 289–311.

Department of Finance (2001), 'Intervention by Minister at ECOFIN on Irish Stability Programme', 12 February.

Deroose, S., Hodson, D., and Kuhlmann, J. (2008), 'The Broad Economic Policy Guidelines: Before and After the Re-launch of the Lisbon Strategy', *Journal of Common Market Studies*, 46/4: 827–48.

de Schutter, O. (2004), 'The Implementation of the EU Charter of Fundamental Rights Through the Open Method of Coordination', New York University School of Law Jean Monnet Working Paper 07/04.

de Vasconcelos, A. (2008), '"Multilateralising" Multipolarity', in G. Grevi and A. de Vasconcelos (eds.), *Partnerships for Effective Multilateralism EU Relations with Brazil, China, India and Russia*, Chaillot Paper No. 9: 11–32.

de Villepin (2005), 'European Council – Statement to the National Assembly', 15 June.

de Witte, B. (2008), 'Legal Instruments and Law Making in the Lisbon Treaty', in S. Grilli and J. Ziller (eds.), *EU Constitutionalism without a Constitutional Treaty* (Vienna and New York: Springer) 79–108.

DG Economic and Financial Affairs (2009*a*), '3rd EU–India Macroeconomic Dialogue', New Delhi, India, 30–31 October (Brussels: DG ECFIN).

—— (2009*b*), 'Joint Statement of the First High Level Brazil-EU Macroeconomic and Financial Dialogue', Brasilia, Brazil, 16 July (Brussels: DG ECFIN).

Drezner, D.W. (2000), 'The Complex Causation of Sanction Outcomes', in S. Chan and A.C. Drury (eds.), *Sanctions as Economic Statecraft: Theory and Practice* (New York: St Martin's), 212–33.

Driffill, J., and Zeno, R. (2004), 'Monetary Policy and Lexicographic Preference Ordering', CEPR Discussion Papers 4247, (London: Centre for Economic Policy Research Discussion Papers).

Duisenberg, W. (2002*a*), 'The Euro as a Catalyst for European Integration', Conference on "One Money, One Euregional Market", Maastricht, 6 February.

—— (2002*b*), 'The Role of the Eurosystem in Prudential Supervision', speech at a conference organized by De Nederlandsche Bank on the 50th anniversary of Dutch banking supervisory legislation, Amsterdam, 24 April.

—— (2003*a*), 'Letter to the President of the Convention Regarding the Draft Constitutional Treaty', 5 June (Frankfurt am Main: ECB).

—— (2003*b*), 'Letter to the President of the Convention Regarding the Draft Constitutional Treaty', 8 May (Frankfurt am Main: ECB).

Dyson, K. (2002), 'Conclusions: European States and Euro Economic Governance', in K. Dyson (ed.), *European States and the Euro: Europeanization, Variation and Convergence* (Oxford: Oxford University Press), 335–66.

—— (2008), 'The European Central Bank: Enlargement as Institutional Affirmation and Differentiation', in E. Best, T. Christiansen, and P. Settembri (eds.), *The Institutions of the Enlarged European Union: Continuity and Change* (Cheltenham: Edward Elgar), 120–39.

—— Featherstone, K. (1999), *The Road to Maastricht: Negotiating Economic and Monetary Union* (Oxford: Oxford University Press).

Eaton, J., and Engers, M. (1992), 'Sanctions', *Journal of Political Economy*, 100/5: 899–928.

—— Sykes, A.O. (2000), 'International Sanctions', in Norman, P. (ed.), *The New Palgrave Dictionary of Economics and the Law* (London: MacMillan), 352–9.

Ecofin Presidency and Commission (2008), 'Statement by the Presidency of the Ecofin Council and the Commission on Hungary', 13 October.

Economist (2001), 'Ireland's Euro-Sins', *Economist*, 17 February.

—— (2009), 'Baltic Brink: Latvia's Troubled Economy', *Economist*, 20 December.

Eichengreen, B. (2006), *Global Imbalances and the Lessons of Bretton Woods* (Cambridge, MA: MIT Press).

Elgie, R. (2002), 'The Politics of the European Central Bank: Principal–Agent Theory and the Democratic Deficit', *Journal of European Public Policy*, 9/2: 186–200.

EU–Brazil Business Summit (2007), 'Joint Declaration of Brazilian and European Business', Lisbon, 4 July.

Eurobarometer (2005), 'The European Constitution: Post-Referendum Survey in France', Flash Eurobarometer, No. 171 (Brussels: DG Press and Communication).

—— (2010), 'Standard Eurobarometer 73 (First Results)' (Brussels: DG Communication).

Eurodad (2006), 'European Coordination at the World Bank and International Monetary Fund: A Question of Harmony?', full text available at: http://www.eurodad.org/uploadedFiles/Whats_New/Reports/Eurodad%20EUIFIgovernance.pdf

Eurogroup (2000), 'Communiqué de l'Eurogroupe', 8 September, Versailles.

—— (2010*a*), *Conclusions of the Eurogroup: Surveillance of Intra-Euro-Area Competitiveness and Macroeconomic Imbalances* (Brussels: Council of the European Union).

—— (2010*b*), *Terms of Reference on Exit Strategies and Near-Term Policy Priorities in the Europe 2020 Strategy: Implications for the Euro Area* (Brussels: Council of the European Union).

—— (2010*c*), *Terms of Reference on Actions Taken by Greece in Response to the Council Decision of 16 February 2010* (Brussels: Council of the European Union).

Eurogroup and Ecofin Ministers (2010), 'Statement', 28 November (Brussels: Council of the European Union).

European Central Bank (2001), 'Annual Report – 2000' (Frankfurt am Main: ECB).

—— (2002), 'Statement of the Governing Council on the Stability and Growth Pact', Press Release, 24 October (Frankfurt am Main: ECB).

—— (2003), Opinion on the draft Treaty establishing a Constitution for Europe (CON/2003/20), OJ C 229, 25.9.2003, 7.

—— (2004), 'The European Constitution and the ECB', ECB Monthly Bulletin 08/2004: 51–64.

—— (2005*a*), 'Statement of the Governing Council on the ECOFIN Council's report on Improving the implementation of the Stability and Growth Pact', Press Release, 21 March (Frankfurt am Main: ECB).

—— (2005*b*), 'The Lisbon Strategy – Five Years On', Monthly Bulletin 07/05 (Frankfurt am Main: ECB).

—— (2005*c*), 'TARGET Annual Report' (Frankfurt am Main: ECB).

—— (2008*a*), Monthly Bulletin (10th Anniversary of the ECB), May (Frankfurt am Main: ECB).

—— (2008*b*), 'Ten Years of the Stability and Growth Pact', ECB Monthly Bulletin, October (Frankfurt am Main: ECB): 53–65.

—— (2010), 'Reinforcing Economic Governance in the Euro Area' (Frankfurt am Main: ECB).

European Economic Community and China (1985), 'Agreement on Trade and Economic Cooperation between the European Economic Community and the People's Republic of China', 19/09/1985 OJ Number L250.

Fallend, F. (2001), 'Austria', *European Journal of Political Research*, 40/7: 238–53.

Federal Ministry of Finance (2006), 'Grasser: EU to Become an Internal Financial Market with Optimum Conditions for Companies and Effective Supervision', Press Release, 7 April.

Fischer, J., Jonung, L., and Larch, M. (2007), '101 Proposals to reform the Stability and Growth Pact. Why so many? A Survey', European Economy, Economic Papers 267 (Brussels: Directorate General Economic and Monetary Affairs, European Commission).

Franco-German Declaration (2010), 'Statement for the France–Germany–Russia Summit', Deauville, 18 October (Paris: Elysee).

Frieden, J. (2004), 'One Europe, One Vote? The Political Economy of European Union Representation in International Organizations', *European Union Politics*, 5/2: 261–76.

G7 (Group of 7) (1999), 'Statement of G7 Ministers and Central Bank Governors', 25 September (Washington, DC, G7).

G20 (Group of 20) (2008*a*), 'The Group of Twenty: A History', full text available at: http://www.g20.org/Documents/history_report_dm1.pdf

G20 (Group of 20) (2008*b*), 'Declaration Summit on Financial Markets and the World Economy', 15 November, Washington, DC, full text available at: http://www.g20.org/Documents/g20_summit_declaration.pdf

—— (2009*a*), 'The Global Plan for Recovery and Reform', London, 2 April, full text available at: http://www.g20.org/Documents/final-communique.pdf

—— (2009*b*), 'Leaders' Statement: The Pittsburgh Summit', Pittsburgh, 24–5 September, full text available at: http://www.g20.org/Documents/pittsburgh_summit_leaders_statement_250909.pdf

Galtung, J. (1967), 'On the Effects of International Economic Sanctions with Examples from the Case of Rhodesia', *World Politics*, 19/3: 378–416.

Garrett, G. (2010), 'G2 in G20: China, the United States and the World after the Global Financial Crisis', *Global Policy*, 1/1: 29–39.

Gianviti, F., Krueger, A., Pisani-Ferry, J., Sapir, A., and von Hagen, J. (2010), 'A European Mechanism for Sovereign Debt Crisis Resolution: A Proposal', Bruegel Blueprint (Brussels: Bruegel).

Goebel, R. (2006), 'Court of Justice Oversight Over the European Central Bank: Delimiting the ECB's Constitutional Autonomy and Independence in the Olaf Judgment', *Fordham International Law Journal*, 29: 600–54.

Goldstein, M., and Lardy, N. (2008), 'China's Exchange Rate Policy: An Overview of Some Key Issues', in M. Goldstein and N.R. Lardy (eds.), *Debating China's Exchange Rate Policy* (Washington, DC: Institute for International Economics), 1–60.

Hall, B. (2009), 'Sarkozy More Likely to Win Than Walk-Out', *Financial Times*, 1 April.

—— Eaglesham, J. (2008), 'Brown and Sarkozy Agree to Seek New Bretton Woods', *Financial Times*, 6 November.

—— Parker, G. (2007), 'Paris Urged to Learn from History', *Financial Times*, 6 June.

—— —— (2008), 'Sarkozy Calls for More Accountable ECB', *Financial Times*, 21 July.

Hall, P., and Soskice, D. (eds.) (2001), *Varieties of Capitalism: The Institutional Foundations of Comparative Advantage* (Oxford: Oxford University Press).

Hallerberg, M. (2004), *Institutions and Fiscal Performance. Domestic Budgets in a United Europe: Fiscal Governance from the End of Bretton Woods to EMU* (Ithaca: Cornell University Press).

—— Bridwell, J. (2008), 'Fiscal Policy Context: Co-ordination and Discipline, The Stability and Growth Pact, and Domestic Fiscal Regimes', in K. Dyson (ed.), *The Euro at Ten: Europeanization, Power, and Convergence* (Oxford: Oxford University Press) 69–86.

—— von Hagen, J. (2005), 'The Past can Teach Germany New Fiscal Lessons', *Financial Times*, 2 November.

—— Strauch, R., and von Hagen, J. (2001), 'The Use and Effectiveness of Budgetary Rules and Norms in EU Member States', Report Prepared for the Dutch Ministry of Finance by the Institute of European Integration Studies (ZEI) (The Hague: Ministry of Finance).

—— —— —— (2004), 'The Design of Fiscal Rules and Forms of Governance in European Union Countries', European Central Bank Working Paper No. 419 (Frankfurt am Main: ECB).

—— —— —— (2009), *Fiscal Governance: Evidence from Europe* (Cambridge: Cambridge University Press).

Hancké, R. (2003), 'The Political Economy of Fiscal Policy in EMU', *European Political Economy Review*, 1/1: 5–14.

Hancké, B., and Soskice, R. (2003), 'Wage-Setting and Inflation Targets in EMU', *Oxford Review of Economic Policy*, 19/1: 149–60.

—— R. Rhodes, M., and Thatcher, M. (eds.) (2007), *Beyond Varieties of Capitalism: Conflict, Contradictions and Complementarities in the European Economy* (Oxford: Oxford University Press) 89–121.

Harney, M. (2001), 'Ireland's Misunderstood Budget: The European Commission is Wrong to Criticise Dublin's Tax and Spending Plans as Inflationary', *Financial Times*, 5 February.

Hatzopoulos, V. (2007), 'Why the Open Method of Coordination Is Bad For You: A Letter to the EU', *European Law Journal*, 13/3: 309–42.

Hayes-Renshaw, F., and Wallace, H. (2006), *The Council of Ministers*, 2nd edition (Basingstoke: Palgrave Macmillan).

Heads of State or Government of the Euro Area (2010), Statement, 25 March (Brussels: Council of the European Union).

Heads of State or Government of the European Union (2010), Statement, 11 February (Brussels: Council of the European Union).

Heeringa, W., and Lindh, Y. (2001), 'Dutch Versus Swedish Budgetary Rules: Comparison', in Banca d'Italia (ed.), *Fiscal Rules* (Rome: Banca d'Italia) 487–514.

Heipertz, M. and Verdun, A. (2010), *Ruling Europe: The Politics of the Stability and Growth Pact* (Cambridge: Cambridge University Press).

Heisenberg, D., and Richmond, A. (2002), 'Supranational Institution-Building in the European Union: A Comparison of the European Court of Justice and the European Central Bank', *Journal of European Public Policy*, 9/2: 201–18.

Helleiner, E. (2008), 'Political Determinants of International Currencies: What Future for the Dollar?', *Review of International Political Economy*, 15/3: 354–78.

Henning, C.R. (2007), 'Democratic Accountability and the Exchange-Rate Policy of the Euro Area', *Review of International Political Economy*, 14/5: 739–45.

—— (2008), *Accountability and Oversight of US Exchange Rate Policy* (Washington, DC: Institute for International Economics).

Hill, C. (1993), 'The Capability–Expectations Gap, or Conceptualizing Europe's International Role', *Journal of Common Market Studies*, 31/3: 305–28.

Hix, S. (1998), 'The Study of the European Union II: The "New Governance" Agenda and Its Rival', *Journal of European Public Policy*, 5/1: 38–65.

—— (2005), *The Political System of the European Union*, 2nd edition (London: Palgrave).

—— (2008), *What's Wrong with the EU and How to Fix it?* (London: Polity).

HM Treasury (2003), 'Fiscal Stabilisation and EMU – A Discussion Paper' (London: HM Stationery Office).

Hodson, D. (2009), 'Reforming EU Economic Governance: A View from (and on), the Principal–Agent Approach', *Comparative European Politics*, 7/4: 455–75.

—— (2010), 'The EU Economy: The Euro Area in 2009', *Journal of Common Market Studies*, 48/s1: 225–42.

Hodson, D., Maher, I. (2001), 'The Open Method as a New Mode of Governance: The Case of Soft Economic Policy Co-ordination', *Journal of Common Market Studies*, 39/4: 719–46.

—— —— (2004), 'Soft Sanctions and the Reform of the Stability and Growth Pact', *Journal of European Public Policy*, 11/5: 798–813.

—— Rahman, M. (2007), 'Understanding the EU's Evolving Economic Relations with India', *EU Political Economy Newsletter*, Fall: 6–10.

—— Simoni, M. (2009), 'Lisbon Through the Looking Glass: The Varieties of Capitalism and Europe's Knowledge Economy', in R. Liddle (ed.), *After the Crisis: A New Socio-Economic Settlement for the EU* (London: Policy Network) 115–28.

Honohan, P., and Lane, P. (2003), 'Divergent Inflation Rates in EMU', *Economic Policy*, 18/37: 357–94.

Hope, K., Tait, N., and Peel, Q. (2010), 'Eurozone Agrees Greek Bail-Out', *Financial Times*, 3 May.

Houlder, V. (2009), 'UK Hails "Beginning of End" for Tax Havens', *Financial Times*, 14 March.

House of Lords Select Committee on the EU (2003), 'The Stability and Growth Pact', Session 2002–03, 13th Report, HL Paper 72, 11 March.

Howarth, D. (2007), 'Making and Breaking the Rules: French Policy on EU Economic Governance', *Journal of European Public Policy*, 14/7: 1–18.

—— Loedel, P. (2005), *The European Central Bank: The New Leviathan* (Basingstoke: Palgrave Macmillan).

Huber, P. (2003), 'National Report for Austria (3rd Round)' (Brussels: GOVECOR), http://www.govecor.org/data/20030917114745_Austrian_Report3.pdf

Hufbauer, G., and Brunel, C. (2008), 'The US Congress and the Chinese Renminbi', in M. Goldstein and N.R. Lardy (eds.), *Debating China's Exchange Rate Policy* (Washington, DC: Institute for International Economics), 219–23.

IMF (International Monetary Fund) (2001), 'Ireland: 2001 Article IV Consultation – Staff Report and Public Information Notice on the Executive Board Discussion', Country Report No. 01/139 (Washington, DC: Ireland).

—— (2009), 'Note to the Group of Twenty', available at: http://www.imf.org/external/np/g20/pdf/020509.pdf

Irish Times (2001), 'Minister Argues Fiscal Strategy was Prudent Given Pressures to Raise Spending', *The Irish Times*, 13 February.

Issing, O. (1999), 'The Eurosystem: Transparent and Accountable or "Willem in Euroland"', *Journal of Common Market Studies*, 37/3: 503–19.

Italianer, A. (1999), 'The Euro and Internal Economic Policy Coordination', *Empirica*, 26/3: 201–16.

Jacquet, P., and Pisani-Ferry, J. (2001), 'Economic Policy Co-ordination in the Eurozone: What Has Been achieved? What Should Be Done?', Sussex European Institute Working Paper No. 40.

Juncker, J.C. (2010), 'Letter from the President of the Eurogroup to Euro Area Finance Ministers, the European Commissioner for Economic and Monetary Affairs and the President of the European Central Bank' (Brussels: Council of the European Union).

Kirshner, J. (1995), *Currency and Coercion: The Political Economy of International Monetary Power* (Princeton, NJ: Princeton University Press).

Kirton, J. (2000), 'The G20: Representativeness, Effectiveness, and Leadership in Global Governance', in J. Kirton, J. Daniels, and A. Freytag (ed.), *Guiding Global Order: G8 Governance in the Twenty-First Century* (Aldershot: Ashgate) 143–72.

—— Guebert, J. (2010), A Summit of Substantial Success: The Performance of the G20 in Washington in 2008' (Toronto: G20 Research Group).

Kohl, H. (2002), 'Supranational Visionary and Builder of Euroland: Former German Chancellor Dr Helmut Kohl on the Euro's Significance for Germany and Its Neighbors', *The Academy of Management Executive*, 16/1: 10–12.

Kohler-Koch, B., and Rittberger, B. (2006), 'The "Governance Turn" in EU Studies', *Journal of Common Market Studies*, 44/s1: 27–49.

Kok, W. (2004), *Facing the Challenge. The Lisbon Strategy for Growth and Employment: Report from the High Level Group Chaired by Wim Kok* (Brussels: European Commission).

Laffan, B. (2001), 'Arrogant, Churlish and Ill-Judged Response to EU', *Irish Times*, 17 February.

Laffer, A.B. (2001), 'Tax Cuts Work – and Ireland Proves It', *Scotsman*, 21 February.

Lambert, L. (2010), 'European Monetary Fund Deserves Examination – Trichet', *Reuters*, 12 March.

Lindberg, L. (1965), 'Decision Making and Integration in the European Community' *International Organization*, 19/1: 56–80.

Luce, E. (2009), 'Handshake Brokered by Obama', *Financial Times*, 3 April.

Maes, I. (2006), 'The Ascent of the European Commission as an Actor in the Monetary Integration Process in the 1960s', *Scottish Journal of Political Economy*, 53/2: 222–41.

Maher, I. (2004), 'Economic Policy Co-ordination and the European Court: Excessive Deficits and Ecofin Discretion', *European Law Review*, 29/6: 831–41.

—— (2007), 'Economic Governance: Hybridity, Accountability, and Control', *Columbia Journal of European Law*, 13/3: 679–703.

Mahieu, G., Ooms, D., and Rottier, S. (2005), 'EU Representation and the Governance of the International Monetary Fund', *European Union Politics*, 6/4: 493–510.

Majone, G. (2005), *Dilemmas of European Integration: The Ambiguities and Pitfalls of Integration by Stealth* (Oxford: Oxford University Press).

—— (2009), *Europe as the Would-Be World Power: The EU at Fifty* (Cambridge: Cambridge University Press).

Mandelson, P. (2007), 'Speech at the EU–China Business Summit', Beijing, 28 November.

Margerum Harlen, C. (2002)' 'Schröder's Economic Reforms: The End of Reformstau?', *German Politics*, 11/1: 61–80.

Martin, L.L. (1992), *Coercive Cooperation: Explaining Multilateral Economic Sanctions* (Princeton: Princeton University Press).

Mashaw, J. (2005), 'Structuring a "Dense Complexity": Accountability and the Project of Administrative Law', *Issues in Legal Scholarship, The Reformation of American Administrative Law*, Article 4.

McNamara, K., and Meunier, S. (2002), 'Between National Sovereignty and International Power: What External Voice for the Euro?', *International Affairs*, 78/4: 849–68.

Menon, A., and Sedelmeier, U. (2010), 'Instruments and Intentionality: Civilian Crisis Management and Enlargement Conditionality in EU Security Policy', *West European Politics*, 33/1: 75–92.

Mersch, Y. (2009), 'Transcript of Interview with Ralph Atkins', *Financial Times*, 26 January.

Meyer, L. (2000), 'The Politics of Monetary Policy: Balancing Independence and Accountability', remarks at the University of Wisconsin, LaCrosse, Wisconsin, 24 October, http://www.federalreserve.gov/boarddocs/speeches/2000/20001024.htm

Meyer, C. (2004), 'The Hard Side of Soft Policy-Coordination in EMU: The Impact of Peer Pressure on Publicized Opinion in the Cases of Germany and Ireland', *Journal of European Public Policy*, 11/5: 814–31.

Mitterrand, F. (1988), *Lettre à tous les Français* (Paris: Parti Socialiste).

Moravcsik, M. (1997), 'Does the European Union Represent an n of 1?', *European Community Studies Association Review*, X/3: 1–5.

Moravcsik, A. (1998), *The Choice for Europe: Social Purpose and State Power from Messina to Maastricht* (Ithaca, NY: Cornell University Press).

—— (2009), 'Europe: The Quiet Superpower', *French Politics*, 7/September–December: 403–22.

Moschella, M. (2010), 'From the Neoliberal to the Regulated Model of Capitalism: The EU and the International Financial Architecture Exercise', paper presented at the ECPR Joint Sessions, Muenster, Germany, March.

Münchau, W. (2010), 'Why Greece Will Default', www.eurointelligence.com 1 April.

Nasra, S., Lesage, D., Orbie, J., Van de Graaf, T., and Vermeiren, M. (2009), 'The EU in the G8 System: Assessing EU Member States' Involvement', Robert Schuman Centre for Advanced Studies Working Papers 2009/45.

Noyer, C. (2009), 'The Macroeconomy and Financial Systems in Normal Times and in Times of Stress', speech at conference jointly organized by the Bank of France and the Deutsche Bundesbank, Chantilly, 9 June.

Obstfeld, M., and Rogoff, K. (2009), 'Global Imbalances and Financial Crisis: Products of Common Causes', paper presented at the Federal Reserve Bank Asia Economic Policy Conference, Santa Barbara, CA, 18–20 October.

OECD (Organization for Economic Cooperation and Development) (2001), *Economic Survey of Ireland: Assessments and Recommendations* (Paris: ECB).

—— (2003), 'Economic Survey of Austria' (Paris: OECD).

Olivier, J.G.J., and Peters, J.A.H.W. (2010), *No Growth in Total Global CO2 Emissions in 2009* (Bilthoven: Netherlands Environmental Assessment Agency).

O'Leary, J. (2001), 'Even We Must Play by EMU Rules', *Irish Times*, 16 February.

O'Sullivan, J. (2001), 'Business People Take McCreevy's Side in New Survey', *Irish Times*, 23 February.

Oye, K. (1985), 'The Sterling–Dollar–Franc Triangle: Monetary Diplomacy 1929–1937', *World Politics*, XXXVIII/October: 173–99.

Padoa-Schioppa, T. (1999), 'EMU and Banking Supervision', lecture at the London School of Economics, Financial Markets Group, 24 February.

Parker, G. (2006*a*), 'ECB Chief Fends off Politicians' Demands for More Dialogue', *Financial Times*, 9 September.

—— (2006*b*), 'Call to End Public Currency Squabbles', *Financial Times*, 11 September.

—— (2007), 'State of Independence: Is the ECB Bowing to Political Pressure?', *Financial Times*, Brussels Blog, 23 January.

Peel, Q. (2010), 'Merkel Insists on EU Treaty Change', *Financial Times*, 27 October.

Persaud, A. (2008), 'The Financial Crisis May Hasten European Integration But Slow Global Banking', www.VoxEU.org 6 October.

Peterson, J. (2004), 'Europe, America, Iraq: Worst Ever, Ever Worsening?', *Journal of Common Market Studies*, 42/s1: 9–26.

—— (2008), 'Enlargement, Reform and the European Commission: Weathering a Perfect Storm?', *Journal of European Public Policy*, 15/5: 761–80.

—— Steffenson, R. (2009), 'Transatlantic Institutions: Can Partnership be Engineered?', *British Journal of Politics and International Relations*, 11: 25–45.

Pisani-Ferry, J. (2006), 'Only One Bed for Two Dreams: A Critical Retrospective on the Debate over the Economic Governance of the Euro Area', *Journal of Common Market Studies*, 44/4: 823–44.

—— (2008*a*), 'Will the Crisis Trigger a Revival in the IMF?', Bruegel Policy Contribution (Brussels: Bruegel).

—— (2008*b*), 'The End of Europe's Long-Standing Indifference to the Renminbi', in M. Goldstein and N.R. Lardy (eds.), *Debating China's Exchange Rate Policy* (Washington, DC: Institute for International Economics) 268–78.

—— Sapir, A. (2006), 'Last Exit to Lisbon', Bruegel Policy Brief (Brussels: Bruegel).

Pollack, M. (2003), *The Engines of European Integration Delegation, Agency, and Agenda Setting in the EU* (Oxford: Oxford University Press).

—— (2005), Theorizing the European Union: International Organization, Domestic Polity, or Experiment in New Governance?', *Annual Review of Political Science*, 8: 357–98.

Pop, V. (2010), 'Van Rompuy Defends Economic Taskforce Against Critics', euobserver.com 22 September.

Posner, E. (2009), 'Making Rules for Global Finance: Transatlantic Regulatory Cooperation at the Turn of the Millennium', *International Organization*, 63/4: 665–99.

Puetter, U. (2006), *The Eurogroup: How a Secretive Circle of Finance Ministers Shapes European Economic Governance* (Manchester: Manchester University Press).

—— (2007), 'Intervening From Outside: The Role of EU Finance Ministers in Constitutional Politics', *Journal of European Public Policy*, 14/8: 1293–310.

—— (forthcoming), 'Europe's Deliberative Intergovernmentalism: The Role of the Council and European Council in EU Economic Governance', *Journal of European Public Policy*.

Quaglia, L. (2008), *Central Banking Governance in the European Union: A Comparative Analysis* (London: Routledge).

—— (2009*a*), 'The 'British Plan' as a Pace-setter: The Europeanisation of Banking Rescue Plans in the EU?', *Journal of Common Market Studies*, 47/5: 1059–79.

—— (2009*b*), 'Political Science and the Cinderellas of Economic and Monetary Union: Payments Services and Clearing and Settlement of Securities', *Journal of European Public Policy*, 16/4: 623–39.

Quaglia, L., Eastwood, R., and Holmes, P. (2009), 'The Financial Turmoil and EU Policy Cooperation', *Journal of Common Market Studies Annual Review*, 47/1: 1–25.

Ramboll Management Consulting (2009), 'Evaluation of the EU Decentralised Agencies in 2009: Final Report Volume III – Agency Level Findings', full text available at: http://ec.europa.eu/dgs/secretariat_general/evaluation/docs/decentralised_agencies_2009_part3_en.pdf

Regling, K. (2007), 'Strengthening the Economic Leg of EMU', contribution to Euro50 Group Roundtable, '50 Years After the Treaty of Rome: Strengthening the Economic Leg of EMU', Rome, 2–3 July.

Rehn, O. (2010), 'Reinforcing Economic Confidence in Europe', speech at the ECON Committee, European Parliament, Strasbourg, SPEECH/10/359, 5 July.

Reinhart, C., and Rogoff, K. (2009), *This Time Its Different: Eight Centuries of Financial Folly* (Princeton NJ: Princeton University Press).

Ricard, P. (2007), 'Le chef de l'Etat répond, lundi, devant l'Eurogroupe aux critiques sur sa politique budgétaire; M. Sarkozy propose un sommet sur l'économie', *Le Monde*, 10 July.

Roederer-Rynning, C. (2010), 'The Common Agricutural Policy: The Fortress Challenged', in H. Wallace, M. Pollack, and A. Young (eds.), *Policy-Making in the European Union* (Oxford: Oxford University Press), 181–206.

Sadeh, T., and Verdun, A. (2008), 'Explaining Europe's Monetary Union: A Survey of the Literature', *The International Studies Review*, 11/2: 277–301.

Sakoui, A., and Hope, K. (2010), 'Market Weighs Up Possibility of Greek Debt Restructuring', *Financial Times*, 20 April.

Sanderson, H. (2007), 'EU Official: China Needs to Open Markets', *Associated Press*, 28 November.

Sarkozy, N. (2007*a*), *Speech to the European Parliament in Strasbourg*, 2 July (Élysée: Présidence de la République).

—— (2007*b*), *Conférence de presse conjointe – Eurogroupe* (Élysée: Présidence de la République).

—— (2007*c*), 'Entretien: Je veux 3% de croissance économique', *Le Monde*, 17 September.

—— (2008), *Discours de M. Le Président de la République Française: 63e Assemblée générale des Nations unies* (Elysée: Présidence de la République).

Savage, J. (2005), *Making the EMU The Politics of Budgetary Surveillance and the Enforcement of Maastricht* (Oxford: Oxford University Press).

Scharpf, F.W. (1987), *Social Democratic Crisis Politics in Europe* (Frankfurt am Main – New York: Campus).

—— (1988), 'The Joint Decision Trap. Lessons from German Federalism and European Integration', *Public Administration*, 66/3: 239–78.

—— (2006), 'The Joint-Decision Trap Revisited', *Journal of Common Market Studies*, 44/4: 845–64.

Schäuble, W. (2010), 'Why Europe's Monetary Union Faces Its Biggest Crisis', *Financial Times*, 12 March.

Schmidt, V.A. (2009), 'Trapped by Their Ideas: French Élites' Discourses of European Integration and Globalization', *Journal of European Public Policy*, 14/7: 1350–763.

Schmitter, P.C., and Grote, J.R. (1997), 'The Corporatist Sisyphus: Past, Present and Future', European University Institute Working Paper (Florence: European University).

Scott, J., and Trubek, D. (2002), 'Mind the Gap: Law and New Approaches to Governance in the European Union', *European Law Journal*, 8/1: 1–18.

Sinn, H.W. (2000), 'Germany's Economic Unification: An Assessment After Ten Years', NBER Working Paper No. 7586.

Sinnott, R. (2001), 'Attitudes and Behaviour of the Irish Electorate in the Referendum on the Nice Treaty', Flash Eurobarometer Report No. 108 (Brussels: TNS Opinion & Social).

Smismans, S. (2008), 'New Modes of Governance and the Participatory Myth', *West European Politics*, 31/5: 874–95.

Snyder, F. (1999), 'EMU Revisited: Are We Making a Constitution? What Constitution Are We Making?', in P. Craig and G. de Burca (eds.), *The Evolution of EU Law* (Oxford: Oxford University Press), 417–73.

Stark, J. (2008), 'Does the Euro Area Need an Economic Government?', statement delivered at the HEC European Executive Campus, Brussels, 22 January.

Staunton, D. (2001), 'Commission Eases Budget Stance but Urges Caution', *Irish Times*, 24 October.

—— (2002), 'Germany, Portugal Escape Censure Over Running High Budget Deficits', *Irish Times*, 13 February.

Stock, M.J., and Magone, J.M. (1997), 'Portugal', *European Journal of Political Research*, 32/3–4: 477–80.

Strange, S. (1971), *Sterling and British Policy* (Oxford: Oxford University Press).

Suiter, J. (2001), 'Diplomatic Offensive Succeeds in Reducing Weight of EU Demands', *Irish Times*, 3 February.

Tabellini, G., and Wyplosz, C. (2006), 'Supply-side Coordination in the European Union', *Swedish Economic Policy Review*, 13: 101–56.

Taskforce to the European Council (2010), *Strengthening Economic Governance in the EU* (Brussels: European Council).

Thatcher, M. (1990), 'HC S: (Confidence in Her Majesty's Government)', 22 November, Hansard HC [181/445–53].

Topolánek, M. (2009), 'Speech to the European Parliament', 2 April, full text available at: http://www.eu2009.cz/en/news-and-documents/speeches-interviews/mirek-topolanek-in-the-european-parliament-13533/

Trichet, J.C. (2003), 'Europe at the Crossroads', speech at the Frankfurt European Banking Congress, Frankfurt am Main, 20 November.

—— (2007), 'Letter to the President of the Council of the European Union', 2 August.

—— (2008*a*), 'Address at the Ceremony to Mark the 10th Anniversary of the European Central Bank and the European System of Central Banks', Frankfurt am Main, 2 June.

—— (2008*b*), 'Interview with De Tijd and L'Echo' (Frankfurt am Main: ECB).

—— (2009*a*), 'Remarks on the Future of European Financial Regulation and Supervision', keynote address at the Committee of European Securities Regulators (CESR), Paris, 23 February.

—— (2009*b*), 'Introductory Remarks' Economic and Monetary Affairs Committee of the European Parliament', Brussels, 30 March.

van den Noord, P., Döhring, B., Langedijk, S., Nogueira Martins, J., Pench, L., Temprano-Arroyo, H., and Thiel, M. (2008), 'The Evolution of Economic Governance in EMU', European Economy Economic Papers 328 (Brussels: European Commission).

von Hagen, J., and Strauch, R. (2001), 'German Public Finances: Recent Experiences and Future Challenges', ZEI Center for European Integration Studies, Working Paper No. B-13.

—— Wyplosz, C. (2008), 'EMU's Decentralized System of Fiscal Policy', European Economy, Economic Papers No. 306 (Brussels: Directorate General Economic and Monetary Affairs, European Commission).

—— Hughes Hallett, A., and Strauch, R. (2001), 'Budgetary Consolidation in EMU', European Commission, Economic Papers No. 148 (Brussels: European Commission).

Van Houtven, L. (2002), *Governance of the IMF: Decision Making, Institutional Oversight, Transparency, and Accountability* (Washington, DC: IMF).

Van Rompuy, H. (2010), 'Europe's Role and Place in the World', speech at the College of Europe, Bruges, 25 February.

Wall Street Journal (2001), 'Green with Envy', *Wall Street Journal*, 14 February.

Wallace, H. (2010), 'An Institutional Anatomy and Five Modes', in H. Wallace, M. Pollack, and M. Young (eds.), *Policy-Making in the European Union* (Oxford: Oxford University Press), 69–104.

—— Pollack, M., and Young, A. (2010), 'EU Policy-Making in Challenging Times: Adversity, Adaptability and Resilience', in H. Wallace, M. Pollack, and A. Young (eds.), *Policy-Making in the European Union* (Oxford: Oxford University Press), 481–502.

Wallensteen, P. (2000), 'A Century of Economic Sanctions: A Field Revisited', Uppsala Peace Research Papers No. 1 (Uppsala University: Department of Peace and Conflict Research).

Watson, R. (2007), 'Europe to Voice Concerns Over Yuan Exchange Rate', *The Times*, 26 November.

Watt, A. (2005), 'Can Reform of the Macroeconomic Dialogue Improve Economic Policy-Making in Europe?', in E. Hein, T. Niechoj, T. Schulten, and A. Truger (eds.), *Macroeconomic Policy Coordination in Europe and the Role of the Trade Unions* (Brussels: ETUI), 237–59.

Weber, A. (2004), 'Speech at His Official Inauguration as Bundesbank President', Frankfurt am Main, 12 May.

—— (2009), 'How to Implement Efficiently the EU Regulatory and Supervisory Package Proposed by the de Larosière Group in the EU and Global Context?', Introductory Statement Eurofi 2009 Panel, 30 September.

Welteke, E. (2003), 'Reforming Europe', Closing Remarks at the European Banking Congress in Frankfurt, 21 November.

Wen, J. (2010), 'Speech at the EU–China Business Summit', Brussels, 6 October.

Werner, P. (1970), *Report to the Council and the Commission on the Realization by Stages of Economic and Monetary Union in the Community* (Luxembourg: Werner Committee).

Wiesmann, G., and Peel, Q. (2010), 'Germany Warms to Giving IMF a Role in Any Greek Debt Rescue', *Financial Times*, 19 March.

Williams, G. (2005), 'Monomaniacs or Schizophrenics? Responsible Governance and the EU's Independent Agencies', *Political Studies*, 53/1: 82–99.

Wilson, D., and Purushothaman, R. (2003), 'Dreaming With BRICs: The Path to 2050', Goldman Sachs Global Economics Paper No. 99.

Woolcock, S. (2007), 'Multilevel Diplomacy: The Case of Investment', in N. Bayne and S. Woolcock (eds.), *The New Economic Diplomacy: Decision-Making and Negotiation in International Economic Relations* (London: Ashgate), 141–62.

Wyplosz, C. (2005), 'Fiscal Policy: Institutions Versus Rules', *National Institute Economic Review*, 191: 70–84.

Zeitlin, J. (2009), 'The Open Method of Coordination and Reform of National Social and Employment Policies: Influences, Mechanisms, Effects', in M. Heidenreich and J. Zeitlin (eds.), *Changing European Employment and Welfare Regimes: The Influence of the Open Method of Coordination on National Reforms* (London: Routledge), 214–45.

Zilioli, C., and Selmayr, M. (2000), 'The European Central Bank: An Independent Specialized Organization of Community Law', *Common Market Law Review*, 37/3: 519–644.

Zimmermann, H. (2004), 'Ever Challenging the Buck? The Euro and the Question of Power in International Monetary Governance', in F. Torres, A. Verdun and H. Zimmermann (eds.), *Governing EMU: Political, Economic, Legal and Historical Perspectives* (Florence: European University Institute), 233–48.

Zohlnhöfer, R. (1999), 'Institutions, the CDU and Policy Change: Explaining German Economic Policy in the 1980s', *German Politics*, 8/3: 141–60.

Index